U0358372

Applied English Writing in Civil Engineering

国际工程应用写作

主　编：杨光辉
副主编：李　程
主　审：李光咸

人民交通出版社股份有限公司
China Communications Press Co.,Ltd.

图书在版编目（CIP）数据

国际工程应用写作 ＝ Applied English Writing in Civil Engineering ：英文 / 杨光辉主编. — 北京 ：人民交通出版社股份有限公司, 2018.8

ISBN 978-7-114-14739-5

Ⅰ. ①国… Ⅱ. ①杨… Ⅲ. ①国际承包工程—英语—写作 Ⅳ. ①F746.18

中国版本图书馆 CIP 数据核字（2018）第 218124 号

书　　名：	Applied English Writing in Civil Engineering　国际工程应用写作
著 作 者：	杨光辉
责任编辑：	李　瑞
责任校对：	张　贺
责任印制：	刘高彤
出版发行：	人民交通出版社股份有限公司
地　　址：	（100011）北京市朝阳区安定门外外馆斜街 3 号
网　　址：	http://www.ccpress.com.cn
销售电话：	（010）59757973
总 经 销：	人民交通出版社股份有限公司发行部
经　　销：	各地新华书店
印　　刷：	北京虎彩文化传播有限公司
开　　本：	787×1092　1/16
印　　张：	15
字　　数：	348 千
版　　次：	2018 年 8 月　第 1 版
印　　次：	2022 年 8 月　第 4 次印刷
书　　号：	ISBN 978-7-114-14739-5
定　　价：	48.00 元

（如有印刷、装订质量问题的图书，由本公司负责调换）

本书参编人员（Authors）

刘聂瑒子（LIU Nieyangzi）　　　　冯霄（FENG Xiao）

谢青（XIE Qing）　　　　　　　　雷蕾（LEI Lei）

陈琳（CHEN Lin）　　　　　　　　吕璞（LYU Pu）

汪帆（WANG Fan）　　　　　　　　易慧（YI Hui）

王溪清（WANG Xiqing）

PREFACE

In today's global market, international trade and cooperation have become common practice benefiting from the fast development of information technology. Whether a multinational company with subsidies all over the world or a local shop around the corner, each has the potential to work with a wide variety of customers. Whether business giants in New York City or a mom-and-pop store on a pacific island, businesses must be prepared to work with both.

In recent years an increasing amount of international companies have come to China for business endeavors and likewise Chinese companies are going abroad for the same reasons. "The Belt and Road" initiative of the Chinese government has encouraged the rapid growth of transportation infrastructure projects all over Asia, Europe, Africa and South America. This trend has created a high demand for civil engineers and project managers with both a technical background and cross-cultural awareness.

However, government agencies and business companies do not always follow the same technical standards and specifications which have caused unnecessary conflicts in many construction projects. Effective business and technical communications among relevant organizations are critical to the success of such international collaborative projects. English, the official language in almost 60 countries, is the most widely used language in the business world. For most Chinese civil engineering students, there is not an adequate English writing textbook that combines the teaching of business correspondences, project management documents, technical reports, theses and engineering drawings.

The Center for Innovative Education (CIE) at School of Highway of Chang'an University has recognized the increasing need for an English writing textbook tailored to Chinese civil engineering students and developed this book from the bilingual teaching experience of international engineering classes over the past ten years. The purpose of this book is to provide students essentials and basic guidelines for effective written communication in engineering related professional and academic fields.

The chief editor of this textbook, Professor YANG Guanghui, has been the founding director of the CIE since 2008. He has an educational background from Chang'an University, University of Florida and Hong Kong Polytechnic University.

Additionally, he has acted as a consultant for many international collaborative civil engineering projects, and he has spent time teaching at Dar es Salaam Technic College in Tanzania as well as Chang'an University. With his extensive experience, both in the field and classroom, Professor Yang understands the importance for students to master effective communication skills. This is what motivated him to gather his colleagues to prepare the Business and Technical Writing course for the bilingual program in Road, Bridge, and River-crossing Engineering of Chang'an University. With the help of the CIE faculty teaching materials, lecture feedbacks, and student observations and reviews, the first edition of the book was finally completed in the fall of 2018.

The chief reviewer of this book, Mr. LI Guangxian, a former graduate from Chang'an University and Appalachian State University, has worked in both business and education fields for many years. Mr. Li has also served as the executive director for United Nations Industrial Development Organization (UNIDO) and industrial subcontracting and partnership program (SPX) from 2008 to 2011. He has also conducted project management training for a number of domestic and international organizations. His rich experience in training and cross-cultural communication has provided insights for the overall organization and detail of this textbook.

There are twelve co-authors of this collective project, most are faculty members in CIE who have graduated from foreign universities and have extensive bilingual teaching experience. Content and authors of each chapter are introduced as follows, respectively. Except for the preface, this book consists of seven chapters. Chapter 1 provides general guidelines for English writing and covers common law and ethics written by Drs. LEI Lei and LI Cheng; Ms. LIU Nieyangzi and WANG Xiqing. Chapter 2 teaches students to select words, use punctuation, and write sentences and paragraphs written by Mr. LI Guangxian. Chapter 3 demonstrates how to write business correspondence such as fax, email, business letter, cover letter and resume written by Drs. XIE Qing and LYU Pu. Chapter 4 explains how to write speeches and prepare PowerPoint presentations written by Drs. CHEN Lin and LI Cheng; and Ms. WANG Fan. Chapter 5 introduces various documents for project management including agreements, contracts, proposals, agendas, and reports written by Ms. LIU Nieyangzi and Dr. YI Hui. Chapters 6-7 are focused on how to write a thesis or dissertation to fulfill the graduation requirements for specific degrees and how to prepare engineering drawings written by Dr. FENG Xiao.

This book can be used as a textbook as well as a reference book, so that students can both study for writing business correspondence, speeches, and research documents as well as refer to the many formatted templates provided for future uses. It is our desire that this textbook will help students master written and oral communication skills and become more confident as professional engineers and researchers in their workplace.

Dr. LIU Yu, the current director of the CIE, deserves special thanks for providing necessary supports to this writing project. Without his encouragement, it would have been difficult to finalize this book. Dr. LI Cheng has contributed greatly in organizing meetings and discussions during the process as well as editing drafts on top of his already busy schedule. On behalf of the entire group, we want to express our appreciation to his devotion and support he committed to the time-consuming preparatory work and detailed maintenance of the text. In addition, special thanks to Ms. Olivia T. Li. As a native English speaker, her proofreading and final editing are essential for this textbook.

August 2018

TABLE OF CONTENTS

CHAPTER 1. WARM UP-JOBS START FROM WRITING

1.1 WHY IS WRITING SO IMPORTANT FOR STUDENTS

Writing is important to all jobs. Upon first contact with a potential employer, your resume and the application letter provide an impression to the company. If you plan to pursue a higher position, writing will be a fundamental part of success. Furthermore, the writing skill is a crucial factor in determining a promotion.

The Associated Press reported in a recent survey that, "Most American businesses say employees need to improve their writing skills." This same report cited a survey of 402 companies identifying writing as "the most valued skill of employees." According to a communication consultant, a business letter costs one hour or more for most people. For those who earn more money, more time is needed to finish a letter. Clearly, writing is an essential skill for anyone in the workplace.

This chapter provides basic knowledge of English writing in today's workplace. It answers questions you may have before you begin writing, which may help you write more effectively.

1.2 WRITING FOR TODAY'S GLOBAL MARKETPLACE

In today's business environment, Internet, teleconferencing, e-mail, and e-commerce have made the world a global village. Thus, it is impossible to run the national business as in old times. Many companies are globalized, which offer positions all over the world. These international corporations may have equipment designed in America, assembled in China, and sold throughout the world. Under the global economy, a country's actions are not isolate but rather bound together by a network of modern communication: the Internet.

Every business, whether large or small, must face the global market more competitively. Take Walmart as an example: it has opened thousands of stores outside the U. S., including Japan, England, China, etc. No matter where your business may be founded physically, you will have to work with customers, vendors, and suppliers all over the world.

If you want to run a successful business you must learn to communicate with people from different cultures and backgrounds. Writing in English is used as the primary tool during the global communcation process.

1.2.1　See the World Through Your Readers' Eyes

It is important to be familiar with cultures of your readers as you begin your writing, for they may not run business as you do in China. They may have different styles of writing or communication. Cultural differences exist not only among countries, but also inside your company. It is naive to assume that your colleagues have the same cultural background as you do. For example, forty to fifty percent of the U. S. workers are immigrants who have different traditions or customs. You need to understand these differences and respect them in the workplace.

1.2.2　Use International English

Whether these international readers are your customers or co-workers, you will have to adapt your writing to respect their language needs and communication protocols. Words, idioms, phrases, and sentences you choose instinctively for the native English speakers may not be appropriate for an audience whose English is not their native language. To communicate with non-native English speakers, you will have to use "international English", a way of writing that is easily understood, culturally tactful, and diplomatically correct. International English simply means that your message is clear, straightforward, and appropriate for readers who are not native speakers of the language. It should be free from complex, hard-to-process sentences as well as the cultural biases.

1.3　ESSENTIALS FOR EFFECTIVE WRITINGS

Effective writing on the job should be carefully planned, thoroughly researched, and clearly presented. Its purpose is often to accomplish a specific goal. Whether you sending a routine e-mail to a co-worker or a special report to the president of the company, you should always ask yourself these questions before start.

1) *Who* will read what I write? (Identify your audience.)

2) *Why* should they read what I write? (Establish your purpose.)

3) *What* do I have to say to them? (Formulate your message.)

4) *How* can I best communicate? (Select your style and tone.)

The questions *who*, *why*, *what* and *how* do not function independently; they are all related. You write 1) for a specific audience 2) with a clearly defined purpose in mind 3) about a topic your readers need to understand 4) in language appropriate for the occasion. Once you answer the first question, you are off to a good start toward answering the other three. Now let us examine each of the four questions in detail.

1.3.1   Identifying Your Audience

Knowing who are your audiences is one of your most important responsibilities as a writer. Throughout the composing process you will need to analyze your audiences.

Keep the following in mind:

1) Members of each audience differ in backgrounds, experiences, needs, and opinions.

2) How you picture your audience will determine what you say to them.

3) Viewing something from the audience's perspective will help you to select the most relevant details for the audience.

You can form a fairly accurate picture of your audience by asking yourself some questions before you write. For each audience for whom you write, consider the following questions.

Who is my audience? What individual (s) will most likely be reading my work?

If it is writing in the workplace,

1) Is your reader a colleague or your boss?

2) What interests, education levels and work experiences does your reader have?

If it is sent to the clients or the customers,

1) What are your readers' interests?

2) Do your readers know you or your company?

How many audiences do I have?

1) Is it just one individual reader or will there be many audiences?

2) Does this message need to be sent to your boss?

Does my audience know English well?

1) Are they native speakers of English? Or do they use it as the second or third language? Or do they know English at all, do they need a dictionary to read your message?

2) Are you connecting with people worldwide?

Does the audience know the topic of my message?

1) Do they need to know as much information as you do or they just need to know a brief introduction?

2) Do they know the technical expressions in this topic? Or easy words need to be used?

Why does my audience need to read the message?

1) Is reading my communication part of their routine duties, or are they looking for information to solve a problem or make a decision?

2) Am I writing to describe benefits that another writer or company cannot offer?

3) Will my readers expect complete details, or just a short summary?

4) Are they reading my work to make an important decision affecting a co-worker, a client, or a community?

5) Are they reading something I write because they must (a legal notification, for instance)?

What are my audiences' expectations about my written work?

1) Do they want a brief e-mail or will they expect a formal letter?

2) Will they expect me to follow a company format and style?

3) Are they looking for a one-page memo or a comprehensive report?

4) Should I use a formal tone or a more relaxed and conversational style?

What is my audience's attitude toward me and my work?

1) Will I be writing to a group of disgruntled customers and/or vendors about a sensitive issue (a product recall, a refusal of credit, or a shipment delay)?

2) Will I have to be sympathetic while at the same time give firm reasons for my company's (or my) decision?

3) Will my readers be skeptical, indifferent, or friendly about what I write?

4) Will my readers feel guilty that they have not answered the earlier message of mine, not paid an overdue bill, or not kept a promise or commitment?

What do I want my audience to do after reading my work?

1) Do I expect my readers to purchase something from my company, approve my plan, or send me additional materials?

2) Do I simply want my readers to get my message and not respond at all?

3) Do I expect my readers to get my message, acknowledge it, save it for future reference, or review it and e-mail it to another individual or office?

4) Does my reader have to take immediate actions, or does he or she have several days or weeks to respond?

Your answers to these questions will demonstrate that you may have to communicate with many different audiences on your job. If you work for a large organization with numerous departments, you may have to write to diverse readers like accountants, engineers, public relation specialists, marketing experts, programmers, and individuals who install, operate, and maintain equipment. On some occasions, you may have to write for multiple audiences simultaneously such as a manager, a buyer, and someone in the legal department.

You need to offer useful and relevant information to different audiences, so you need to know their expectations.

1.3.2 Identifying Your Purpose

The purpose of writing will guide you to communicate more effectively. The most important rule in writing is to accomplish your goal in the most direct and clear manner. Such as,

I would like to offer an orientation about the campus for new students.

The audiences need to be notified at the beginning of your message, such as e-mail, memo, letter, and report.

This e-mail will acquaint new students in the Departments of Engineering, Arts, and Archeology.

1.3.3 Formulating Your Contents

There are two kinds of information which need to be included in your contents:

1)Scope, which restricts the amount of information you will provide.

2)Details, the key points for readers to help them finish their jobs.

Your content needs to be organized and tailored for different readers. For example, if your reader is a technician your message should include every detail pertaining to his expertise and an appendix is expected at the conclusion of the report.

1.3.4 Choosing Your Styles

Style is how your message is expressed. It determines whether your communication is effective or not; how much information your readers receive. It includes the following information:

1)Paragraph constructions

2)Length and patterns of your sentences

3)Words chosen

You need to review and revise your message considering the purposes and the readers. For instance, the vocabulary you use should be tailored to your audience. If all your readers are specialists of the information, choose technical words or symbols to more clearly communicate your message. However, if your readers are non-specialists, you may need to use words common to the general public.

1.4 PRACTICAL GUIDELINES FOR JOB-RELATED WRITING

Job-related writings have six requirements: 1) providing useful information,

2)providing facts, not impressions, 3)providing visuals to help understanding, 4)providing accurate measurements, 5)providing responsibilities precisely, and 6)providing recommendations. These requirements may help you to understand what kind of writing you are working on.

1.4.1 Providing Useful Information

Job-related writings require a here's-what-you-need-to-do method. The first kind of method is action-oriented. You need to let the readers know how to do something whether it is how to assemble furniture, how to drive a car, or how to cook a dish. The second method is knowledge-oriented: to help the readers to understand something whether it is what causes rain or how to solve a problem. An example of knowledge-oriented practical writing is a letter from a manufacturer to customers explaining a product recall or an e-mail to employees concerning changes in their company health insurance.

1.4.2 Providing Facts, Not Impressions

Job-related writings include things that can be seen, heard, felt, tasted, or smelled. You, as the writer need to identify specific details and facts rather than how you feel or what you assume.

The following example is a discussion about the sources of oil spills and their effects on the environment. The facts are illustrated without anger or tears.

Major oil spills occur as a result of accidents such as blowout, pipeline breakage, etc. Technological advances coupled with stringent regulations have helped to reduce the chances of such major spills; however, there is chronic low-lever discharge of oil associated with normal drilling and production operations. Waste oils discharged through the river systems and practices associated with tanker transports dump more significant quantities of oils into the ocean, compared to what is introduced by the offshore oil industry. All of this contributes to the chronic low-lever discharge of oil into world oceans. The long-range cumulative effect of these discharges is possibly the most significant threat to the ecosystem.

1.4.3 Providing Visuals to Clarify and Condense Information

Visuals are indispensable partners of words in conveying information to your readers. On-the-job writing makes frequent use of tables, photographs, flow charts, diagrams, and drawings. Visuals are important at work. A photo can help customers better understand the instructions and properly use a product. A visual can significantly improve efficiency of a communicated message.

1.4.4 Giving Accurate Measurements

Much of your work involves measurements such as meters, calories, and degrees. This quantifiable information will make your message more substantial and convincing. For example, the discussion below is about mixing colored cement for wall construction; it is clear that without the included measurements, there would be confusion.

The topping mix should range in volume between 1 part Portland cement, 14/1 parts sand, and 14/1 parts gravel or crushed stone and 1 part Portland cement, 2 parts sand, and 2 parts gravel or crushed stone. Maximum size gravel or crushed stone should be 3/8 inch.

1.4.5 Stating Responsibilities Precisely

Writing in the workplace needs to be clear concerning what the writer could express or offer. Misunderstandings can waste time and cost your business money.

Other kinds of writings in the workplace concern responsibility. For instance, *"Tomorrow I will meet with the district sales manager to discuss (1) July's sales figures, (2) the necessity of redesigning our website, and (3) next fall's production schedule. I will e-mail a short report of our discussion by August 5, 2009."*

1.4.6 Persuading and Offering Recommendations

Writing in the business world is about persuading customers to buy a product or to agree with the plan promoted by your company. Not only will you have to attract new customers, you will also have to persuade previous ones to continue purchasing your company's product and/or service. You will have to convince readers that you (and your company) can save them time and money, increase efficiency, reduce risks, and improve their images.

Expect to be called upon to write convincingly about your company's image, as in the case of product recalls and discontinuations, customer complaints, or damage control after a corporate mistake.

To be persuasive you will need to get your readers' attentions so that they understand your message and believe what you say. Many persuasions support claims with evidence, thus research is needed. Logical arguments, examples, relevant information should be provided for your readers.

Writing for colleagues will require you to develop the skill of persuading. You will need to give recommendations to the employer by evaluating various plans through research and then promote the most appropriate one.

You can be also expected to write about problems that your company faces. For example, when a market has dropped and your employer wants to know what can be done to improve the company's situation or when a product your company relies on becomes too costly you must know how to communicate these issues clearly.

1.5   PROCESS FOR WRITINGS

This session provides practical tips about the writing process. It includes how to gather information, how to turn ideas into written form, and how to organize, revise, and edit this written form so that it is appropriate and clear to the readers.

1.5.1   Do Your Homework Before Researching

Research is an important part of the writing process and needed before any writing starts. Information collected must be correct and sufficient.

It is not wasting time to think twice before writing rather than beginning to write immediately. Actually, if you do not clearly understand your topic, it will take you much more time to edit with a rush start. Below are listed the recommended procedures.

First, make sure that the purpose of your message is what the reader expects. Then, clarify the details and do the research to collect relevant and useful information. Your research may include:

1) Interviewing people;
2) Doing laboratory studies;
3) Preparing some appropriate questions;
4) Contacting with colleagues;
5) Conducting a survey;
6) Literature review and evaluating those information;
7) Collecting feedbacks from sales, technical staff, or customers.

However, research is not limited to the beginning of the writing process, which can and should continue throughout the entire writing.

1.5.2   Making a Writing Plan

In this step, you need to transform all your ideas into written from. This step perhaps is the most challenging for beginning writers. But once it is done, it will make your ideas more concrete and your writing will be more fluent. Here are some tips for you:

1. Clustering

First, write down big-picture topic words that concern your writing. Second, write words that are related to these topic words, and connect those related words with its sources.

2. Brainstorm

Write down the topic words, and then list all the information you can think of about these words as quickly as possible. Here are some tips for brainstorming.

1)Don't stop to delete during this process.

2)Don't worry if your spelling or grammar is correct.

3)Restart this process after having a rest.

3. Outlining

This step may be easier for some writers. This will serve as an outline which will need to be revised many times. It is for your personal aid only so it does not matter if your outline is brief or messy.

1.5.3 Drafting

When you finish the procedures above, the next step is to draft your writing. In this step you will need to transform the outlines you have created as clustered maps into more organized phases. You will find some redundant information from the materials you have listed and this is where you can do much of your editing to ensure fluid outline.

When you start drafting, the following questions need to be answered:

1)Is the information too much or too little?

2)Is the relationship between connected words appropriate?

3)Is this point necessary or redundant?

4)Is there any contradiction?

5)Does the writing end appropriately?

During this answering process, more research may be needed and more ideas may come up.

1.5.4 Revising

Revision is the next stage during the writing process and may require more time for you to go through your writing several times. Do not skip this stage even if you think you have written your message carefully. This step determines the quality of your writing that will be sent to your readers.

1. Revise your writing with enough time

This step cannot be finished in rush need to plan enough time to do it thoroughly.

2. Revision is rethinking

During this stage, you will think through your message once again, largely repeating the process of your earlier work.

3. Questions when you revise

1) Content

· Is all the information included correct?

· Is there any missing or redundant information?

· Is the evidence persuading?

2) Organization

· Is the key point pointed out and explained clearly?

· Is the current order appropriate?

· Is there any useless information which should be removed?

· Is the related information been put in the same section?

3) Tone

· What tone or attitude do I need to express?

· What impression may the readers have after reading my message?

1.5.5 Editing

Editing is the last step for writing. During this step you should check the following items: sentences, vocabulary, grammars, clarity, and word spelling. Do not skip this step; accuracy and style expression will influence your readers significantly. If your message is hard to read or includes mistakes, your work could be questioned and you may lose credibility.

Here are the procedures for you to edit your message:

1. Guidelines for writing lean and clear sentences

The most frequent readers' complaints about poorly edited writing in the workplace are:

1) The sentences are too long. I could not follow the writer's meaning.

2) The sentences are too complex. I could not understand what the writer meant the first time I read the work; I had to reread it several times.

3) The sentences are unclear. Even after I reread them, I am not sure I understood the writer's message.

4) The sentences are too short and simplistic. The writing seemed immature.

Wordy, unclear sentences frustrate readers by forcing them to reread. However, if there are improper simplistic sentences, they also frustrate readers with the lack of sophistication. Writing appropriate sentences is not easy, and it takes not only time but genuine effort. The investment will be worth it as it has the potential to save your readers time and deliver your information more persuasively. The suggested procedure below would help your editing phase:

1) Do not use long sentences: Divide one long sentence into several short but

readable sentences.

2) Do not use choppy sentences: Both simplistic and choppy sentences can make your message immature.

3) Edit sentences into subject-verb-object (s-v-o) pattern.

4) Use verbs rather than verb phrases: Verb phrases may make you sound bureaucratic.

5) Do not put too many modifiers before nouns.

2. Suggestions for removing unnecessary words

People may think the more words, the better. However your readers are busy and unnecessary words would waste their time. Simplify your expression as much as possible while making sure that your ideas are still clear and readable. For example, the phases on the left in the following table could be replaced with the words on the right.

Wordy	Concisely Edited
Look something like	Resemble
Show a tendency to	Tend
With reference to	Regarding; About
With the result that	So
End result	Result
Final conclusions/Final outcome	Conclusions/Outcome
First and foremost	First
Full and complete	Full; Complete
Over and done with	Over
Tired and true	Tired; Proven

Another kind of wordiness comes from using redundant expressions; saying the same thing a second time in different words. For example, "fellow colleague", "component parts", "corrosive acid" and "free gift". Thus, be careful of repeating expression within one sentence.

An example of unedited e-mail with redundant expressions and the final version after careful editing is presented below. The writer removed wordy expressions and cut out duplication making this e-mail more readable and clear.

A wordy and unedited email

Due to the Inescapable reliance on technology, specifically on Emall and Internet communication, with in our company, I believe it would be beneficial to look into the possibility of issuing smartphones, such as BlackBerry, Apple iPhone, Nokia E62, or Palm Treo, to our employees. Issuing smartphones would have a variety of positive implications for efficiency of our company. Unlike normal cell phones, these smartphones have many new features that will help our employees in their daily work. Since they combine cellular phone technologies with e-mail and document transfer capabilities, as well as many other important features. The employees could increase their efficiency due to the fact that they could constantly keep track of appointments on their schedule for each day. The employees would also benefit from smartphones by having access to their contacts even when they are out on the road traveling, whether they are at local office meetings or on cross-country business trips. By means of smartphones I feel quite certain that our company's correspondence would be deal with much more speedily. Since these devices will allow our employees to access their e-mail at all times, I think it would be absolutely essential for the satisfaction of our customers and to the ongoing operation of our company's business today to respond fully and completely to the possibility such a proposal afford us. It would therefore appear safe conclude that with reference to the issue of smartphones that every means at our disposal would be brought to bear on issuing such smartphones to our employees.

The email edited for conciseness

Because our sales force spends so much time out of the office, I think we should issue smartphones, such as BlackBerry and Apple iPhone, to increase productivity and efficiency. Combining laptop and cell phone technologies, smartphones will allow employees to e-mail clients about appointments, to access accounts, and to transfer documents anywhere, thus increasing customer satisfaction.

I think switching to smartphones is both a necessary and cost-effective investment. With your approval, I will obtain more information from vendors to prepare a proposal to request bids.

1.6 ETHICAL AND LEGAL ISSUES FOR ENGINEERING WRITINGS

1.6.1 Plagiarism

Plagiarism is when an individual takes another person's work and claims it as his/her own original work whether it is in thought, language, ideas, or expressions from websites, books, articles, television programs, or other medium. It is illegal to use another person'ss work without properly indicating the source of the information. Just listing the sources at the end of your work is not enough, even improper citation, quotation or acknowledgment of others' words or ideas within an internal citation is considered plagiarism. It is especially important for students when writing research papers that plagiarism can occur frequently due to incorrect citation or forgetting to cite the reference. The following are common forms of plagiarism:

1) Submitting others' works as your own.

2) Directly or indirectly presenting others' ideas as your own.

3) Rewriting others' work without properly citing sources.

4) Copying or pasting text and images without indicating the source.

5) Taking passage from your own previous work without citing.

6) Interweaving various sources together in one work without citing.

7) Using quotation but not citing the source.

8) Summarizing information without citing the source.

9) Inaccurately citing the source.

Plagiarism can be both intentional and inadvertent. Intentional plagiarism means the purposeful use of others' words or ideas as your own, while inadvertent plagiarism means improper but accidental use of others' ideas or words without identifying the source or citing incorrectly. The former one is generally considered worse due to the consciousness of the decision.

1.6.1.1 *Types of Plagiarism*

It is important for students to identify the different types of plagiarism because students most frequently plagiarize due to ignorance or carelessness rather than intent. The following are the different types of plagiarisms:

1. Complete plagiarism

Submitting an essay or report that has been written by other people. This is the most severe form of plagiarism.

2. Direct plagiarism

Copying the exact words from someone else's writing without using quotation marks or without indicating the source.

3. Paraphrased plagiarism

Changing a few words or phrases of someone else's writing without acknowledging the source.

4. Mosaic plagiarism

Borrowing ideas, phrases, and paragraphs from various sources and joining them together without indicating their sources.

5. Self-plagiarism

Self-plagiarism is when an author uses his or her previous work in a new one without referencing the earlier one, either entirely or partially.

1.6.1.2 *Consequences of Plagiarism*

Plagiarism is considered a serious academic dishonesty. People who plagiarize may face serious consequences. Many universities ask students to sign declaration to promise not to plagiarize and use plagiarism check software to check students' writing assignments.

If a student is found guilty of plagiarism, some severe consequences may follow. For example,

1) Get expelled from the course;

2) Result in your work being destroyed, such as a dissertation or thesis;

3) Result in expulsion from your academic institution;

4) Result in legal action;

5) Destroy your professional or academic reputation.

1.6.1.3 *How to Avoid Plagiarism*

When using sources in your papers, you can avoid plagiarism by providing a reference to the source in order to indicate where the original information came from.

1. Paraphrasing

When you find some useful information that you would want to include in your own paper, you must be sure that you understand the original information and then restate the information in your own words. This is called paraphrasing. It is important to retain the original ideas of the material you paraphrased and to cite the original sources correctly. Only changing a few words or revising the structure or phrases in a sentence is not considered good paraphrasing.

2. Summarizing

A summary is like an overview of another's work, which contains only key points without unimportant details or examples. Remember, the original sources should be cited.

You can follow the below steps for summarizing:

1) Read the original materials thoroughly and completely understand the information;

2) Write brief summaries for each paragraph as an outline;

3) Identify the key points;

4) Write a draft of summary including all key points in your own words;

5) Review and revise your summary; and

6) Include correct citations to indicate the sources.

1.6.2 Proper citation and quotation

1.6.2.1 *Citation*

As discussed in the previous section of the book, when you want to use another author's work in your own paper, you need to cite the original work no matter if it is a quote, an idea or the fact. Below shows some items need citations.

1) Sentences or sections copied directly from a text; cite with quotation marks.

2) Paraphrased text that is not common knowledge.

3) Data, numbers, and facts that have been published.

4) Theories, methods, and ideas.

5) Images, graphs, and illustrations.

1.6.2.2　*Quotation*

Generally, there are three types of quotations. Below are some examples for each of the three types.

1. In-Text Quotations

The author's last name and the year of publication of the source should appear in the text and a complete reference should appear in the reference list.

Coleman (2013) *compared reaction times*

In a recent study of reaction times (*Coleman*, 2013)

2. Short Quotations

Quotations that include less than 40 words are considered short quotations and double quotation marks should be used to indicate them. If punctuation is a part of the quotation, including question and exclamation marks, it needs to be included within the quotation marks. A complete reference is also required in the reference list.

She stated, "The placebo effect disappeared when behaviors were studied in this manner" (*Miele*, 1993, *p.* 276), *but she did not clarify which behaviors were studied.*

According to Miele (1993), *"The placebo effect disappeared when behaviors were studied in this manner"* (*p.* 276).

Miele (1993) *found that "the placebo effect disappeared" in this case* (*p.* 276), *but what will the next step in researching this issue be?*

3. Long Quotations

Quotations longer than 40 words should be stated in a separate paragraph but the quotation marks can be omitted. The parenthetical citation should come after closing punctuation mark. A complete reference is required in the reference list.

Miele's 1993 study found the following: The placebo effect disappeared when behaviors were studied in this manner. Furthermore, the behaviors were never exhibited again, even when real drugs were administered. Earlier studies conducted by the same group of researchers at the hospital were clearly premature in attributing the results to a placebo effect. (*p.* 276)

There are some things like common knowledge, historical dates, well-known arguments or theories, and universal proverbs that do not need to be cited. Descriptions of the citation and reference styles are detailed in next section.

1.6.3   References

Referencing in the writing process consists of the act of referring to your sources of information. As a writer, you refer to books, articles, and various materials while writing. As a matter of fact, you would include some references in the pages of your thesis in the form of footnotes. The footnotes contain the reference passages taken from the relevant books and journals from which you quote them. At the end of each chapter you would give the corresponding books and journals from which you have picked the quotations mentioned in the footnotes, which is what is referred to as "References" or "Works Cited".

Your reference list should include all the works (books, articles, internet sites, etc.) you have quoted, paraphrased or otherwise used to create your paper. Usually references are included at the end of every chapter of a thesis or towards the end of the thesis. The purpose of a reference list is to let readers of the thesis know the various books from which you have quoted, so that readers should be able to gather this information from the list at the end of your thesis or footnotes.

How works are internally cited and the specification of how the citations are arranged in the "Works Cited" page will be determined by where your work is submitted. The forms of citations and references subscribe to one of the generally accepted styles, such as the Chicago, Oxford, Harvard, Modern Language Association (MLA), American Sociological Association (ASA), American Psychological Association (APA), because their syntactic conventions are widely known and easily interpreted by readers. Each of these styles has its advantages and disadvantages. Editors often specify which style to use. The APA, MLA and the Chicago Manual of Style are three commonly used reference styles. Detailed descriptions of the three styles can be easily found online.

1.6.4   Annotated Bibliographies

1.6.4.1   *Annotated Bibliographies*

An annotated bibliography is a list of annotations. It provides a way to help readers assess whether the annotated works would be useful. Students often misunderstand an annotated bibliography and believe it is a collection of copy-pasted abstracts or conclusions of the work. The two mains reasons why people prepare annotative bibliographies are for personal use or publication. The annotated bibliographies prepared for personal use are less formal and may range from notes written on the book to a spreadsheet with different fields (e. g. , author, key points, and comments). The point is to track material so that you may use it in the future. Material from an informal annotated bibliography is very useful for preparing annotated bibliographies for publication. Below is a sample of a formal annotated bibliography. Students can find and read the full article based on the below reference.

Example

  This article presents an application of geostastistics as an improvement over the use of univariate statistics in quantifying and characterizing spatial non-uniformity of compacted layers using roller-integrated compaction monitoring data. Two case studies are described in this paper. One case study describes how geostatistical semivariogram can be used to detect non-stationarity in the data and separate the sections for analysis and acceptance. Another case study describes how geostatistical semivariogram analysis can guide a roller operator to identify localized poorly compacted areas and prioritize areas of rework to improve uniformity. This approach represents a paradigm shift for future implementation of earthwork compaction and quality control specifications. However, this approach would require automating the process and training field engineers and roller operators. The authors documented analytical/numerical pavement performance models, and a key element of their ongoing research is to link the semivariogram parameters with the performance models to provide new insights into the effect of uniformity on long-term pavement performance.

  Keywords: geostatistics, semivariogram, soil compaction, quality control, earthwork, intelligent compaction.

  Source: Vennapusa, P., White, D. J., and Morris, M. (2010). "Geostatistical analysis of spatial referenced roller-integrated compaction measurements." J. Geotech. Geoenv. Engrg., ASCE 136(6), 813-822.

1.6.4.2   *General Characteristics of an Annotation*

The general characteristics of an annotation are:

1) Very concise (150-200 words);

2) Summarizing special or unique features of the work;

3) The central idea(s) and/or evaluate a conclusions;

4) Discussing how the work is or is not consistent with other work;

5) Comparing the work with your conclusions or observations;

6) Generally including these key elements:

  · a complete citation using certain citation styles;

  · a summary of the work's purposes, conclusions, and/or observations;

· an analysis of the work's limitations;

· a description of the relevance or applicability of the work to your research topic.

1.7 EXERCISES

1. Paraphrase the below paragraph.

Students frequently overuse direct quotations in taking notes, and as a result they overuse quotations in the final [research] paper. Only about 10% of your final manuscript should appear as directly quoted matter. Therefore, you should strive to limit the amount of exact transcribing of source materials while taking notes. Lester, James D. Writing Research Papers. 2nd ed. (1976): 46-47.

2. Find examples of APA reference style and MLA reference style.

3. List out the differences between the APA and MLA reference styles for citing a journal article.

1.8 BIBLIOGRAPHY

1. MERGES R, MENELL P, LEMLEY M. Intellectual Property in the New Technological Age [M]. 4th ed. New York: Wolters Kluwer, 2007.

2. YOUNGER J. Citation Formats for Bibliographies and Notes [OL]. [2018-05-04]. http://www. people. ku. edu/ ~ jyounger/fn + bibformats. html.

3. VENNAPUSA P, WHITE D J, MORRIS M. Geostatistical analysis of spatial referenced roller-integrated compaction measurements[J]. J. Geotech. Geoenv. Engrg. , 2010, 136(6): 813-822.

4. University of Leicester, Referencing and bibliographies [OL]. [2018-05-04]. https://www2. le. ac. uk/offices/ld/resources/writing/writing-resources/ref-bib.

5. Academic Referencing[OL]. [2018-05-04]. http://www. skillsyouneed. com/learn/academic-referencing. html#ixzz4UghoUdA8.

CHAPTER 2. HOW TO CHOOSE WORDS AND WRITE SENTENCES AND PARAGRAPHS

If you received a writing assignment you probably will do some research for that topic, get some facts for the content, and perhaps draw a picture demonstrating what the article will look like, even more draft an outline for the article. However, for most nonnative English speakers, which most international students are, very often they will still be frustrated when starting the first line, the first sentence and the first paragraph.

We often hear that: "I know the meaning in my own native language, but I can not find a proper word in English to describe it", "I did spell these words correctly. Why does the computer still mark it in red?" or "Did I express myself clearly and concisely? Can it be understood correctly?" and even more, "Should I put these topics in the same paragraph? What sequences should I write about these topics?" All of these questions are very common for international students when they start to learn how to write in English, especially for those major in civil engineering fields.

This chapter will give you some basic instructions on how to choose words, check spelling, use punctuation marks correctly, and how to formulate a sentence and construct a paragraph.

2.1 CHOOSING WORDS PROPERLY

2.1.1 How Many Words You Need to Know

Students often ask how many words they need to know in order to write well, and some experts have said that only 2,000 words are sufficient. For international students of civil engineering, no more than 3,000 to 5,000 words are needed. Of course, some may not agree with this estimate and some may think it is impossible. For a nonnative speaker, if you know more than 3,000 English words, you will not have any problems living or working in an English-speaking society. That is to say, the number of words you need to know for writing well in English is far less than you think. It is also not as difficult as you would think; the strange words you have memorized from dictionaries will probably never be used.

For example, in the works of Shakespeare, one of the most wonderful wordsmiths the world has known, there are an enormous number of 15,000 different words used in his writings however almost 10,000 of them are obsolete or meaningless today.

In today's latest edition of large dictionaries, there are about 200,000 words included. The most commonly used English dictionary in China, A New English-Chinese Dictionary, has about 100,000 entries included. Webster's New World Dictionary has about 60,000 entries and even a Concise English-Chinese/Chinese-English Dictionary has more than 20,000 entries. That is to say a large vocabulary found in a dictionary will probably never be used in your lifetime. As a student of civil engineerings you will focus your learning on the specific vocabularies related to different engineering fields.

2.1.2   Parts of Speech

All the words in the English language are divided into nine classes – parts of speech. They are the Article, Noun, Adjective, Pronoun, Verb, Adverb, Preposition, Conjunction and Interjection.

The noun is the most important among them, as all the others are more or less dependent upon it. A noun signifies the name of any person, place, or thing, and in fact anything which we can have either thought or idea. For example, *Chang' an University*, *Xi' an*, and the personal name *Linda* are all nouns.

An article is a word placed before a noun to show whether the latter is used in a the particular or general sense. There are but two articles, *a* or *an* and *the*.

An adjective is a word which qualifies a noun; it shows some distinguishing marks or characteristics belonging to the noun. For example, Linda is a *beautiful* girl from China. Golden Gate bridge is a *unique* landmark for San Francisco.

A pronoun is a word used instead of a noun to keep us from repeating the same noun too often. For example, Mr. Li has borrowed my car and *he* drove it to take *his* family to Beijing last month. I copied that book which *he* has asked *me* to do.

A verb is a word which implies action or the doing of something. It may be defined as a word which affirms, commands, or asks a question. For example, Dr. Chen *speaks* very good English and Chinese. Mary *travelled* across China last summer.

An adverb is a word that modifies a verb, an adjective, or another adverb. In the example—"Tom writes *well*," the adverb shows the manner in which the writing is performed; in the examples—"Mary is *remarkably* diligent" and "James works *very* faithfully," the adverbs modify the adjective "diligent" and the other adverb "faithfully" by expressing the degree of diligence and faithfulness.

A preposition serves to connect words and to show the relation between the objects that the words express. A preposition connects words, clauses, and sentences together and shows the relation between them. "John puts his book *on* the desk" shows the relation between book and desk.

A conjunction joins words, clauses, and sentences; as "Linda *and* Mary," "My sister *and* brother have come, *but* I have not seen them yet." The conjunctions in most general use are: *and*, *also*; *either*, *or*; *neither*, *nor*; *though*, *yet*; *but*, *however*; *for*, *that*; *because*, *since*; *therefore*, *wherefore*, *then*; *if*, *unless*.

An interjection is a word that expresses surprise or some sudden emotions of the mind. In the examples —"*Ah*! There he comes". "*Alas*! What shall I do?" *Ah*, expresses surprise, and *alas*, expresses distress.

2.1.3 Mastering the Fundamentals of Grammar

In order to write correctly, we need to understand the fundamental principles of grammar. If we do not know the underlying principles of correct formation of sentences and the relation of words to one another, we will misunderstand the meaning of what is said. If we do not understand the grammar of the language, we may be making disgraceful blunders while writing.

As nonnative English speaker, most international students may have studied English in high school and some may have started since elementary school. During the first year of college in China, students of civil engineering will take 6 hours of English classes and 2 hours of oral English taught by a native English-speaking teacher. Students should have studied fundamental principles of the English grammar prior to an oral speaking class. Therefore, in this book, we are not going to repeat that content but rather just summarize the basics as reference.

INDICATIVE MOOD		
Present Tense		
	Sing.	Plural
1st person	I ask	We ask
2nd person	You ask	You ask
3rd person	He asks	They ask
Past Tense		
	Singular	Plural
1st person	I asked	We asked
2nd person	You asked	You asked
3rd person	He asked	They asked

Future Tense

	Sing.	Plural
1st person	I shall ask	We shall ask
2nd person	You will ask	You will ask
3rd person	He will ask	They will ask

Present Perfect Tense

	Sing.	Plural
1st person	I have asked	We have asked
2nd person	You have asked	You have asked
3rd person	He has asked	They have asked

Past Perfect Tense

	Sing.	Plural
1st person	I had asked	We had asked
2nd person	You had asked	You had asked
3rd person	He had asked	They had asked

Future Perfect Tense

	Sing.	Plural
1st person	I shall have asked	We shall have asked
2nd person	You will have asked	You will have asked
3rd person	He will have asked	They will have asked

SUBJUNCTIVE MOOD

Present Tense

	Sing.	Plural
1st person	If I ask	If we ask
2nd person	If you ask	If you ask
3rd person	If he asks	If they ask

Past Tense

	Sing.	Plural
1st person	If I asked	If we asked
2nd person	If you asked	If you asked
3rd person	If he asked	If they asked

Present Perfect Tense

	Sing.	Plural
1st person	If I have asked	If we have asked
2nd person	If you have asked	If you have asked
3rd person	If he has asked	If they have asked

Past Perfect Tense

	Sing.	Plural
1st person	If I had asked.	If we had asked
2nd person	If you had asked.	If you had asked
3rd person	If he had asked.	If they had asked

CONJUGATION OF PASSIVE VOICE
AND INDICATIVE MOOD

Present Tense

	Sing.	Plural
1st person	I am asked	We are asked
2nd person	You are asked	You are asked
3rd person	He is asked	They are asked

Past Tense

	Sing.	Plural
1st person	I was asked	We were asked
2nd person	You were asked	You were asked
3rd person	He was asked	They were asked

Future Tense

	Sing.	Plural
1st person	I shall be asked	We shall be asked
2nd person	You will be asked	You will be asked
3rd person	He will be asked	They will be asked

Present Perfect Tense

	Sing.	Plural
1st person	I have been asked	We have been asked
2nd person	You have been asked	You have been asked
3rd person	He has been asked	They have been asked

Past Perfect Tense

	Sing.	Plural
1st person	I had been asked	We had been asked
2nd person	You had been asked	You had been asked
3rd person	He had been asked	They had been asked

Future Perfect Tense

	Sing.	Plural
1st person	I shall have been asked	We shall have been asked
2nd person	You will have been asked	You will have been asked
3rd person	He will have been asked	They will have been asked

SUBJUNCTIVE MOOD

Present Tense

	Sing.	Plural
1st person	If I be asked	If we be asked
2nd person	If you be asked	If you be asked
3rd person	If he be asked	If they be asked

Past Tense		
	Sing.	Plural
1st person	If I were asked	If we were asked
2nd person	If you were asked	If you were asked
3rd person	If he were asked	If they were asked
Present Perfect Tense		
	Sing.	Plural
1st person	If I have been asked	If we have been asked
2nd person	If you have been asked	If you have been asked
3rd person	If he has been asked	If they have been asked
Past Perfect Tense		
	Sing.	Plural
1st person	If I had been asked	If we had been asked
2nd person	If you had been asked	If you had been asked
3rd person	If he had been asked	If they had been asked

2.1.4 Checking the Meanings and the Usages of Words

No matter what you are writing, if you are not sure about the meanings and the usages of your chosen words, even the commonly used words, it is better to put in the effort to make sure you understand them correctly before using them.

The best way to check the meanings and the usages of words is to look them up individually using dictionaries. A good dictionary will not only give the meaning of a particular word but also list the word group and phrases it belongs to, and examples are also provided for their uses. For Chinese students and scholars, *the New English-Chinese Dictionary* has been the most commonly used English-Chinese dictionary for several decades and is still popular on almost every college campus. This dictionary includes more than 80,000 words entries and provides definitions in Chinese.

Using your native language to explain the meanings of English words may not be enough especially when faced words with similar meanings like, "infer" vs. "imply", "assure" vs. "ensure", "simulate" vs. "imitate", "intelligent" vs.

"brilliant", "research" vs. "investigate", "response" vs. "reaction", "convince" vs. "persuade", and so on. These words may have similar meanings but there are differences you must be aware of when you use them and sometime these differences are subtle.

Imply means to suggest by inference or association, while *infer* means to reach a conclusion from facts or circumstances. *Assure* should be used only in reference to person, e. g. , "I assure you I am telling the truth." *Ensure* means to make certain or guard against loss, e. g. , " It will ensure better safety." *Convince* means to lead someone to believe or understand, e. g. , "I am convinced that we have made a wrong assumption." *Persuade* means to win someone over, e. g. , "John has been trying to persuade me to accept his idea."

So, when you come across these similar words and are not sure of the meanings or usages of them, take the time to look it up in the English-English dictionary. *Funk & Wagnalls Standard Dictionary* or *Webster's New World Dictionary* may prove useful for you.

The following list consists of frequently misused words by international students, so be sure to use the right word with the right meaning in the right context.

Accept (v.) to receive, to acknowledge: Our company has accepted your application.

Except (prep.) excluding, but: The entire class attended the meeting except you.

Advice (n.) a recommendation: Dr. Chen has given me some good advice about this proposal.

Advise (v.) to counsel: Our Lawyers advised us not to sign this agreement.

Affect (v.) to change, to influence: This decision will affect our plan for the whole semester.

Effect (n.) result or (v.) to bring about: What was the effect of this new policy?

Attain (v.) to achieve, to reach: The expected results have been attained from these experiments.

Obtain (v.) to get, to receive: The students can obtain the application form by requesting on line.

Complement (v.) to add to, enhance: Mr. Li's presentation complemented his report of the action plan.

Compliment (v.) to praise: The teacher complimented John's report.

Continually (adv.) frequently and regularly: My car makes strange noise continually during the summer.

Continuously (adv.) constantly: Those two boys have been talking continuously during the entire class.

Discreet (adj.) showing respect, being tactful: The speaker was very discreet in answering those questions.

Discrete (adj.) separate, distinct: These two discrete figures are not related to the result directly.

Eminent (adj.) prominent, highly esteemed: Dr. Yang is the most eminent professor in our university.

Imminent (adj.) about to happen: It seems that different opinions about this proposal are imminent.

Foreword (n.) preface, introduction to book: The foreword of this book gives a summary of the scientist's findings.

Forward (adj.) toward a time or place; in advance: We have to move forward in spite of many difficulties ahead.

Forward (v.) to send ahead: I have forwarded your email to Dr. Chen.

Lay/laid/laid (v.) to put down: He has laid aside that task for almost two months.

Lie/lay/lain (v.) to recline: I have to lay down for a while before I start my afternoon work.

Lose (v.) to misplace, to fail to win: Don't lose your mobile phone when you get on the bus.

Loose (adj.) not tight: The safety belt in my car is too loose to be used.

Personal (adj.) private: Dr. Wang did not attend the meeting for personal reason.

Personnel (n.) staff of employee: All personnel must participate the meeting on Tuesday.

Perspective (n.) view: From the author's perspective, these topics are not important in this book.

Prospective (adj.) expected, likely to happen or become: This prospective report will be evaluated during our next meeting.

Precede (v.) to go before: An opening remark will precede the presentation.

Proceed (v.) to carry on, to go ahead: We will proceed no matter how difficult the situation is.

Principal (adj.) main, chief: Writing skills for international students of civil engineering are the principal topics for this book.

Principal (n.) the head of a school: He was a high school principal before he started his own training center.

Principal (n.) money owed: He has paid off the principal and the interest for his loan that he has borrowed from the bank.

Principle (n.) a policy, a belief: We have to follow the principles when dealing with these problems.

Serial (adj.) arranged in sequence: You have to give the serial numbers when you file a complaint for your computer.

Serials (n.) journals/magazines published at regular intervals: Certain numbers of articles are required to be published in serials.

Stationary (adj.) not moving: Tom usually rides a stationary bike for his workout.

Stationery (n.) writing supplies, such as paper and envelops: There are several stationery stores nearby our school.

Waiver (n.) international relinquishment of a right, claim, or privilege: I received a waiver from the government, so I can work when I studied overseas.

Waver (v.) to shake, to move: At this time, we will not waver in our commitment to safety.

If we are careless or ignorant of the various meanings or usages of words, our writings could lead to confusing communication, and even more cause discriminatory issues in cross-cultural environment. These issues are often not thought of by international students when they write. For example, when you refer to women as adults it should be worded as such, "the men and women" not "the men and girls"; "the guests and spouses" not "the guests and wives"; "Mr. Li and Ms. Sparks" not "Mr. Li and Laura"; "his or her, or their" not just "his."

In the areas of handicap bias, and racial or ethnic discrimination, the following vocabulary is recommended:

Use "speech and hearing impaired" not "deaf and dumb"; use "the guest of honor" not "the blind guest"; use "the African-American" not "the black American"; use "the Mexican-American" not "the nonwhite people", etc.

Under most international circumstances, especially in a cross-cultural environment, equal treatment and equal opportunity are strongly enforced. Carelessness and ignorance of choosing words for speech and writing may lead to misunderstanding and mistrust, cause ethical or legal disputes, and cause economic loss or political problems.

As an international student of civil engineering, you may either work for an international company in your own country or work on a construction project in a foreign country and if you are invited to deliver a speech or assigned to write a letter or report, it is your duty to check the meanings and usages of your words carefully to avoid errors and abuse. A good suggestion given by an experienced writer is to choose simple words to communicate a clear message rather than big, pretentious ones to impress.

2.1.5　Choosing the Simple Words

The purpose in writing is to communicate with someone. Either you want to inform, to persuade, to request something or to obtain information, the secret behind successful writing is to make your readers' life easier. Effective written communication is to help your readers understand your message in as few words as possible. Be short, clear, and concise! It all starts from choosing the simple words.

Many nonnative students and scholars like to choose some awkward and uncommon words for their writing. This is not to criticize scientists and researchers using their technical terminology when publishing their professional studies. On the other hand, it does not imply that professionals like lawyers should write in simple languages for their lawsuits. Here we are just talking about our English writing classes for international students.

From high schools to colleges there are unfortunately tendencies to teach students to memorize enormous vocabularies, some of which may not be used even in their lifetime. Some terms perhaps are used only for show-offs to a degree, believing it reflects greater intellect and higher professional status.

In today's social and business world, brief, clear and concise passages are strongly encouraged for writing. Many well-known speakers and writers are appreciated because their speeches and writings are simple and easy to understand. Effectiveness comes from understanding; if you want to communicate effectively, simplicity is the key.

It sounds so easy-simple, yet your message must also be clear and concise, what a dilemma! Let's see some examples below.

· Original: After giving due consideration to each design, we have made a choice.

Preferred: After considering each design, we have made a choice.

· Original: The project will be carried out as per your suggestions.

Preferred: The project will be carried out according to your suggestions.

· Original: Please return the attached file at your convenience after reviewing it.

Preferred: Please return the attached file by Tuesday, February 6, 2018 after reviewing it.

· Original: Your complaint about our products has been duly forwarded to our service group.

Preferred: We have sent you complaint about our products to our service group.

　・Original：Enclosed please find our latest catalog.

Preferred：Enclosed is our latest catalog.

　・Original：I am enclosing my resume for your consideration.

Preferred：I am enclosing my resume.

　・Original：Please be advised that the deadline is Thursday, February 15, 2018.

Preferred：The deadline is Thursday, February 15, 2018.

　・Original：This letter is for the purpose of inviting your suggestions.

Preferred：Please send me your suggestions.

　・Original：We regret to inform you that your order is unavailable.

Preferred：We are sorry that your order is unavailable.

Now you have some ideas of what is simple, clear, and concise. Usually letters, memos, faxes, emails are short messages of one or two pages so using simple words are essential. You may find it difficult to write economically, but that should not discourage you. What you need to do after you finish your writing is to read it and then rewrite. Remember your purpose for writing is to communicate a clear message so make it easier for your readers to understand.

The followings are some preferred words for your writing.

Preferred	**Not Preferred**
Much	A great deal of
Most	A majority of
About	A number of
Like	Along the line of
About	As to
Later	At a later date
When	At a time when
Because	Due to the fact that
If possible	If at all possible
During	In the course of
In the event that	If
Clearly	It is clear that

Preferred	**Not Preferred**
January	Month of January
Occasionally	On a few occasion
Friend	Personal friend
Before	Prior to
Except	With the exception of
End	Terminate
Meet with	Interface with
Hurry	Expedite
Begin	Initiate
Total	Aggregation
Use	Utilize
Try	Endeavor
Genuine	Bona fide
Praise	Commendation
Slowly	At a slow rate
Now	At this point in time
Agree	Be in agreement with
Conclude	Bring to a conclusion
Because	Due to the fact that
Affirm	Express an opinion that
For	For the period of
So that	In such a manner that
Tend	Show a tendency to
Regarding	With reference to
So	With the result that

Of course, the list could be longer. For students just beginning to learn to write should focus on, "simple, clear and concise" phrasing.

2.2　SPELLING WORDS CORRECTLY

Needless to say, spelling words correctly is the basic requirement for dealing with any writing materials of either native or nonnative speakers. A misspelled word or a typing error is disturbing in any written works, whether an employment application, letter, or report. Spelling errors will not only look careless and uneducated to a client or a supervisor but will also discredit the quality of your work and your capability. These mistakes can ultimately decrease the credibility of your organization.

I still remember today that when I studied for my MBA in the 1990s, my professor told the whole class that he would mark any writing assignments with misspellings and errors with a "C" right away no matter how good the content was. I have benefited from this strict teaching method in my career even today.

A widely spread story about Henry Kissinger tells the importance of careful writing. Once Kissinger asked his staff to write a report and a few days later one of his staff came to turn in his report. Kissinger asked, "Is this the best work you can do?" The staff answered, "If I have few more days, I could do it much better. " Kissinger asked his staff to go back and rewrite it. And again, after few days, Kissinger asked the same question when the staff came to turn in the report, the staff again said he could do it better if he had more time. In the end, when the staff finally turned this report to Kissinger and said, "This is the best work I can do. " Then Kissinger said, "Now I will read it. "

This story demonstrates that even for high-profile politicians, carefulness and correctness of writing are the top priority for daily work. So as a student, spelling correctly is a basic standard when we are studying how to write.

Many international students treat spelling mistakes as a small matter and often overlook them. Much of this comes from the wide use of computers and other electronic devices to help with assignments. Students have become heavily dependent on spell checkers of the word processing program and are not aware of that spell checkers can only recognize certain misspelled words and actually make mistakes. An uncommon name or infrequently used word may be flagged as an error though it is spelled correctly. Moreover, it will not differentiate between homonyms as "too" and "two" or "there" and "their". For example, if you spell "four" as "for," spell checkers will not notice it. So, do not rely exclusively on computer spell checkers to take care of your spelling mistakes.

Consulting a dictionary for your spelling is always a good choice. As we mentioned above, a good dictionary like *Merriam-Webster Dictionary*, or *a New English-Chinese Dictionary* could be very handy for any spelling and word-choice problems.

2.3 USING PUNCTUATION, ABBREVIATIONS, AND NUMBERS ADEQUATELY

Punctuation marks are used in the writing system to clarify the structure and meaning of sentences. To some degree, using punctuation is associated with certain grammatical elements in a sentence. In some cases, to punctuate the same sentence differently may cause a different interpretation of the text. In other cases, with equal correctness and clarity, different writers may use punctuation marks differently.

Abbreviations are commonly used for business and technical writings such as, "etc. , i. e. , e. g. , No. ". They are used to save space, avoid repetition of words and phrases, and reduce keystrokes for writers. Many abbreviations are adapted, especially for technical literature of civil engineering.

Usage of numbers varies considerably in writing. In most formal writings, the numbers are likely spelled out, and in scientific and technical contexts numbers are likely to be expressed as figures.

2.3.1 Punctuation

1. Ampersand

An ampersand is typically written "&", and it represents the word "and"; its function is to replace the word when a shorter form is desirable.

Such as, *AT&T, R&D, Wang & Li.*

2. Apostrophe

1) Apostrophe is used to indicate the possessive case of nouns and indefinite pronouns, such as: *children's clothing, consumers' confidence, someone's book.*

2) Apostrophes are used to mark omissions in contractions of two or more words that are pronounced as one, such as: *didn't, o'clock, you're, get 'em while you can.*

3) Apostrophes mark the omissions of numerals, such as: *class of '85, news in the '90s.*

3. Colon

1) A colon introduces a clause or a phrase that explains, illustrates, amplifies, or restates what has gone before, e. g. , *The sentence was poorly constructed: it lacked both unity and coherence. Time is running out: a decision has to be made.*

2) A colon directs attention to an appositive, e. g. , *The question is: how can we get the money? He has only one pleasure: playing.*

3)A colon is used to introduce a series, e. g. , *UN security council consists of five nations: U. S, Russia, Britain, France and China.*

4)In transcriptions of dialogue, a colon follows the speaker's name.

John: Have you had lunch?

Laura: No, I have not.

5)A colon follows a brief heading or an introductory term.

NOTE: The library will be closed on 7th due to repairing.

6)A colon separates elements in biblical citations, which in fixed formulas used to express ration and time such as, *4:10, 8:30 pm, a ratio of 3:7.*

7)A colon separates titles and subtitles such as, *The Great Depression: A History Being Forgotten.*

8)A colon follows the salutation in formal correspondence such as, *Dear General Washington:, Dear Mr. Xi:, Ladies and Gentlemen:.*

9)A colon punctuates memo and subject lines in business letters.

To:

Subject:

Date:

Reference:

4. Comma

The comma is the most frequently used punctuation mark in English writing.

1)A comma separates main clauses joined by conjunction (as and, but, or, nor, so, yet and for).

· *She has contributed to this task greatly, and she did not boast about it.*

· *We knew very little about this topic, so we cannot give you any advice.*

· *We have requested this product many times before, yet have not gotten any reply.*

· *He looks very sad, for he knows he has failed this test.*

2)If a sentence is composed of three or more clauses, the clauses may be separated by commas.

· *The market seems to have changed quickly, the economy is uncertain, the technology seems to have impacted every aspects of the industry.*

3)Adverbial clauses and phrases that precede a main clause are usually set off with commas.

· *To understand the situation, you must be familiar with the background.*

· *In 2016, he left home and came to Xi'an to study civil engineering.*

· *Having made that decision, he turned his attention to other matters.*

4)Commas are used to set off an adverbial clause or phrase that fall between the subject and the verb.

· *The transportation, from cars to buses, is arranged for all the guests.*

5) Commas are used to set off a word, a phrase, or a clause that is in apposition to a noun and that is nonrestrictive.

· *My English teacher, Ms. Laura, is also teaching music in our school.*

· *George Washington, the first president of the U. S, is admired by many people around the world.*

· *We were most impressed by the last speaker, the one who gave many examples and showed her art works during her presentation.*

6) Commas set off transitional words and phrases (as finally, meanwhile, indeed, on the other hand, and after all).

· *Indeed, these two books are very similar.*

· *We are eager to start the project right away; however, the raw materials have not yet arrived.*

· *Finally, we finished all exams for this semester.*

7) Commas are used to set off words or phrases that introduce examples or explanations.

· *This experiment proves at least three factors, namely, pressure, temperature, and volume are crucial to the outcomes.*

· *We have to stress that the balance of the entire structure of this bridge, which is used to judge the quality of designs, needs to be considered seriously.*

8) A comma is used to set off contrasting expressions, within a sentence.

· *This project needs to be done in six weeks, not six months.*

· *We are hiring her because of her attitude toward work, not her appearance in front of people.*

9) Words, phrases, and clauses joined in a series are to be separated by commas.

· *This project requires students to be careful, intelligent, and hardworking.*

· *Men, women, and children rushed on the crowded bus.*

10) A comma is used to separate two or more adjectives, adverbs, or phrases that modify the same word or phrase.

· *Her teaching style is interactive, clear, and interesting.*

· *This highway project obtained a good reputation because of its excellent design, timely construction, and special materials used.*

11) A comma separates a direct quotation from a phrase identifying its source or speaker.

· *"We are leaving now," our teacher said.*

· *"I got to go now," Mr. Yang said, "even if you want me to stay."*

12）A comma is used to set off the individual elements of an address.

· *Mr. Wang can be reached at* 112 *South Street, Beijing, China.*

· *He was born in Xi'an, China.*

13）Commas are used to set off the year from the day of the month.

· *On October* 1, 1949, *the People's Republic of China was established.*

· *In December* 2017, *Mr. Li was appointed as the chairperson of this department.*

5. Dash

In many cases, the dash functions like the comma, colon, or a pair of parentheses. Dash is usually considered to be a less formal equivalent of the colon and parenthesis, which frequently takes their place in advertising and other informal contexts. Nevertheless, dashes are prevalent in all kinds of writing even the most formal documents, and the choice of using it is usually a matter of personal preference.

The dash exists in a number of different lengths. In most general use, dash is approximately the width of two hyphens.

1）The dash marks an abrupt change or a suspension in the flow of a writer's thought or in the structure of a sentence.

· *If I had kept my receipts—and I really wish I had—I would be able to give you the exact amount.*

· *Nature has hidden in the earth, and how much of it is—or will become—accessible, and the fact that different countries use different methods of estimation.*

· *That equipment was so expensive—well, never mind how expensive it is – and we use it very carefully.*

2）Dashes are used to emphasize certain materials and make them to stand out clearly from the rest of the sentence.

· *In order to get paid, you will have to comply exactly with it—there is no tolerance！*

· *There are two ways to create a workable system—you should use both.*

· *Which do you want—Northern Ireland or the Republic of Ireland？*

· *This framework thus provides a method of exploring culture differences—both within and between countries—guiding us through different approaches: observation, questioning, and interpretation.*

3）Dashes are used to introduce defining and enumerating phrases and to link clauses, especially when one clause explains, summarizes, or expands upon others.

· *Mr. Williams—who is the director of the association—emphasizes that the importance of technical progress for the economy lies primarily in its capacity to increase productivity and reduce costs.*

　· *More than three-quarters of that increase—1 ,200 millions people—will be added to urban populations in a little more than 15 years.*

　· *Updated and revised database—with—1 ,600 additional entries.*

　· *Indeed , many nations control trade the right to import or export goods to or from another country—as a political tool.*

　· *The commission acted quickly to determine the cause—apparently the birds died from the industrial dumping of either chromium or red dye—and made recommendations in order to protect other migratory birds.*

　4) Dashes often set off parenthetic or amplifying material introduced by phrases as for example, namely, that is, such as, e. g. , and i. e.

　· *Typically, these forms leave room on the front so the parties may insert important contract terms—such as price, quality, or ship date.*

　· *Titles of convenience—namely, director or vice president—bestowed temporarily by the company can help women or young executives in status-conscious societies.*

　· *Two European countries are somewhat better—that is, Sweden and Denmark, at 45 and 47 percent, respectively.*

　5) A dash precedes the name of an author or source at the end of a quoted passage.

　· *"If you want to go places you' ve never been before—you have to think in ways you' ve never thought before. "*

　—Ken Blanchard, co-author of THE ONE MINUTE MANAGER

　· *"Maxwell has another great one here. . . An important topic that doesn' t get discussed enough. "*

　—Tim Flanagan Jr. , vice president, MUTUAL FINACIAL GROUP

　· *"A comprehensive, authoritative, and beautifully written biography. "— National Review*

　6) Dashes are used frequently as elements in page design.

　· *Composing Successful Letters*

　—Developing style and the right tone

　—Determining word usage and sentence length

　· *Required documents are :*

　—Personal ID

　—Diploma

　—Health Report

　6. Ellipsis Points

Ellipsis points or ellipses are used usually as three spaced dots within a sentence to indicate where words have been omitted from quoted material.

· *One book said, "The Internet, which has existed for many years, has exploded into prominence in business world, mainly because of the new capabilities of the World Wide Web to transmit... ands contains links to other pages of information."*

· *Teachers often tell the students that, "your colleagues or supervisors will count on you to take responsibility for a variety of international tasks without offering you much training or information except... things go wrong."*

7. Hyphen

1) Hyphens are used to link elements in compound words, e. g. , *two-thirds majority, heavy-duty machine, city-state, player-manager, hand-held device, step-by-step, country-by-country.*

2) A hyphen indicates that a word element is a prefix, suffix, or medial elements, e. g. , *self-, anti-, -ship, -o-.*

8. Parentheses

1) Parentheses enclose words, phrases, and clauses that provide definitions, translations, explanations, or supplementary facts.

· *Officers (president, treasurer, and secretary) of student union are elected and approved at last meeting.*

· *Even though they liked that restaurant (their Thai food was awesome), they never went back again.*

· *Gong-Fu (martial art) is very popular in this country.*

2) Parentheses enclose abbreviations occurring after those words or the spelled-out word occurring after the abbreviations.

· *The speaker mentioned many times about the company—China Merchant Bank (CMB).*

· *The best seller in last year's auto market is Nissan SUV (Sport Utility Vehicle).*

3) Parentheses are used to set off bibliographical or historical data and to cite books, articles, or other published works.

· *His articles are influenced by several of Mr. Hu's essays including, "The Engineering Structure of an International Project" (2009).*

· *Another book about this topic is The Competitive Edges (Apple Press, MYM11. 98).*

· *Textbooks are available at the bookstore for all courses. (see Page 23 for details.)*

· *The diagram (Fig. 5) illustrates the results of this experiment.*

4) Parentheses enclose Arabic numerals that confirm a spelled-out number in a

text.

· *Products will be delivered in twenty* (20) *days.*

· *Students are expected to finish this exam in forty-five* (45) *minutes.*

5) Parentheses enclose numbers or letters in a series within running text.

· *We must start to* (1) *find the right persons*, (2) *build a good team*, *and* (3) *provide enough resources in order to finish this task on time.*

· *This article should include* (a) *the main idea*, (b) *evidences to support the idea*, *and* (c) *the conclusion.*

6) Parentheses are used in combination with numbers for several purposes, such as grouping elements in mathematical expressions and indicating losses in accounting.

· $5(a+b) + 9(a+b) = 14(a+b)$

· *Operating Profits* (*in thousands*)

Sales of Goods	98. 45
Costs	(32. 20)
Salaries	(12. 86)
Overheads	(23. 50)
Profit (*Loss*)	29. 89

9. Period

1) A period terminates a sentence.

· *We are very successful so far.*

· *Thank you very much for your consideration.*

2) A period is used for some abbreviations and individual's initials, e. g. , *Dr. Wang*, *Ph. D.* , *No.* , *Corp.* , *Inc.* , *J. Ford*, *i. e.* , *R. S. V. P.* , *W. J. Ling.*

3) A period follows Roman and Arabic numerals and letters when they are used without parentheses in outlines.

· *Objectives*

A. *Short term*

a) *Increased sales*

b) *Lower expenses*

c) *Reduced overheads*

B. *Mid-term*

· *Required readings are*:

a) *Page 23—40 for Chapter One*

b) *Page 45—59 for Chapter Two*

10. Question Mark

1) The question mark terminates a direct question.

· *Who was that young lady last night*?

· *What kind of results are you expecting from these experiments?*

2）The question mark indicates a person's or a subject's uncertainty about a fact.

· *Scott Powell, English Scientist （? —1889）*

· *This technology is invented in 1905?*

11. Quotation Marks

Quotation marks are used to enclose quoted words, sentences, and even paragraphs. Sometimes they are used to set off translations of words or single letters within sentences.

1）Quotation marks enclose direct quotations.

· *Article 6 of the CISG states, "The parties may exclude the application of this Convention or ... derogate from or vary the effect of any of its provisions."*

· *In his famous speech "I Have a Dream," Martin Luther King Jr. observes that: "One hundred years later, the Negro still is not free."*

· *"I will be back," he said, " and this will not take too long."*

· *"To be or not to be, that is a problem."—Shakespeare*

2）Quotation marks enclose words or phrases borrowed from others, words used in a special way.

· *Please send a copy of your resume, or as some people may say, "biodata summery or vita."*

· *The maintenance of harmony placed on personal dignity stresses the importance of not causing others to "lose face" in Chinese culture.*

· *No matter how high your official position is, the public display of strong emotion will label you as a "peasant."*

· *"One Belt & One Road" is a suggested read by the Chinese government in recent years in order to promote international cooperation and develop overseas market.*

3）Quotation marks are used to enclose translations of foreign or borrowed terms.

· *"ESSE QUAM VIDERI" comes from the Latin word, meaning "to do is better than to say."*

· *Zizhiqu is a Chinese word, meaning "autonomous regions."*

4）Single quotation marks enclose a quotation within a quotation.

· *The student explains, "I definitely heard the teacher says, 'Don't be late.'"*

· *The teacher said to the class, "I don't like to hear that 'I don't know' from anyone."*

12. Semicolon

1）The semicolon is used in ways that are similar to those in which periods and commas are used. It is considered as either a weaker period or a stronger comma.

· *He has been wandering around for about an hour*; *he couldn' t make up his mind.*

· *The purposes of the UN are*:

a）*To maintain international peace and security. . .* ;

b）*To develop friendly relations. . .* ;

c）*To achieve international cooperation in solving. . .*

· *In many cases the conference sessions are much too long*; *the breaks between them, much too short.*

· *This report is incomplete*; *it does not reflect all facts*; *it misleads the readers.*

2）A semicolon joins two clauses when the second begins with a conjunctive adverb, such as accordingly, besides, consequently, furthermore, hence, however, indeed, moreover, namely, nevertheless, otherwise, still, then, therefore, and thus.

· *It won' t be easy to improve your writing skills*; *however, if you keep practicing you will get there.*

· *Many international students often ignore the importance of being culturally sensitive*; *nevertheless, they will either learn it from the others or their own experience and usually the hard way.*

· *This book is well-written*; *therefore I recommend that all students should read it.*

3）A semicolon is sometimes used before expressions（as for example, for instance, that is, namely, e. g. , or i. e. ）that introduce expansions.

· *This project is considered very successful*; *that is, it costs less and takes short time.*

· *There are a lot of terms in this chapter that are not used very often*; *for example, ampersand, apostrophe, ellipsis and semicolon.*

13. Slash

1）A slash represents the word *per* or *to* when used with units of measurement or when used to introduce the terms of a ratio.

· 5 ,000 *tons/year*

· *price/earning ratio*

· 45km/hr.

· 20/80 *principle*

2）A slash separates alternatives and it usually represents the words *and/or*, e. g. , *his/her, black/white, oral/written.*

3) A slash replaces the word and in some compound words, e. g. , *in the Sept. /Oct. issue*, 1989/90 *binder.*

2.3.2 Fonts, Sizes, Capitals and Italics

As we stated above, effective communication is to present your purpose clearly and to help your readers to understand you more easily. Your writing in English should follow here: when you choose letter fonts, sizes, capitals, and italics for your English writings, you should always ask yourself, "Is this going to make it easier for the readers?"

Generally speaking, there are no strict rules about using letter fonts and sizes for writing in English. However, in the business world there are some common practices accepted by professionals and scholars. Here we recommend our international students to adapt these for your writing studies.

There are many fonts available on any word processing software but only few are used for formal writings, such as Arial, Times New Roman. Why? Because they can be easily read. Other fancy and cursive fonts are usually not used in business correspondence and technical reports. Although these fancy types may look clever or innovative, they are more difficult to read and will cause frustration to your readers.

Use 10—14 point sizes for main body text; 14—20 for main headings, bold or normal; and 12—14 for sub-heading bold.

Be consistent! After you choose certain fonts and sizes for heading, sub-heading, and body text, keep it the same throughout your entire writing. This principle is especially important for longer reports, proposals, and books.

Do not always use CAPITAL LETTERS—even for headings. Words formed of capital letters are difficult to read because they don't have word-shapes. Readers recognize the meaning of a word by its shape much quicker than individual letters.

The following are some examples where capitalized letters are used.

1) The first word of a sentence is capitalized.

· *Thank you very much for your help.*

· *No! That is not what I mean.*

· *Are you going to the USA this summer?*

2) The first word of a direct quotation is capitalized; however, if the quotation is interrupted in mid-sentence, the second part does not begin with a capital.

· *The teacher said,* "*We have rejected his application for this scholarship.* "

· "*I have accepted his apology,*" *the manager said,* "*and I think he made that mistake by accident.* "

3) The first word of a sentence contained within parentheses is capitalized;

however, a parenthetical sentence occurring inside another sentence is not capitalized unless it is a Complete Quoted Sentence.

· *The meeting is still going on. (No one knows the results.)*

· *After waiting in line for about one and half hour (Why Do We Do That?) , then we left.*

4) The first word following a colon may be capitalized especially it introduces a fairly lengthy sentence or a series of sentences.

· *Consider the following steps: A team has to be formed. New sources of revenue are being explored. And several candidates have been interviewed.*

· *The overall meeting is held successfully: The university decides to improve the quality of the food service and students will have more choices on campus.*

5) The first word in an outline heading is capitalized.

· *I. Preface*

  II. Chapter One

    a) Reading text

    b) Spelling words

    c) Writing essays

· *Meeting agenda*

  a) Discussing problems

  b) Evaluating alternatives

  c) Making decisions

  d) Forming action plan

6) The first word of the salutation of a letter and the first word of a complimentary closing are capitalized.

· *Dear Mr. Li:*

· *Ladies and Gentlemen:*

· *Sincerely yours,*

7) The first word and each subsequent major word following SUBJECT and TO headings (as in a memorandum) are capitalized.

· *SUBJECT: Summer Studies Overseas*

· *TO: All Teachers and Students*

8) Abbreviated forms of proper nouns and adjectives are capitalized, just as the spell-out forms would be.

· *Dec. for December*

· *Wed. for Wednesday*

· *Vol. for Volume*

9) Names, names of academic degrees, names of awards, honors, and prizes are capitalized.

- *Tiger Woods*
- *Doctor of Laws*
- *Master of Civil Engineering*
- *Noble Peace Prize*
- *Academy Award*
- *Emmy*
- *New York Drama Award*

10) Words designating global, national, regional, or local political divisions are capitalized.

- *The British Empire*
- *The United States of America*
- *The People's Republic of China*
- *Ministry of Science*
- *United Nations Industrial Development Organization*

11) The names of streets, monuments, parks, landmarks, well-known buildings, and other public places are capitalized.

- *Xi'an, China*
- *Chicago, Illinois*
- *The Middle East*
- *The Southwest*
- *New York City*
- *Wall Street*
- *Golden Gate Bridge*
- *Himalaya Mountain*
- *Fifth Avenue*
- *Xi'an High-tech Development Zone*

12) The names of conferences, councils, expositions and specific sporting, historical and cultural events are capitalized.

- *The Chinese New Year*
- *The Olympic Summer Game*
- *The Yalta Conference*
- *The Congress of Vienna*
- *The San Francisco Earthquake*

13) Names of firms, corporations, schools, and organizations are capitalized.
- *Chang' an University*
- *Air China*
- *The City University of New York*
- *China Mobile*

14) Words designating languages, nationalities, peoples, races, religious groups, and tribes are capitalized.

- *Latin*
- *Canadians*
- *Muslims*
- *Christians*

15) The pronoun I is capitalized.

- *He and I are longtime friends.*

16) The names of computer languages, services, and databases are usually capitalized.

- *BASIC*
- *FORTRAN*
- *PASCAL*
- *COBOL*

17) Registered trademarks, service marks, collective marks, and brand names are capitalized.

- *Band-Aid*
- *Coca Cola*
- *Kleenex*
- *Pepsi*
- *HUAWEI*

18) Full capitalization of words or phrases is used for emphasis.

- *SEASONAL SALES COMING SOON*!
- *NO SMOKING*!
- *MIND YOUR STEP*!

In general, italics are used to emphasize or draw attention to a word or words in a sentence. Sometimes they are used to indicate there is something out of the ordinary about specific words or phrases or maybe about the way in which they are being used.

- The **pro forma** invoice should not be confused with the commercial invoice, which is the final bill for the goods accompanies the request for payment.
- Foreign words and phrases are italicized especially for those which have not been adopted into English language. However, any word that appears in a dictionary vocabulary section does not need to be italicized.
- They looked up this place as a **cordon sanitaire** around the city.

Unfamiliar words that have specialized meanings are set in italics.

- Another method is the **direct-to-consumer** transaction.
- When this occurs, lawyers call it a **battle of the forms**.

· A *certificate of origin* may be required by customs regulations in buyer's country.

As we mentioned above, italics are more difficult to read, so only use them where they are necessary. Do not use italics frequently otherwise they will create difficulties for readers and lose their effectiveness.

2.3.3 Abbreviations

Originally abbreviations are used for typewritten or printed material to save space, avoid repetition of long words and phrases, and to reduce keystrokes for typists and thereby increase their outputs. The usage of abbreviations is directly related to the nature of the material. Technical literature such as those in the fields of engineering, data processing, and medicine, features many abbreviations. Business writings depending on the nature of the business, employs many abbreviation uses. The styling of abbreviations has developed as such there is no set of rules that can cover all the possible variations. Abbreviations somewhat depend on the writers' preferences or the organization's writing policy.

In the following paragraphs we are going to introduce some broad principles that apply to abbreviations in general. For international students of civil engineering, we suggest that you should conform to the conventional usage of abbreviations and do not try to create your own styles. Whenever you are not sure about the usage, it is better to spell out the full words and to consult a dictionary.

1. Abbreviations are usually capitalized when formed from the initial letters of the words or word elements.

CAD—computer aided design
TESOL—teaching English to speakers of other languages
FOB—free on board
CIF—cost, insurance and freight
PC—personal computer
CPU—central processing unit
ICU—intensive care unit
TM—trademark
JV—joint venture
FYI—for your interest
TBD—to be decided
R&D—research and development
UNIDO—United Nations Industrial Development Organization

2. A period follows most abbreviations that are either formed by omitting all but the first few letters of a word or letters from the middle of word.

Fig. —figure

Nov. —November

Sat. —Saturday

Mfg. —manufacturing

Mr. —Mister

Inc. —incorporated

Co. —company

Ltd. —limited

3. Punctuated abbreviations of single words are pluralized by adding -s before the period; if the abbreviation stands for phrases or compounds they are pluralized by adding -'s after last period. Unpunctuated abbreviations that represent phrases and compounds are usually pluralized by adding -s to the end of the abbreviation.

Bldgs. —buildings

Figs. —figures

Mts. —mountains

Blvds. —boulevards

Ph. D. 's—doctors of philosophy

M. B. A. 's—masters of business administration

CPUs—central processing units

UFOs—unidentified flying objects

4. Possessive uses of abbreviations are formed in the same way as those of spelled-out nouns: the singular possessive is formed by the addition of -'s, the plural possessive simply by the addition of an apostrophe.

· *Intel Corp. 's annual sales*

· *the CPU's memory*

· *Turner Bros.' earnings*

· *most CPUs' memories*

5. The choice of the article *a* or *an* before abbreviations depends on the sound with which the abbreviations begins. If an abbreviation begins with a consonant sound, *a* is normally used; if it begins with vowel sound, *an* is used.

· *a B. A. degree*

· *an M. B. A. degree*

· *a UN agency*

· *an IRS report*

· *an SAT score*

6. The names of agencies, associations, and organizations, or articles, laws, treaties, and agreements are usually abbreviated after they have been spelled out on their first occurrence in a text.

· *Known as the Uniform Commercial Code (UCC), it is the primary body of commercial law for domestic transactions in the US. The purposes of UCC are...*

· *For international transactions, the UCC is being gradually supplanted by the United Nations Convention on Contracts for the International Sale of Goods (CISG). The CISG is the uniform international sales law in countries that accounts for over two-thirds of all world trade.*

7. The names of days and months are usually spelled out in running text, but when referring to a specific day or days or used in tables or notes, they are commonly abbreviated.

· *We plan to visit your family in August.*

· *We are going to arrive on Dec. 12th, 2018.*

8. Except for a few academic degrees with highly recognizable abbreviations (as B. A. , M. B. A. , and Ph. D.), the names of degrees and professional ratings are spelled out in full when first mentioned in running context.

· *He is pursuing the Master of Science (M. S.) in civil engineering field.*

9. Words and phrases derived from Latin are commonly abbreviated in context but not capitalized, and usually not italicized.

· *etc. —et cetera*

· *e. g. —exempli gratia (for example)*

· *i. e. —id est (that is)*

10. For personal names, first names are not abbreviated. For some famous persons, initials are used in place of their full names.

· *George W. Bush*

· *JFK—John F. Kennedy*

· *FDR—Franklin D. Roosevelt*

11. Measures and weights may be abbreviated in a figure plus unit combination; however, if the numeral is written out, the unit should also be written out.

· 12 *cu. ft.*

· 18 *ml*

· 25 *km*

· 7 *ft.*

· 4 *sec.*

· 30 *min.*

· *Twenty-five cubic feet*

12. Versus is abbreviated as *v.* in legal contexts; it is either spelled out or abbreviated as *vs.* in general context.

· *Smith v. Vermont (in a legal context)*

· *Honesty versus dishonesty or honesty vs. Dishonesty (in a general context)*

2.3.4 Numbers

The treatment of numbers in any written material varies considerably and there are many conventions to follow. The major decision for writers is whether to write out numbers as words or to express them in figures. In general, the more formal writing the more likely that numbers will be spelled out. These formal writings include proclamations, legal agreements, and other types of formal documents. In scientific, technical, or statistical contexts, numbers are usually expressed as figures.

In this section, the most commonly used conventions are described as general principles for international students of civil engineering, especially those related business correspondence and technical writings. When you apply these conventions to your own writing, there are three things you need to be reminded of: 1) Is this styling of numbers easier for readers to understand your writing? 2) Is this usage complying with rules accepted by previous publications, industrial norms, or company policies? 3) Be consistent. Either expressing numbers as words or figures, writers should follow one or the other and stay with it throughout your entire writing material.

The following are some general principles for the treatment of numbers in writing materials.

1. The most commonly accepted rule is that to use words for numbers ten and below and exact numbers for those greater than ten.

· *The Winter Olympic has lasted for* 15 *days and Chinese players won seven medals.*

· *This new book will consist of* 20 *chapters and each writer will be at least responsible for four chapters on average.*

2. Numbers that begin a sentence are written out.

· *Twenty-five students attended the last Friday's meeting and they made three decisions about the coming events.*

· *One hundred thirty-six books are selected for after-class readings and I only finished five of them.*

3. Two separate sets of figures should not be adjacent to one another unless they form a series, in such case, the figure that is shorter and more easily read will be changed into written form.

· *By the end of* 2018 , *two hundred small businesses will close their doors.*

· *There are twenty-seven* 9-inch *plates available for us to use.*

· *During this meeting, there will be fifteen* 5-minute *presentations given by* 24 *students.*

4. Numbers that form a pair or a series referring to comparable quantities should be treated consistently and usually styled alike.

· *There are about 50 to 65 houses destroyed during the storm.*

· *These three projects will take 7, 10 and 50 days to finish, respectively.*

5. Numbers between one and ten followed by hundred and thousand may be spelled out or expressed in figures. Numbers of one million and billion and above may be expressed as figures. If a more exact number is required, especially in technical writing the whole amount should be expressed as numerals.

· *Chinese culture has more than five thousand years history.*

· *By the year of 2016, China has about 1.38 billion people and India has about 1.32 billion; these two countries together counts up 37% of the world's population.*

· *Last year, this company achieved over $ 8.35 million in sales.*

· *At the time of its opening in 1937, the Golden Gate Bridge was the longest and the tallest suspension bridge in the world with a main span of 4,200 feet (1,280m) and a total height of 746 feet (227m).*

6. In technical writing, all ordinal numbers are written as figure-plus-suffix combinations. When using *second* and *third*, they may be written with figures as 2nd, 3rd, 32nd, 83rd, and 102nd.

· *This is the 14th year for him to teach English in China.*

· *This experiment has taken almost five years and at the 147th try, he finally succeeded.*

· *In both the 7th and 11th chapters, this topic is discussed in detail.*

· *During the last Olympic Game, in terms of the number of gold medals, UK and China got the 2nd and 3rd positions.*

7. For lengthy figures, each group of three digits may be separated by a space counting from the decimal point to the left and the right. They can also be separated by a comma instead, however, if commas are used, neither commas nor spaces are placed to the right of the decimal point.

· *a fee of RMB 52,000*

· *23,000 units*

· *65 960 346*

· *43 980.231 763*

· *321,43.432657*

8. Hyphens are used with written-out numbers between 21 and 99.

· *five hundred twenty-three*

· *fifty-four*

· *the twenty-fifth day*

9. A hyphen is usually used between the numerator and the denominator, especially when the fraction is used as a modifier. If either the numerator or the denominator is hyphened, no hyphen is used between them.

· *the two-thirds majority of the class*

· *three fifths of her total income*

· *thirty-five hundredths*

· *seven three-hundredths*

10. Numbers that form the first part of a compound modifier expressing measurement are followed by a hyphen. An exception is that when the second part of the modifier is the word *percent.*

· *a 39-mile drive*

· *a 9-pound weight*

· *an eight-pound baby*

· *a 850-acre farm*

· *a 65 percent increase*

11. Inclusive numbers—those which express a range—are separated either by the word *to* or by a dash. But a dash is not used in combination with the words *from* or *between*, instead, they are written as "from 1949 to 1979" or "between 1970 and 1990."

· *pages 35 to 78*

· *pages 23—74*

· *8—14 months*

· *the years 1949—1976*

12. Units of measurement expressed in words or abbreviations are usually used only after the second element of an inclusive number. Symbols, however, are repeated.

· *traveling 5,000 to 8,000 miles every year*

· *ten to sixteen dollars*

· *$ 65— $ 70 millions*

· 15-28 ℃

· 7' —9' *long*

In technical writing, numbers used with units of measurement—even numbers below ten—are expressed as numerals.

When units of measurements are written as abbreviations or symbols, the adjacent numbers are always figures, and this is true in both general and technical texts.

Roman numerals are also used occasionally in some specific situations, such as names, headings, volumes in collection, and technical terms. Here we will not provide any extra examples and leave those for students to explore beyond this textbook. A list of Roman numerals and their Arabic equivalents is given in the following table as reference.

Name	Arabic Numeral	Roman Numeral
zero	0	
one	1	I
two	2	II
three	3	III
four	4	IV
five	5	V
six	6	VI
seven	7	VII
eight	8	VIII
nine	9	IX
ten	10	X
eleven	11	XI
twelve	12	XII
thirteen	13	XIII
fourteen	14	XIV
fifteen	15	XV
sixteen	16	XVI
seventeen	17	XVII
eighteen	18	XVIII
nineteen	19	XIX
twenty	20	XX
twenty-one	21	XXI
twenty-two	22	XXII
twenty-three	23	XXIII

Name	Arabic Numeral	Roman Numeral
twenty-four	24	XXIV
twenty-five	25	XXV
twenty-six	26	XXVI
twenty-nine	29	XXIX
thirty	30	XXX
thirty-one	31	XXXI
thirty-two	32	XXXII
forty	40	XL
forty-one	41	XLI
fifty	50	L
fifty-five	55	LV
sixty	60	LX
seventy	70	LXX
eighty	80	LXXX
ninety	90	XC
one hundred	100	C
one hundred one	101	CI
one hundred two	102	CII
two hundred	200	CC
three hundred	300	CCC
four hundred	400	CD
five hundred	500	D
eight hundred	800	DCCC
nine hundred	900	CM
one thousand	1,000	M
two thousand	2,000	MM

Besides the general principles described above, there are some specific types of situations involving numbers that students must be aware of. In the following paragraphs these specific styles are introduced for students to either use them in writing or refer to as helpful hints for reading.

1) For all building, house, apartment, room, and suite numbers, Arabic numerals are used except for *one*, which is written out.

- 118 *Chang' an Road*, *Beilin District*, *Xi'an*
- *Suite* 12, 1865 *Fremont Street*
- *Room* 1208, *Jinshi Building*, *the 2nd South Ring Road*

2) Arabic numerals are used for highways and even country roads.

- *Highway* 182
- *Interstate* 95 *or I* 95
- *U. S. Route* 66

3) Full dates (month, day, and year) are commonly styled as the month-day-year sequence.

- *January* 28, 2018
- *December* 15, 2017

4) In technical writing, figures are generally used for quantities expressed in degrees. The degree (°) rather than the word degree is used with the figure.

- *a* 45° *angle*
- 8°6′15″N
- 32 ℃
- 85° F

5) In vertical enumeration, the numbers are followed by a period. There is no terminal punctuation following the items unless at least one of the items is a complete sentence, in which case a period is used for each item.

- Requirements for this job are:

CET-4 *or CET*-6

Master Degree of Civil Engineering

Graduated from 211 *or* 985 *University*

- Application should follow the procedure:

Send your resume and cover letter.

Fill out the application form.

Enclose two recommendation letters.

6) Outlines make use of Roman numerals, Arabic numerals, and letters.

I. Activities on campus

a) In-door discussion

b) Out-door practice

Warm-up

Five-minutes exercise

Thirty-minutes game

II. Events off campus

a) Preparation

Documents

Clothing

Luggage

b) Travel Arrangement

Tickets

ID and visa

Detailed schedule

c) Sum-up meeting

7) In running text, fractions standing alone are usually written out and when used with units of measurement, they are expressed in figures.

· *two thirds of the class*

· *¾ km*

· *¼ mile*

8) Mixed fractions (fractions with a whole number, such as $3\frac{1}{2}$) and fractions that form part of a unit modifier are expressed in figures.

· *taking 3¾ hours*

· *a 3¼-kilometer bridge*

· *2¾ million population*

9) Decimal fractions are always set as figures. In technical writing, a zero is placed to the left of the decimal point when the fraction is less than a whole number.

· *The test drive took 0.675 sec. to hit the target.*

· *The result of the experiment is 1.7832 mg/kg for this kind of mixture.*

10) When the sums of money can be expressed in one or two words, it is usually written out. But if several sums are mentioned in the sentence or paragraph, all are expressed as figures. When written out, the unit of currency is also provided. If the sum is expressed in figures, the symbol of the currency unit can be used.

· *Thirteen dollars was spent for this book.*

· *I got twenty-five dollars for my birthday gift.*

· *We spent $150 for transportation, $200 for hotels, and $160 for food on this trip.*

· *Tickets for this show were* $15 *for each entry, and* $25 *for all day.*

11) In technical writing, specific percentages are styled as the figure plus the sign (%). The word percent is used in nonscientific text.

· 15. 7%

· *The cost of this material has increased* 13 *percent in the past two months.*

12) Ratios expressed in figures use a colon, hyphen, dash, or the word *to* as a means of comparison. Ratios expressed in words use a hyphen, or the word *to*.

· *a* 5 : 1 *chance*

· *a* 10-1 *vote*

· *a* 20/80 *principle*

· *a ratio of ten to six*

· *a fifty-fifty chance*

13) The time of day is usually spelled out when expressed in even, half, or quarter hours. Figures are used to delineate a precise time.

· *We plan to leave at a quarter after five tomorrow.*

· *His flight will arrive in Xi'an at* 19:15 *this evening.*

14) When the time of day is used in conjunction with the abbreviations *a. m.* and *p. m.* , figures are preferred. These abbreviations should not be used in conjunction with the words *morning* or *evening*; and the word *o' clock* should not be combined with either *a. m.* or *p. m.*

· *The train is leaving at* 3:10 *p. m.*

· *I usually got up at eight o' clock in the morning.*

2.4 FORMING SENTENCES

A sentence is a complete thought or idea that contains both a subject and predicate, begins with a capital letter, and ends with a punctuation mark. It consists of a group of related words arranged to convey a meaning. Sentences 1) express a statement; 2) asks a question; 3) express a request or a command; or 4) express an exclamation.

There are three main types of sentences based on their structure: simple, compound and complex.

2.4.1 Simple Sentences

The simple sentence expresses a single thought and consists of one subject and one predicate.

1. Basic Types of Simple Sentences

There are seven basic types of simple sentence.

1) Type 1. Someone (or something) does an activity.

· *The dog is sleeping.*

· *I am reading a book.*

· *He will win.*

In these sentences, there is one actor or a group of actors engaged in a particular activity.

2) Type 2. Someone (or something) does an activity to another person or object.

· *He designs this bridge.*

· *Mr. Wang has taught us English writing.*

· *This highway was built by a Chinese company.*

In these sentences, there is one actor or group of actors acting on something or someone else.

3) Type 3. Someone (or something) acts on himself.

· *He shaved himself.*

· *The air conditioner turned off itself.*

· *John hurt himself.*

4) Type 4. Someone (or something) is identified.

· *Mr. Li is the manager of this project.*

· *Dr. Yang is the group leader.*

· *This is a suspension bridge.*

5) Type 5. Someone (or something) is described.

· *Hannah is a pretty girl.*

· *This computer is very helpful.*

· *This book is very interesting.*

In these sentences, a quality of the person or object is stated.

6) Type 6. Someone (or something) is possessed.

· *This book is mine.*

· *That schoolbag is John's.*

7) Type 7. The location of someone (or something) is stated.

· *Your letter is on the desk.*

· *The bus stop is half mile down the street.*

· *Mr. Zhang's office is on the 5th floor.*

2. Multiply the Basics

Once you have mastered the basic types of the simple sentence then you are ready to practice modifications to them. There are four ways to multiply the basics. The examples of these modifications are given below.

1) Multiply by Negation.

· *I am not reading a book.*

· *Mr. Wang has not taught us English writing.*

· *The air conditioner did not turn off itself.*

· *This is not a suspension bridge.*

· *That schoolbag is not John's.*

· *This computer is not very helpful.*

· *Your letter is not on the desk.*

2）Multiply by Questions.

· *Who was reading that book?*

· *What has Mr. Wang taught?*

· *Did the air conditioner turn off itself?*

· *What kind of bridge is this?*

· *Whose schoolbag is this?*

· *Why isn't this computer helpful?*

· *Where is your letter?*

3）Multiply by Emphasis or Exclamation.

· *Oh my, how did you do that?*

· *What a beautiful bridge this is!*

· *Look at it, what a big house!*

· *How come, I could not believe this can happen!*

4）Multiply by Instructions or Commands.

· *Please pay attention to this chapter.*

· *Be brave; do not hesitate to try it out.*

· *Come on, you are all invited to join the party.*

· *Be there on time, otherwise you will miss the bus.*

3. Combination and Flexibility

Of course, these modifications can be combined and furthermore flexibility can also be achieved by replacement, expansion, and rearrangement. It depends on what meaning you want to express and after all what you want your readers to understand.

Certain parts of sentences can be replaced with other various words, and sometimes a replacement will require a change in other parts of the sentence especially when tenses change.

1）Mr. Li teaches English writing.

→ Mr. Li is teaching English writing.

→ He will teach English writing.

→ He has taught English writing.

→ That teacher taught English writing.

The basic sentence can be expanded by adding modifiers and other phrases.

There are many things that can be added to different parts of a sentence.

2) Mr. Li teaches English writing.

→ Mr. Li, the best teacher I ever had, has taught English writing for the last three years.

→ Mr. Li, our best teacher in this school, will teach us English writing for the next three years.

→ Mr. Li and Ms. Wang, two good teachers, both have taught English writing in our school for many years.

The sentence can be rearranged by interchanging the order of its parts.

3) Mr. Li teaches English writing.

→ Mr. Li, who has taught English writing for many years, is the best teacher in our school.

→ As the best teacher in our school, Mr. Li will teach us English writing next year.

2.4.2 Compound Sentences

The compound sentence consists of two or more simple sentences of equal importance. These simple sentences can have the same actor or different actors and the events can occur at the same time, sequentially, or at different times. Usually these sentences are linked with the words *and*, *but*, and *or*. These sentences can make sense standing alone and they do not depend on one another.

· *The men work in the fields and the women work in the household.*

· *I could drop by your office on Friday, or just send you an email before Monday.*

· *Most of the teachers have Ph. D, but some of them only have M. A or M. B. A.*

· *Our teacher designed this project, organized and led it, later he finished it by himself.*

2.4.3 Complex Sentences

The complex sentence consists of two or more simple sentences combined so that one depends on the other to complete its meaning. One of the compound sentences is the main clause which must contain a subject and a verb; it can stand alone as a complete sentence. The others are dependent (or subordinate) clauses that may also contain subjects and verbs, but they do not make complete sense by itself and cannot stand alone. A dependent clause usually has a conjunction—before, after, although, because, since, if, where, when, unless—at the beginning of the clause. These conjunctions make the clause dependent for meaning and completion on an independent clause. There is typically a time relationship between the clause, or sometimes a relationship like purpose, cause and effect, condition, or desire.

· *When Dr. Wang returns, I will take a leave and go on my vacation.*

· *If you have mastered the skills in this book, you could become a good writer.*

· *The meeting just started when the rest of students walked in.*

· *We are very glad to have you as our client, so we hope that you call on us whenever you need help.*

Needless to say, comparing with the simple sentence and the compound sentence, the complex sentence is more difficult to write; it is easier to make mistakes when writing a complex sentence. The following are some suggestions for you to avoid mistakes and misunderstandings.

1)Be clear about what you want to say, that is, make sure that your sentences say exactly what you mean. What you want your readers to understand from these sentences is what you should express with these clauses.

2)Understand the relationship between the main (or independent) clause and the subordinate (or dependent) clause. When choosing the conjunctions, you should remember that a rational and logical ordering of the sentence is to guarantee that the material will be understood clearly.

3)Sentences should form complete grammatical units containing both a subject and a verb. Furthermore, subject and verb should agree in your sentence.

The subject-verb agreement errors are the most popular mistakes in any writings. There are some rules to follow in order to avoid these mistakes.

· Recognize the subject and its verb of the main clause and ignore any words that come in between them.

· If the subject is a compound word (connected by *and*), it requires a plural verb.

· When a compound subject contains *neither...nor* or ei*ther...or*, the verb agrees with the subject closest to it.

· Use a singular verb after collective nouns (such as *class*, *committee*, *crew*, *department*, *group*, *organization*, *staff*, *team*) when the group functions as a single unit.

· Use a singular verb with indefinite pronoun (such as *anyone*, *anybody*, *each*, *everyone*, *everything*, *no one*, *somebody*, *something*).

· Words like *scissors* and *pants* are plural when they are the true subject.

· Some foreign language plurals (*curricula*, *data*, *media*, *phenomena*, *strata*, *syllabi*, *alumni*) always take a plural verb.

· Use a singular verb with fractions.

· When a sentence with one verb has two or more subjects denoting different things, connected by *and*, the verb should be plural; When the subjects denote the same thing and are connected by *or* the verb should be singular.

· When the same verb has more than one subject of different persons or numbers, it agrees with the most prominent in thought.

Place the adverb as near as possible to the word it modifies. Instead of saying, "He walked to the door quickly," say "He walked quickly to the door."

Unnecessary or unexpected grammatical shifts will interrupt the train of thought and complicate your material. Balanced sentence structure not only maintains an even, rhythmic thought flow but also helps the sentences remain understandable.

· Not preferred: Any information you can provide will be greatly appreciated and we assure you that discretion will be exercised in its use.

· Preferred: We will appreciate any information that you can provide and we assure you that we will use it with discretion.

· Not preferred: Because of the current shortage and we are experiencing a strike, we cannot take any orders now.

· Preferred: Because of the shortage and a strike, we cannot take any orders now.

Variety of styles can keep the readers' attentions and make the materials more interesting and diversified. The main point can be either placed at the beginning or suspended until the very end. Interrupting elements or a reversal of sentence order can also be used for different purposes.

2.5 CONSTRUCTING PARAGRAPHS

Any written communication should be clear, coherent, and logical in progression so as the readers can understand your message. A paragraph is the basic underlying structure for a piece of writing that should consist of one or more sentences arranged in a logical order with proper information provided on one topic.

A paragraph usually conveys a central thought or an idea and sentences contribute to the overall meaning of that thought or idea. Each paragraph should contain a topic sentence that expresses the central thought or idea, and supporting information will explain this topic sentence.

A topic sentence may be placed either at the beginning or at the end of a paragraph. A lead-in topic sentence presents the main idea and sets the initial tone of the material that will follow. A terminal topic sentence is often an analysis, conclusion, or summation of what was written previously.

A carefully structured paragraph should stick to one topic only. Every sentence in the paragraph will support, explain or prove this one central idea. A unified paragraph includes only relevant information and excludes unnecessary or irrelevant comments.

In a paragraph all sentences should flow smoothly and logically. They should follow one train of thought and each sentence should be connected as the link of a chain. The following words can be used for connection or transition between sentences.

· Addition: *again*, *additionally*, *along with*, *as well as*, *also*, *besides*, *furthermore*, *in addition*, *moreover*, *together with*, *what's more*.

· Cause/effect: *accordingly*, *as a result*, *because of*, *consequently*, *due to*, *hence*, *on account of*, *therefore*, *thus*.

· Comparison/contrast: *conversely*, *equally*, *however*, *in contrast*, *in the same way*, *likewise*, *on the contrary*, *on the other hand*, *similarly*.

· Conclusion: *altogether*, *as we saw*, *at last*, *finally*, *in brief*, *in conclusion*, *in short*, *in summary*, *on the whole*, *to conclude*, *to summarize*, *to wrap up*.

· Condition: *although*, *depending*, *even though*, *of course*, *provided that*, *to be sure*, *unless*.

· Emphasis: *above all*, *after all*, *as a matter of fact*, *as I said*, *for emphasis*, *indeed*, *in fact*, *in other words*, *obviously*, *surely*, *unquestionably*.

· Illustration: *for example*, *for instance*, *in effect*, *in particular*, *specifically*, *that is*, *to demonstrate*.

· Place: *across from*, *adjacent to*, *at this point*, *behind*, *below*, *beyond*, *in front of*, *next to*, *under*, *wherever*.

· Time: *afterward*, *at the same time*, *at times*, *beforehand*, *currently*, *formerly*, *hereafter*, *later*, *meanwhile*, *presently*, *previously*, *simultaneously*, *subsequently*.

Your readers will view any writings consisting of more than one paragraph as a whole so each paragraph should be linked or interrelated. Paragraphs should not be organized as isolated entities and mechanically lined up without transitions in between. Rather, they should be tightly interlinked and interact in a sequential development of a major idea or cluster of ideas.

Depending on the message, purpose, content, and style you wish to present, the development of paragraphs may follow any of the directions below.

1) Paragraphs may flow from the general to the specific, or vice versa.

2) Paragraphs may demonstrate an alternating order of comparison and contrast.

3) Paragraphs may chronicle events in a set of temporal order, from the beginning to the end, or vice versa.

4) Paragraphs may describe something in a set of spatial order, from near to far, or vice versa.

5) Paragraphs may follow a sequence with the least important facts and examples presented first and lead to the most important facts and examples. For example, facts or issues that are easy to understand and accept may be set first and followed by those more difficult ones. By this way, the easier material prepares readers to comprehend or accept the more difficult points later on.

6) When writing a persuasive article, usually the most powerful arguments will be set first so that it will make the strongest influence to the readers and then the rest of the arguments follow gradually.

A well-written paragraph should state the purpose clearly with its topic sentence. Effective writers usually place this main sentence at the beginning of the paragraph with a fairly concise sentence. Then the rest of the paragraph is constructed as the elaboration around this main idea. These remaining sentences should help to illustrate, confirm, and enforce the general thought or purpose of this topic sentence. These sentences should be interrelated and the transitions should be natural and obvious. At the end of the paragraph, good writers will use the last sentence to reinforce the main idea of the paragraph and make a conclusion; a restatement, counterpart, or application of the beginning.

Similarly, paragraphs should also follow a certain pattern, logically arranged according to the flow of thought. The very first paragraph sets the initial tone and introduces the subject or topic under discussion; it leads into the thrust of communication. It should immediately attract the readers' attentions and interests. The last paragraph should tie together all of the ideas and points that have been set forth in the writing and reemphasize the main conclusions, solutions, suggestions, or statements of opinion.

The following questions are used to test if paragraphs are well written.

1) Do these paragraphs communicate the purpose clearly?

2) Are these paragraphs properly developed, or do they confuse the readers or raise other questions?

3) Are these paragraphs logically arranged and each of them interrelated coherently? Is there easy and clear transition between paragraphs?

4) Does one paragraph just simply repeat words and ideas that have been expressed before?

5) Is the structure or organization of these paragraphs adequate? Do they need to be rearranged or regrouped in order to be more effective?

In this chapter, we have discussed how to choose words at the beginning of your writing, including topics like how much vocabulary is necessary, parts of speech, fundamentals of grammars, checking definitions and usafes of words, and using simple words. Then we emphasized the importance of spelling checker for writings. We also talked about the usage of punctuation, abbreviations, and numbers in our writing. A guideline for choosing fonts, sizes, capitals and italics were provided. At the end of the chapter, forming sentences and constructing paragraphs were discussed. The purpose of this chapter is to provide basic ideas and knowledge to students of civil engineering to be able to write basic sentences and paragraphs.

The last suggestion we want to give is that no one can become a good writer without enough practice. So for the beginner of writing in English, the best approach is to practice and practice more.

2.6 EXERCISES

1. Divide the following words into groups as Article, Noun, Adjective, Pronoun, Verb, Adverb, Preposition, Conjunction and Interjection.

up, *struggle*, *against*, *an*, *told*, *to*, *excellent*, *absolutely*, *but*, *nevertheless*, *why*, *oops*, *congratulation*, *driver*, *similar*, *large*, *scientific*, *economy*, *economics*.

2. Use the words *tell*, *love*, and *teach* to practice the fundamentals of English grammar, see how they are used in different moods and tenses.

3. Compare the words in each pair and use each one of them to write a sentence; be sure to pay attention to their meanings and usage.

Affect vs. *Effect*, *Attain* vs. *Obtain*, *Foreword* vs *Forward*, *Personal* vs. *Personnel*, *Lose* vs. *Loose*, *Proceed* vs. *Precede*, *Principle* vs. *Principal*

4. Rewrite the following sentences and keep in mind, to "be short, clear and concise."

1) After many meetings of discussion, students from different groups finally made an agreement on the topic they are going to work on as the group project.

2) Collecting information, searching for references, and reading journals about the similar topics, then you can start to prepare for your writing for this assignment.

3) If you conduct this experiment under the same conditions, you will probably get the same conclusion of these results, and even more to prove that it is repeatable.

4) There are many transportation methods you can choose to travel by, air plane, train, bus and car, whichever is faster and safer. People usually choose the way of travel according to which is cheaper, more comfortable and convenient.

5. Write three sentences for each of the following sentence types: simple sentence. Compound sentence and complex sentence. Compare these sentences and understand their differences.

6. Read the following paragraphs about "Free Writing," then choose a topic or no topics and just start to practice your free writing.

"Free Writing" could be defined as "writing without rules." It is proven technique for generating ideas and for curing writer's block. Free writing is considered a good prewriting exercise. It can be a useful step in producing written work of high quality.

You can use this technique for a given subject. Or you can start without having a subject in mind. Choose an amount of time that you will keep your pen to paper. This could be five minutes or more. Then begin writing. Do not worry about what you write. You can write, "I have nothing to write about," or "There is nothing to say." As words flow, do not worry about grammar and punctuation. Just let the ideas out. Your writing can be refined later. Or it can be thrown in a wastebasket and never used again. Have you managed to put something on paper? Have you simply been a writer for those five minutes? Then the goal of free writing has been achieved.

7. Choose one of the topics below and write some paragraphs, bring your writings and share them with the class.

1) About your hometown, your family or your school;

2) About your favorite book, movie or sport;

3) About a project you have done, a trip you took, or an interesting experience you have had before.

2.7 BIBLIOGRAPHY

1. BREWSTER E T, BREWSTER E S. Language Acquisition Made Practical: Field Methods for Language Learners [M]. 1st ed. Lingua House, 1976.

2. DEVLIN J. How to Speak and Write Correctly [M]. 1st ed. Audible Studios, 2012.

3. GOODALE M, SCHELL M. Managing Across Cultures: The Seven Keys to Doing Business with a Global Mindset [M]. 1st ed. McGraw-Hill Education, 2009.

4. FEARON G, Fearon's Practical English (The Pacemaker Curriculum) [M]. 2nd ed. Fearon/Janus/Quercus, 1995.

5. DEVRIES M A. The New American Handbook of Letter Writing and Other Forms of Correspondence [M]. 2nd ed. Wings Book, 1994.

6. SHAFFER R, EARLE B, AGUSTI F. International Business Law and Its Environment [M]. 10th ed. Cengage Learning, 2017.

7. ATKINSON T. Merriam-Webster's Guide to International Business

Communications［M］. 2nd ed. Merriam Webster, 1996.

8. KOLIN P C. Successful Writing at Work: Concise Edition［M］. 4th ed. Cengage Learning, 2014.

9. MERRIAM-WEBSTER. Webster's New Business Writers Guide［M］. Smithmark Pub, 1998.

CHAPTER 3. BUSINESS CORRESPONDENCE

Business correspondence is the exchange of information in a written format. It can take place between people within and outside the organization, in the process of business activities performed for the commercial benefit of the organization. Business correspondence is generally conveyed by widely accepted formats such as letters, faxes, emails and notices, which are acknowledged and followed universally.

3.1 LETTER, MEMO FAXE, AND EMAIL

3.1.1 Letter

A letter is usually a form of written communication for exchanging information and processing business matters between companies, companies and customers, or clients and other external parties. Letters are framed for a variety of purposes, for example, to request specific information or action from the letter's recipient, to place an order from a supplier, to complain about a bad experience, to apologize for a wrong doing, or to express appreciation to the recipient. The overall style of letter is framed depending on the relationship between the sender and the recipient. Sometimes, a letter is particularly useful and taken more seriously by the recipient than other forms of communications, because it can produce a permanent written record.

3.1.1.1 *Structure of a Letter*

A letter generally consists of the following components:

1. Letterhead

The letterhead of a company often includes the basic information of the company: name, address, telephone, fax, email, Internet address and/or logo, etc of an organization. Normally a company provides specialized stationery at the top of which the above information is printed on. The quality of the stationery and the design of the letterhead should be kept in good condition so that they can present the image of the company well. Particularly, the letterhead should be practical, attractive, and decent.

2. Date

The date of when the letter was written is placed one line or two lines below the letterhead. How to write the date in English is noteworthy. There are generally two writing styles, i. e. US style and UK style.

For example,

May 20, 2016 (US style);

20 May 2016 (UK style);

May the 20th, 2016 (UK style);

May 20th, 2016 (Both US and UK style);

The 20th day of May 2016 (The most formal style).

It should be noted that sometimes the date is also written in figures, e. g. , 10/6/2017. However, it may cause confusion concerning the month and the date could be read as October 6, 2017 or June 10, 2017. Consequently, the date should be written as clearly as possible in a formal letter. Abbreviation of month, e. g. , Oct. (short for October), is not recommended.

3. Reference Number (optional)

Considering classification, archiving, and access of documents, letters sent are normally identified using a reference number. For example,

Ref. No. CRCG-CUAD-01-259

in which

Ref. —Reference

No. —Number

CRCG— China Railway Construction Group Co. , Ltd. (the name of the company).

CUAD—Abbreviation of the name of the project.

01—The code of the PIC (people in charge) to whom the letter is sent.

259—The number of the letter sent to the PIC.

4. Addressee's Name/Attention Line

Addressee's name appears at the attention line, which is usually placed one line or two lines below the date and is used when the letter needs to be directed to a recipient in an organization. The person's title and position should also be given here. For example,

Mr. Alison Lau, Sales Manager.

Dr. Eric Grey, The Head of the Service Department.

5. Inside Address

Identify the recipient's address, which should appear immediately after the attention line. For example,

Miss Renee Wong

Chief Executive Officer

Unique Design Limited

16/F Sunshine Tower

27 Hennessy Road

Causeway Bay

Hong Kong

6. Salutation

A salutation is a greeting used in a letter. Its formality depends on your relationship with the recipient. The commonly used salutation in an English letter is *Dear* followed either by an honorific and a surname or by a given name.

· Use his/her name directly if you know the recipient well, for example, "Dear Eric". Use the last name with his/her executive or professional title to show respect, for example, "Dear Mr. Shepherd" "Dear Dr. Xie".

· Use "Dear Sir/Madam" if the gender of the reader is unknown.

· Use "To whom it may concern" if you do not know the specific recipient and/or wish to convey that the reader should forward the copy to a person who is more suitable to receive or respond appropriately.

A comma normally follows the salutation and name except that a colon is used instead in U. S. business correspondence. The salutation is often placed one line or two lines below the inside address.

7. Project (optional)

For the letter regarding an international engineering project, it needs to indicate the project name before the subject. The full project name should appear the same as what is written in the contract. For example,

Project: Shannxi Road Development II Project

8. Subject or Re.

The Subject or Re. line of a letter clearly indicates what the letter is about or its purpose. It should be concise and specific enough to convey this. The first letter of the non-function word is usually capitalized, and all following words are in bold for attention. For example,

Subject: Subscription Renewal

Re: About Your Promoting Projects

It is noteworthy that "Subject:" and "Re. :" can sometimes be omitted.

9. Body of the Letter

As the core of the letter, the body conveys the message you would like to deliver. Following are some points for attention:

· You should be familiar with the recipient's cultural background, religion, beliefs, and customs in order to use appropriate and polite written expressions.

· The content to be delivered should be clear and well organized. It is recommended that only a single subject is involved in each letter.

· It is highly recommended to choose brief and clearly understood written words rather than rarely used and ambiguous words.

· Try to avoid using lengthy sentences that may cause misunderstanding and unnecessary inconvenience.

· Choose suitable language and tone. Even in letters of urging payment you should be careful when using extreme phrases.

10. Complimentary Close

The commonly used phrases in formal letters are: Yours sincerely, Sincerely yours, Yours (very) truly, Regards, etc. The level of formality depends on your relationship with the recipient. For example, use "Best regards" "Regards" or "Best wishes" for closer relationships while use "Yours" "Respectively" "Faithfully" "Sincerely" "Truly", and "Cordially" for a formal relationship.

11. Signature Area

The writer's signature, typewritten name, and business title are included in signature area. The signature often needs to be handwritten.

12. Enclosure

The enclosure notation indicates additional items included, if any. The written forms are as follows.

1) Full words:

Enclosure.

or

Attachment.

2) Abbreviated:

Enc.

or

Att.

3) Full words with the title of the specific enclosure:

Enclosure: Form A.

Enclosure: 1 catalogue

1 price list

4) The title of the specific enclosure:

Annual Report (December 2017):

2 hard copies and 1 soft copy.

13. Mailing Notation

This part provides a record of how the letter was sent, e. g., delivery, facsimile, special delivery, or registered mail and appears after the signature area or enclosure notations, whichever is last and before copy notations.

14. Copy Notation

cc is short for "carbon copy" which indicates making the copies of the letter/ attachment to other recipients. For example,

cc to Dr. Martin Smith

cc: Mr. Nan Ge

Copy/copies to Mr. Shepherd

15. Postscript (P. S.)

Postscript (P. S.) is often placed after the signature area to supplement what is omitted in the body part. It is more commonly used in informal personal letters. For example,

P. S. Enclosed are some pictures taken during your visit to Xi'an.

3.1.1.2 *Layout Plan of a Letter*

```
                                              XXXXXXXXXX
                                              XXXXXXXXXX
                                               XXXXXXXX (1)
XXXXXXXXXX (2)

XXXXXXXXXX (3)
XXXXXXXXXX (4)
XXXXXXXXXX
XXXXXXXXXX (5)

XXXXXXXXXX (6)
                    XXXXXXXXXXXXXXXXXXXXXX (7)
             XXXXXXXXXXXXXXXXXXXXXXXXXXXXXXXXXXXXXXXXXXXXXXXXXXX
XXXXXXXXXXXXXXXXXXXXXXXXXXXXXXXXXXXXXXXXXXXXXXXXXXXXXXXXXXXXXXXX
XXXXXXXXXXXX (8)

XXXXXX (9)

(signature)
XXXXXX (10)

XXXXXX (11)
XXXXXX (12)
XXXXXXXXX (13)
```

It should be noted that if the letter extends beyond one page, plain paper with the same form including the quality and color as the first page is used for the text beyond the first page. The top or bottom margin of the second page should include the page number.

3.1.1.3 *Sample Letters*

Sunshine Publications Ltd

26 October, 2017

Mr. Daniel Choi
Chief Executive Officer
Excellent Architectural Design Limited
23/F Special Tower
27 Hennessy Road
Causeway Bay
Hong Kong

Dear Mr. Choi,

Subscription Renewal

Thank you for your subscription of Design Monthly Magazine, the widely received leading information source of the architectural design industry. This is a gentle reminder that your subscription expires at the end of this year. To continue to stay ahead in the architectural design industry, remember to renew your subscription of the magazine that gives you "access to opportunity and advancement".

Simply complete the leaflet enclosed and fax it to us at 8000 1235 or call our customer services hotline at 8000 1234 anytime from 9:00am-5:00pm, Monday to Friday and 9:00am-1:00pm, Saturday. Alternatively, you can also send the completed leaflet in the self-addressed return envelope to us.

We look forward to continuing to serve you.

Yours faithfully,

SherryDong

Sales Executive

19/F, Sunshine Mansion, 36 Sunshine Road, Hung Hom, Hong Kong
Tel: 8000 1234 Fax: 8000 1235, Email Address: sales@ sunshine.com.hk

3.1.1.4 *Addressing an Envelope*

Sherry Dong
Sunshine Publications Ltd
19/F, Sunshine Mansion
36 Sunshine Road
Hung Hom
Hong Kong
(Address of addresser)

Stamp

Mr. Daniel Wong
Chief Executive Officer
Excellent Architectural Design Limited
23/F Special Tower
27 Hennessy Road
Causeway Bay
Hong Kong
(Address of Recipient)

3.1.2 Faxes

Fax, short for facsimile and sometimes called telefax or telecopying, is the telephonic transmission of scanned printed material (both text and images), to the receiver normally identified by a telephone number and connected to a printer or other output device. The original document is first scanned with a fax machine (or a telecopier), which processes and converts the content including both text and images from a single fixed graphic image into a bitmap, then it is transmitted through the telephone system in the form of audio-frequency tones. These tones are sent to the receiving fax machine where they are interpreted and those images are reconstructed, finally a paper copy is printed out.

In most cases, a company has a fixed fax format. Thus, what you need to do is clearly fill out the letterhead and draft the content, and then you will be able to fax it to the recipient.

Some commonly used abbreviations in faxes are given as follows:

Ref. : reference (it denotes the reference number of the fax)

Our Ref. : the addresser's reference number

Your Ref. : the recipient's reference number

Attn. : the recipient

cc. : make a copy to other recipients

Fax Format 1

To: Hongxing Company   Attn: Ms. Jones
From: Mr. Zhang   Date: 20180325
Fax No.: 1234567   Ref No.: MZ1827-02
Pages: 1

Subject: About Your Promoting Project

Dear Ms. Jones,

    It was a great pleasure meeting you this Monday and learning of your interest in our promoting project.

    Please find enclosed detailed information of our special promotion package for the May issue.

    As the final deadline is approaching, your prompt confirmation would be highly appreciated.

    Thank you for your kind attention and I am looking forward to your prompt reply.

Kind regards.

(Signature)

Fax Format 2

To: Hongxing Company
From: Mr. Zhang
Fax No.: 1234567
Attn: Ms. Jones
Date: 20180325
Ref No.: MZ1827-02
Pages: 1

Re: About Your Promoting Project

Dear Ms. Jones,

    It was a great pleasure meeting you this Monday and learning of your interest in our promoting project.

    Please find enclosed detailed information of our special promotion package for the May issue.

    As the final deadline is approaching, your prompt confirmation would be highly appreciated.

    Thank you for your kind attention and I am looking forward to your prompt reply.

Kind regards.

(Signature)

Sample fax

Asian Development Bank

FAX

East Asia Department
Transport Division (EATC)
6 ADB Avenue, Mandaluyong City
1550 Metro Manila, Philippines
Tel (632) 632-4444
Fax (632) 636-2426, 636-2444

Page 1 of 1

To:	Mr. Ma Jiahua Chairman of the Board XXXX Expressway Construction Co. Ltd. Yundu, Guangxi, PRC	Date:	27 January 2012
		Fax:	+86 123 456789
Originator:	Daniel Smith Transport Specialist, EATC	Approved by:	Nigel Roberts Director, EATC

Dear Mr. Ma,

Subject: Loan 2008-PRC: Guangxi Road Development II Project
- Increase in ADB Financing and Utilization of Loan Savings

Please be informed that ADB has approved the increase in ADB financing of the civil works-expressway contracts from 38% to 43% to utilize the expected loan savings of $9.66 million. The increased financing will be applied retroactively to past disbursements and to any future disbursements until the ADB loan of $124.0 million is fully utilized. For this purpose, please advise us the remaining disbursements to be made under the loan for all loan categories. As the loan closing date is due on 31 January 2012, please submit to ADB the last withdrawal application on or before 29 February 2012.

Sincerely yours,

Nigel Roberts
Director
Transport Division
East Asia Department

cc: Mr. Wang Changyu, Assistant Chairman of the Board of Directors, CMCD
     Yundu, Guangxi, PRC (Fax No. 86-123-456789, 2234222)

/tet

3.1.3 Emails

Email, short for electronic mail, is a method of exchanging information between two or more people by virtue of electronics. It has been widely used by individuals, businesses, and organizations in most countries. As a result of the "e-revolution" in business communication, email has key benefits to businesses and organizations:

· Email provides a method to exchange messages without set-up costs.

· Sending an email is not as expensive as sending postal mail.

· Email is much more efficient than most of the alternatives.

· Unlike a telephone or in-person conversation, e-mail by its nature can be stored electronically, which records detailed communication, including email addresses of the sender and recipient, and the date and the exact time when the message was sent or received.

Although email possesses more advantages over the traditional mail, it is normally regarded as less formal, and you also need to choose appropriate formality in style and carefully proofread your message, similar to what you do with the printed correspondence.

Sample Email

> Dear Dr. Zhang:
>
> My name is Yinan Qiu in your course— CAD for Civil Engineer. Please find my assignment in the attachment.
> Thank you for your time.
>
>
> Best regards,
> Yinan Qiu
> Department of Civil Engineering
> University of Tokyo

3.1.4 Notes

A note is a short form of letter that can be used for specific purposes. For example, you can write a note when you want to leave a message, express your thanks/appreciation, or make an apology, an appointment, or an invitation. These normally consist of one or a few sentences in a rather informal style, while the surname of the writer and the intended reader usually do not appear. Typically, there are four steps for writing a note:

1. Write the date when the note is written in the upper right corner;

2. Write the name of the reader followed by a comma or nothing;

3. Write the body of the note;

4. Sign your name.

Leaving Messages

> May 2
>
> Dr. Wang,
>
> A student named Edward Lau called you for something urgent. When you return, please call him back at 56023370 a. s. a. p.
>
> Emily Zhang

Expressing Thanks

> Feb. 26
>
> Hong and Guiyang,
>
> We are writing to thank you for inviting us to the wonderful and unforgetable Chinese New Year party. Your kindness and friendship made us feel at home in this country.
>
> Thank you once again!
>
> Jean and Rod

Expressing Apologies

> July 7
>
> Dear Lucy,
>
> I'm so sorry I wasn't able to get to the theater in time for a terrible traffic jam. I wish you enjoyed the opera without me.
>
> Andy

Appointments

> Sept. 10
>
> Dear Prof. Wang,
>
> I have some problems in finishing the homework. Could I make an appointment with you for a tutorial this week?
>
> Your student,
>
> Li Lei

Informal Invitations

June 3

Dear Leonard,

This Friday evening we'll have a party to celebrate the 2nd anniversary of our Modern Poetry Club in Room 201. The party is expected to last from 19:00 to 20:30.
We would be happy if you could attend it.

Meredith

3.2 COVER LETTER, AUTOBIOGRAPHY AND RESUME

3.2.1 Cover Letter

The goal of a cover letter is to send your application to let a potential employer know what value, skills, and expertise you will bring to the company, and if you are a perfect fit to the position. A cover letter is professional as it is sent along with your personal resume; an elegant, personal, and inviting document with one-page as an introduction to show your passion and attract others'attentions in different ways. You can send a cover letter along with your resume even if the potential employer doesn't ask you to do so.

There are some key points for writing a cover letter which include:

· Greeting: name the person you sent your cover letter to.

· Opening: compose an opening paragraph to show that you are the best person for the work, and how your skills and your enthusiasm will benefit the company.

· Hook: write a personal hook paragraph that indicates your achievements in the past related to the job you are applying for.

· Skills: briefly highlight your additional experience and skills related to the job, for instance, the second or third language you can use, computer skills and so on.

· Close: reemphasize your advantages and value for the job and recap your personal contact information.

Here are some general tips that you may need to compose a cover letter.

First, your cover letter should fit to your applications for each position. You should pay attention to the description of the employment information that contains important keywords of the job to let you know the position type and the company's requirements for this position. It is better to write a cover letter using these same keywords used in the employment description.

Secondly, you should tell the company you want this job, that you are the best person to match their needs, and that your experience and skills will bring significant value to the company.

Thirdly, be sure to emphasize what kind of research you have done as you have studied the company's current situation and problems. It will be helpful if you provide a solution to the problem associated with your potential job. In your cover letter, you can clarify how you will contribute to the company if you get this job. For instance, if you are a professional manager, be sure to explain your management experience; if you are applying for an IT position, indicate that you have efficient professional skills in the IT field.

Finally, your cover letter should be checked carefully in terms of the grammar and spelling. Be sure that every word is properly written even if you use the spell-checker, it will still be helpful to let others proofread your cover letter again.

Cover Letter Sample 1

Your Address

[your name]

[your full address]

[your phone number]

[your email address]

Date

[month] [day], [year]

Recipient's Address

[name of hiring manager]

[hiring manager's title]

[company]

[company's full address]

Salutation

Dear [insert name of hiring manager],

Body

First paragraph: Mention the job you're applying for and where you found the job listing. Middle paragraphs: Discuss your qualifications. These paragraphs should be specifically tailored to requirements posted in the job listing. You might also consider including why this specific company interested you in the first place. Limit this section to two to three paragraphs.

Final paragraph: Discuss the next steps. If you are going to follow up in one to two weeks, mention a specific date. If you would prefer to leave the ball in their court, say that you look forward to discussing your qualifications further. Also provide your email address and phone number. Don't forget to thank them for their time.

Close

Best,

[your handwritten signature]

[your typed name]

[your title, if applicable]

Cover Letter Sample 2

[Date]

Ms. XXXXXX

Customer Service Manager

XXXXXX Inc.

Second Ring Road.

Xi'an, Shaanxi, 710061

Dear Ms. XXXXXX:

I was excited to see your opening for a customer service rep, and I hope to be invited for an interview.

My background includes serving as a civil engineer associate within both highway and transportation. Most recently, I worked on the customer service desk for Discount-Mart, where my responsibilities included handling customer merchandise returns, issuing refunds/store credits, flagging damaged merchandise for shipment back to vendors and providing back-up cashiering during busy periods.

I am also being proficiencies in using MS Word, MS Excel and CRM database applications and 4 year of college (civil engineering major). Please see the accompanying resume for details of my experience and education.

I am confident that I can offer you the customer service, communication and problem-solving skills you are seeking. Feel free to call me at XXXXXX to arrange an interview. Thank you for your time—I look forward to learning more about this opportunity!

Sincerely,

XXXXXX

Enclosure: Resume

3.2.2 Autobiography

At some points in your education or career, you may be asked to give a speech about yourself or write an autobiography. Biographers often rely on a wide variety of documents and opinions and may be based entirely on the author's memory of his or her life story.

Your autobiography should contain a basic framework: an introductory paragraph with a thesis statement, a body containing several paragraphs, and a conclusion.

When starting to write your life story, your goal is to figure out what makes your family or experience unique and to build a story around it. Here are some clues you can study:

· The time and place of your birth.

· What is interesting about the region where you were born.

· An overview of your personality.

· Your likes and dislikes.

· The special events that shaped your life.

Take a look at your own life from an outsider's point of view and establish the theme; there are two main elements you should research.

1. Consider your childhood and culture

You may not have the most interesting childhood in the world, but everyone has some memorable experiences. The idea is to highlight the best parts when you can. Some of your childhood experiences will always be unique to others; you need to take a step back and act as if they know nothing about your geography or culture. You might think of your family celebrating or observing certain days or events, and you may consider certain festivals, customs, or the food you eat as unique. Clothes you wear and games you play can also be identifying factors of your life. With special phrases, tell your audience about some special times.

2. Think about your educational experience

Considering the education experience in life, generally, people usually focus on their applications (such as a bad semester), or the self-defined topic they need to discuss, such as political reasons.

Your personal statement about education is worth including:

· Attendance of the first year or an advanced seminar, assuming that the seminar is academic and requires you to produce meaningful work and something deliverable.

· Past academic scholarships and your criteria for obtaining these scholarships, especially if they are competitive national awards;

· Any cooperation or work experience directly related to graduate study, especially if your work is integrated into advanced research;

· Study in more than one school or study abroad, especially if you are proficient in multiple languages;

· Honorary education course or honorary degree thesis;

· Complete a bachelor/master program to discuss project details;

· Complete a graduation thesis, especially if there are some aspects of the research that can be continued in graduate school;

· Education training through military or professional certification programs, emphasizing the relevance of postgraduate study;

· Transfer or return to school after leaving school, emphasizing the lessons learned from experience and providing evidences of achievements and motivations.

Once you have thought through this, you will be able to select the most interesting elements from your notes to create a theme. You can spend an ordinary day in your life and turn it into a topic worth writing about. You can also use an event in your life as a topic. One day in your life can have such a big impact that it can be portrayed as a main subject.

Whether you think that your life story is a single event, a single feature, or a day, you can use an element as a theme. You will define this topic in your introductory paragraph.

Then you should create an outline with some activities related to your central theme and turn them into the body paragraphs of your story. Finally, summarize all your experiences and explain the theme of your life.

3.2.3 Resume

The purpose of a resume is to describe your qualifications for a particular job. A resume is not the history of your life. The purpose of a resume is to prove that you are qualified for a particular type of work, and that you will be a competent and responsible employee who communicates effectively. Your format can either be traditional or innovative as long as the information is accessible and organized to highlight the most important items (from an employer's perspective). Your style should be formal, but you do not need to use complete sentences, rather use concise and positive statements.

The order and content of each person's resume will not necessarily be the same. However, the format is somewhat standardized, so that employers can easily find the information they are looking for. After your title, rank the information on your resume from the most important to the least in order to support your goals.

3.2.3.1 *Heading*

· Your full name: Use the form of your name as it appears on academic records and other documents. There should be no confusion that documents belong to the same person.

· Telephone: If you only use one phone number, you can put it under your name or use the mailing list.

· Email address (es): You can put it under your name or by mail. Use your full name as an alias, as in Matthew. broderick@ vt. edu. The "edu" extension lets E-mail recipients know you are connected to a university.

· Mailing address: Undergraduate students should provide university and permanent address. Make them accurate and easy to find you.

If you have a job sample online for employers, make it easily accessible, however, do not assume employers have time to visit them.

3.2.3.2 *Objective*

The objective is to tell your prospective employer what type of work you are currently working on. The rest of your resume should be designed to support your goals most effectively.

If you are using your resume to apply for a scholarship, graduate school, etc. , make sure to state it in your goals. State your purpose succinctly; there is no need to have a lengthy statement.

For a job search, do not let an employer guessing what you want to do. Therefore:

· Make sure the employer knows either the industry you want to work in, the type of work you want to do, the skills you can apply, or a combination of these. For example, marketing position in sports or sports promotion, interest in using writing and public speaking skills.

· Avoid broad statements like, "position which utilizes my skills and abilities" without specifying your skills and abilities.

· Avoid "position related to (name of your major)". when your major does not describe a job or career field, it is too vague to be meaningful. For example, "position in business" is far too vague to give an employer an idea of what you want to do.

If you want to find an internship, summer job, or any other temporary position, illustrate this point, so employers don't misunderstand you and assume you are graduating and seeking a long-term job.

If you have several different goals, create more than one resume. Each version of your resume can be slightly different to support one of your specific goals.

It is not necessary to list the name of the employment organization in your goals.

3.2.3.3 *Education*

Your education department should always follow your purpose statement. This is because your education is your current pursuit or the most recent achievement, usually related to your goals. Even if your major is not clearly tied to your goals, you will want your employer to know that you are completing (or working toward) a college degree.

The education information should include:

· Degree(s),

· Major/program,

· Option or minor,

· Graduation month/year,

· Institution,

· City/town, and

· State.

Example 3.2.1

> Bachelor of Science, Civil Engineering, Transportation; Psychology Minor, expected July 2018, Chang'an University, Xi'an, Shaanxi.
>
> Bachelor of Arts, English; Math Minor, expected July 2018, Chang'an University, Xi'an, Shaanxi.

Here are some suggestions for a list of degrees and majors:

· If you have more than one degree, list the most recent one first.

· If your major and choice/focus/secondary names are short, you can put them on the same line as your major.

· If the name for your major, choice, minor, etc., is long, try putting options, attention, and/or adverbs in the second line.

· You can use the full name of the university, an official nickname, or both.

Example 3.2.2

> ONE degree, ONE major, ONE minor AND/OR option
>
> Bachelor of Science, Civil Engineering, Transportation; Psychology Minor, expected July 2018, Chang'an University, Xi'an, Shaanxi.
> OR
> adding option (too long to fit one line with major):
>
> Bachelor of Science, Civil Engineering, Transportation, expected July 2018
>
> Exercise and Health Promotion Option, Psychology Minor
>
> Chang'an University, Xi'an, Shaanxi.

Bachelor of Arts, English; Math Minor, expected July 2018

Chang'an University, Xi'an, Shaanxi

OR

Bachelor of Arts, English, expected July 2018

Math Minor

Chang'an University, Xi'an, Shaanxi.

Example 3. 2. 3

ONE degree, TWO majors

Bachelor of Science, Civil Engineering and English, expected July 2018

Chang'an University, Xi'an, Shaanxi

Example 3. 2. 4

Degrees from different institutions

Master of Science, Civil Engineering, Transportation, expected July 2018, Chang'an University, Xi'an, Shaanxi

Bachelor of Science, Biology, July 2014, Tongji University, Shanghai

Example 3. 2. 5

Undergraduate and graduate degrees from same institution

Master of Science, Computer Engineering, expected July 2018

Bachelor of management, Engineering Management, July 2014

Chang'an University, Xi'an, Shaanxi

You could repeat the institution name under each degree, as in the example above where degrees are from different institutions, but listing the institution once saves space if you have other good content filling your resume.

Optional items include:

· Overall and/or major GPA.

· Honors, or events and honors. If you have an important academic award, scholarship, academic achievement and/or a particularly outstanding academic honor, list it here.

· Class projects or independent research. This could also be a major heading section. A class project can be an entry for relevant experience and you can show how these details pertain to your topic, work, research, accomplishments, and your presentations.

3.2.3.4 *Publications*

This may also be a major heading section. Undergraduates usually do not have publications but if you do have any, include them here; it will be significant. Many graduate students participate in the writing of publications.

3.2.3.5 *Coursework*

Consider these guidelines:

· Be sure to have courses related to your goals or the employer may not know you have been educated on the topic. For example, if you are a civil engineering student, and have taken four computer science classes, these courses should be listed here.

· If your major (or minor) does not include these courses, then be sure to include courses that are important to your career goals.

· If you find the job description or other information offered by the employer indicating that they want to know if you have taken a particular course, include the relevant courses.

· You can list the advanced electives of your major (or related to your career goals). Do not include lower-level courses or basic prerequisites for the advanced courses.

· Don't add to your major or minor courses that will not add value to your resume and will not help you stand out from other candidates. It is better to use your space on more relevant information.

· In most cases, do not list your high school education. If you are in college, it is assumed that you have graduated from high school.

· If you are a freshman or sophomore and attended a well-known high school, you may have an exception. In your junior year, however, you need to demonstrate your college grades and through graduate school, list the work of university and graduate level.

· The other exception is that if you apply for a teaching position and went to the high school in the same district you are applying for, you will want to express your familiarity with the community.

3.2.3.6 *Experience* (*Related experience or Other experience*)

Use relevant experience to support your goals if possible. It can be paid or unpaid, it can be an internship or a big project, a volunteer position or a club position, etc.

However, your experience does not have to be relevant. This will allow you to include any skills, knowledge, or abilities that you have learned of the type of work you are looking for.

If your experience is divided into two categories, "relevant" and "other", you can use these two headings to divide your experience. Details of "other experience" can be added under "relevant experience" sections.

If you do not have relevant experience, you should list your employment background, this will signify that you understand basic professional ethics and have acquired specific skills. Demonstrating skills such as responsibility, teaching ability, customer service, time management, show the company your preparedness for employment.

In general, list your experiences in chronological order in each category.

Include these basic elements in the title: Titles and/or the organization name; anything that looks the most useful. However, if everything is bold, nothing will stand out so use the bold font sparingly.

· Your current job title (what you did).

· Organization name (e. g. , world health organization).

· Operative/daily (current) month & year, or school/season and year.

Briefly describe your accomplishments under this heading. Use phrases or incomplete sentences.

Example 3. 2. 6

Transportation Consulting Center Volunteer, Xi'an, Shaanxi

Worked 5-10 hours per week; September 2014 — May 2015

— Learned about transportation resources for various citizen needs.

— Scheduled other volunteers for telephone hotline shifts.

Editing & Reporting Internship, Summer 2016, Library, Chang'an University, Xi'an, Shaanxi

— Reviewed copies and suggested edits under supervision of events editor.

— Etc.

---

3. 2. 3. 7 *Activities, Honors, and Leadership*

Sort them on your resume.

If you have several activities related to your career goals, list your activities at the top of your resume and honors at the end.

If you are likely to belong to these two types of projects, use the combination section.

If you have a project under the "honor" category, it would be redundant to put a project under a plural title.

If you have a particularly outstanding academic honor, you may want to list it under your education heading.

When the list is organized:

Use full names instead of abbreviations.

· Example: China Road and Bridge Corporation (CRBC).

If the nature or purpose of the organization is unclear, provide a brief explanation.

· Example: ABC, Asian bank

Do not add "members of...", if you list an organization, the employer knows you are a member; the name of the organization is sufficient.

Please indicate the position you are in (including month/year or school year) and/or the activities you attend (you can clearly express your accomplishments in the interview).

If you have a leadership position, you can simply list or describe your accomplishments (as you did in your work experience). Emphasizing activities or skills that support your career goals. Please refer to the section on experience above; you may want to include activities under "relevant experience" if applicable.

Date of appointment (month/year or school year) and leadership role.

Example 3. 2. 7

Comedy Club, 20XX   present

President, 20YY   20ZZ

Events Chair, 20XX   20YY

· Scheduled venue and coordinated publicity and acts for twice-yearly performances.

· Served as liaison with university officials for compliance with policies and facility rules.

---

3. 2. 3. 8 *Skills*

Most resumes list skills. Titles may be described as "Skills", including writing skills, computer skills, foreign language skills, lab skills, and more.

If you have several skills you can include the subtitle of your classification, such as "computer skills", "laboratory skills", "language skills", "organizational skills", and so on.

If your skills and career goals are more relevant than the rest of your background, put this section on the resume page, not the other relevant sections.

3.2.3.9 *Certifications / Licenses*

If you have a certification or license related to your career goals, provide this information in this section. Write this in the main section of your resume instead of with any other relevant information.

A list of other items related to your target authentication or license may be listed in education, especially if your training is to ensure its security. You can also put it under the heading of "relevant experience and qualifications".

Target with you, to own certification is important to this part, but it is also a useful information, such as emergency cardiopulmonary resuscitation (CPR). It can be listed in another category with an appropriate title such as "other activities", or "activity and certification."

3.2.3.10 *Availability*

Students seeking an occupation with an education should have availability. For example, the fall semester of 2018 and/or the spring semester of 2019. The location of the collaboration can start any semester, and the employer will not know when you are going to start unless you provide the information.

Students looking for internships or related summer jobs should demonstrate this in their job objectives. Therefore, there will be no need to explain the date of availability—your goal means you are available. However, if you are applying for a position in which the employer asks for a specific date of employment, you can provide it on your resume or cover letter.

Undergraduate students do not need a statement of availability date unless your availability is not apparent on your degree completion date. For example, if you use June 2022 as your degree month, but you cannot start working until September, explain it.

Graduate students may want to specify an availability date, especially if you have some flexibility in this area. For example, if you plan to complete your thesis or thesis defense in February 2012, you can start work in January 2012 and this can be included in a brief statement. You might point out that your availability is flexible between January and March 2012.

3.2.3.11 *Resume Sample* 1

Xiaoming Li xiaoming@chd.edu.cn (540) 111-2345	**Permanent Address:** 1234 Second Ring Road Xi'an, Shaanxi, 710061

OBJECTIVE Cooperative Consulting position related to civil engineering

EDUCATION
B.S. Civil Engineering, Expected graduation with co-op: July 2018
Minor: Statistics
Chang'an University, Xi'an, Shaanxi.
GPA: 3.2/4.0

COMPUTER SKILLS

SOFTWARE:		LANGUAGES:	
AutoCAD	MiniTab	Fortran	PowerC
TK solver	Mathematica	Visual Basic	C++

EXPERIENCE

Transportation Consulting Center Volunteer, Xi'an, Shaanxi
September 2014 - May 2015
— Learned about transportation resources for various citizen needs.
— Scheduled other volunteers for telephone hotline shifts.

Editing & Reporting Internship, Library, Chang'an University, Xi'an, Shaanxi
Summer 2016,
— Reviewed copy and suggested edits under supervision of events editor.

ACTIVITIES
Student Engineers Council (SEC), Membership Committee Chair, 20XX-20XX
High School Varsity Volleyball Team, 20XX-20XX
High School Symphonic Band, 20XX-20XX

HONORS
Distinguished student Scholar, Chang'an University, 20XX
Scholar Athlete Award, 20XX-20XX

AVAILABILITY
Fall semester 2018, Summer 2019, Spring2019*(Note: this information could be placed with "objective" which would take less space on the page.)*

Features of this resume：

· Includes high school activities，because this student is a sophomore；by junior year，generally remove high school activities unless they are rare or show a long track record of interest or involvement in your chosen field.

· Availability is included, because this is for a co-op position with multiple work terms; employers won't automatically know when are available to work, so tell them.

· When you don't have career-related experience (yet) your other jobs show employers things like work ethic and customer service experience—qualities important in all work settings.

3.3 BUSINESS LETTER

In this session, several commonly used types of business letters are presented, including letter of inquiry or request, letter of acknowledgment, sales letter, order letter, letter of urging payment, letter of payment confirmation, letter of complaints and the replies to complaints, letter of recommendation, letter of invitation, follow-up letter, letter of appreciation or thanks, apology letter, and letter of intent.

3.3.1 Letter of Request or Inquiry

A letter of inquiry is written to request specific information. For example, you can request for promotional material or for specific information of a product or service. Although the recipient may or may not be as motivated to respond promptly, you should always write the letter in a friendly and professional manner; try to be as straightforward as possible to identify the information you request.

Write a letter of inquiry in the following format:

· In the first paragraph, identify yourself by providing your position and organization if appropriate.

· In the second paragraph, provide details about the request subject by briefly explaining why you are writing and how the requested information will be used. Offer to keep the information confidential if it seems reasonable.

· List the specific information you are requesting. You can phrase your requests as a list of specific items or questions and do your best to make each item clear and discrete.

· At the end of the letter, offer some motivations to the recipient for a prompt response.

If you need the information by a particular deadline, mention it in the letter. Punctuation, spelling, and grammatical errors should be carefully checked. Below is a letter of inquiry written by a marketing representative who has requested specific information about organic fruit promotion.

September 9, 2016
Mr. Robert Cruise
Organic Fruit Growers Association
Company, Address
Dear Mr. Robert,

I am Mr. Keith Lieberman, marketing representative of Wellcome Supermarket. We are interested in purchasing and selling your product, organic fruits, in our market. We read your promo materials regarding the products that are currently being sold at special discounted prices.

We would like to inquire some details about your product:

1. Where are the fruits grown and how do you ensure that they are organically grown?
2. Would you be able to supply fruits that you do not have now but we would specify?
3. Would you be able to provide a regular supply of fruits delivered fresh everyday?
4. How much are the wholesale prices of the fruits and how much discount can we avail?

I would be happy to talk to you about the details of your product as we hope to add organic fruits to our supermarket soon. Please contact me at 020 8805 8367.
Thank you.
Sincerely,
Mr. Keith Lieberman

3.3.2 Letter of Acknowledgment

A letter of acknowledgment is a formal letter written by one party to another, providing proof that specific documents, goods, or a specific request has been received. These letters normally start with a brief sentence stating with "this is, indeed, a letter of acknowledgment". Some phrases you can use are as follows:

· I hereby acknowledge the receipt of the following documents. . .

· I am writing to acknowledge the receipt of. . .

For the remainder of the letter, you should specifically explain what you are acknowledging in one or two paragraphs. In your conclusion, you can offer your help if needed by using phrases such as: "If I may be of further assistance, please do not hesitate/feel free to contact me."

Sample Letter

Joseph Smith
ACEM Communication Bank
5555 S. Main Street
Anywhere, New York 90001
March 18, 2018

Re: Loan No. 2018

Dear Mr. James Chan,

Because Mr. Doug Walsh is on a business trip for the next week, I hereby acknowledge the receipt of your letter dated March 15, 2018. It will be brought to his attention immediately upon his return.

If I may be of any assistance during Mr. Walsh' absence, please do not hesitate to call me at 0123 4567.

Yours sincerely,

Joseph Smith

3.3.3 Sales Letter

A sales letter is a piece of direct mail designed to persuade the reader to purchase a specific product or service in the absence of a salesman. Different from other direct mail techniques such as leaflet distributions, the sales letter typically sells a single product, product line, or service (due to its price) considered a purchase at medium or even high value (typically tens to thousands of dollars). Sales letters prefer to be mainly textual than graphically based. A sales letter is often, although not exclusively, the last stage of the sales process before the customer places an order and it is designed to ensure the prospect is committed to becoming a customer.

Before writing a sales letter, gather facts about your product or service. Ask yourself the following questions: If your product is a tangible one, what is its size, shape, composition, etc.? Does it compare favorably with your competitor's product in durability, efficiency, appearance, safety, or in terms of price? What human needs or wants does it fulfill?

With your product or service in mind, you are ready to identify central selling features that will fulfill specific customer needs. End-users are usually interested in comfort, performance, appearance, and safety, while dealers are more interested in turnover and profit.

The purpose of any sales letter is to sell; many companies depend on them to boost their sales. These are unsolicited letters, so it is important to ensure that your sales letter does not go unnoticed.

The principle of *AIDA* in writing sales letter:

To draw or capture customers'*Attention*.

To arouse their *Interest*.

To create their *Desire* for a product.

To encourage their *Action* of purchase.

Following the *AIDA* principle, the structure and strategies in writing a sales letter are naturally formed.

1. Paragraph 1—Drawing Attention

This paragraph is the most crucial paragraph in a sales letter and must get the client's attention.

Here, you will demonstrate why the client needs your company's product/ service. For example, many sales letters often remind readers of a "pain point" — a problem that a person needs to solve, and then introduce a product or service which will provide the solution.

It is very important to move quickly to your sales pitch in the letter, as most readers will soon understand that you are just advertising. Keep it short and crisp.

It should be interesting, but at the same time it should not be overstated. Refrain from exaggeration, e. g. do not try to make the client believe that his company is in a crisis. It is best to stick to facts as everybody appreciates honesty.

If this is the first time you have contacted the customer, or if your company is unknown to the client, start the letter by briefly introducing yourself and your company.

The following are some useful key phrases and examples for writing the first paragraph of a sales letter.

Useful Key Phrases:

· Would you like to see the speed of your computer increase by 10% or more?

· Wouldn't you prefer to have your wedding ceremony planned by a leader in the field?

· Are you having trouble. . .

· In 2015 we helped over 20 software companies like yours increase their productivity.

· This is why it is important to have. . .

· At Best Company, we have the techniques and experience to. . .

Examples

It has been an honor to write to your company Sunny Fresh Foods on behalf of SF Express. One of the most important and crucial aspects of any business is the distribution and delivery that crafts the success path of any company. Our company has been providing the best available shipping and distributing solutions that will ensure the faith and trust of the clients in your company.

It is my pleasure to introduce you an user-friendly software that can act as an assistant to reduce your workload. I have been visiting various offices and creating awareness over the past few months. As a result of this, many accounting firms have accepted and embraced this software. I would be happy to help make your work easier and reduce your operational costs.

Have you ever worn a sweater that was both thin and warm? Believe it or not, this enclosed sample of wool is used in our new HYX sweater that will offer you such a feeling.

2. Paragraph 2—Building Interest and Desire

In the second paragraph, convince the reader of the value of your product. Once you have captured the reader's attention, you must hold that attention. The best way to maintain your client's attention is to build interest by describing your product in a way that the client have a virtual experience.

Use colorful and descriptive words to show the reader that he/she either:

· needs your product (e. g. , a bicycle);

· could use your product (e. g. , an robot cleaner);

· would benefit from your product (e. g. , water purifier);

· OR should not be without your product (e. g. , insurance).

You must emphasize the superiority of your product/service over others without speaking ill of your competitors. Adhere to the facts without making unrealistic promises.

Examples

Our company, located in Harbin, produces a wide variety of wool sweaters for men, women, and children. These sweaters are of the highest quality, popular with customers, and sold well. Our total production averages 5 million per year, 40% for the domestic market and 60% for export.

We are pleased to announce that we now offer the same service to large-scale companies like yours. From our office in Hangzhou, the heart of low cost and good quality silk products, we can supply your company with whatever kind of silk apparel you would like.

3. Paragraph 3—Convincing the Reader to Purchase

If the reader has read your letter to this point, it means that he/she has some interests in your product. Thus, the third paragraph aims at convincing the reader to buy your product.

You can indicate what your product would bring to the reader and go the extra mile by offering benefits. Keep it personal and imagine you are speaking to a specific person who represents your customer base. A promotional gift or discount can be surprisingly persuasive.

Examples

We cooperate with a wide range of Chinese furniture companies and can ensure that you will get any furniture style you may be looking for. Whether antique or modern, American style or Chinese style, and office furniture or kids furniture, we can offer you the quantity you need at the best possible price. In addition, our quality control staff ensures the furniture is well made.

Fast-computation Software will not interfere with other computational software installed on a computer. This software provides audio instructions for installation. The entire setup procedure takes less than 5 minutes. For only $ 899, you can provide a network version of this valuable software to all your students.

4. Paragraph 4—Directing Favorable Action

In the fourth paragraph that will also be the last paragraph, you must instruct the reader how to get the product or sign up for the service. Give the exact directions that you want him/her to follow. If the desired plan for your client is to go to your website and get more information, hopefully your client will contact you for further inquiries or place an order. It is worth noting that even the most highly motivated and excited customer will not act if the action you are requesting is inconvenient. Thus, make your desired action easy to understand and follow. Here are some recommendations for writing the last paragraph:

At the very least, provide some way the reader can get in touch with you, e. g. , a phone number, an e-mail address, a URL, or a reply form.

Your call to action should stand out in some way. You can do this by making it bold, making it a headline, or placing it somewhere the reader is likely to see.

One way to further encourage the reader's action is to imply a sense of urgency stating that quantities are limited or the time is limited.

Examples

To place an order, please log on to our website at www. xxxxxxx. com, or fill out the enclosed order form and send it by fax or post to our office in Harbin. Before you know it, you will be wearing this fashionable and anti-cold sweater— feeling like royalty in winter.

If you would like to take advantage of the Fast-computation Software, please go to our website at www. xxxxx. com or contact us by phone at (12/345) 8789666 and fax at (12/345) 1234 000. Thank you for your interest and we look forward to hearing from you.

Our company is expanding its market to the Mainland China and we look forward to work with your company. Enclosed is our product catalog and a price list that presents the wide range of our products. We would like take this opportunity to introduce our swimsuit to you. For more information or to place an order, please kindly visit our website at www. xxxxxx. com.

Samples of sales letter

Workwell Software
3700 Stewart Avenue
Phone 31-555-3127
http://www.workwell.com

June 7, 2010

Ali Jen, Manager
Circuit System
7 Tyler Place
Oklahoma City, OK 73101

Dear Ali Jen,

Do you know how much money your company loses repetitive strain inquiry? Each year employers spend millions of dollars on employee insurance claims because of black plans, fatigue, eye strain and carpal tunnel syndrome.

Workwell can solve your problems with its easy-to-use Exercise Program Software that will automatically monitor the time employees spend at their computers and also measure keyboard activity. After each hour, Workwell Software will take your employees through a series of exercises that will help prevent carpal tunnel syndrome and strains.

Workwell's Exercise Program Software will not interfere with busy schedules. Each of the 15 minutes is demonstrated on screen with audio instructions. The entire program takes less than 3 minutes and is available for windows EX and windows Vista. For only $1499, you can provide a network version of this valuable software to all of your employees.

To help your employees stay at work efficiently in a safe work environment, please call us at 1-800-555-WELL or contact us at http://www.workwell.com to order your software today.

Thank you.

(signature here)

Cory Soufas
Sales Manager

Business Asia Review
G.P.O. Box 123
Hong Kong
27 June 2017

Dear Executive

Business intelligence that you need

The rise of China is changing our world. If you want to be among those savvy few in the business world who profit from Asia's power, you need a reliable, on-the-ground, round-the-clock source of intelligence.

The REVIEW delivers you all of Asia's business investment, marketing and sales information every week.

Let the REVIEW work for you and you'll get:

- the advice of 100 experts with deep roots in Asia;

- an extensive business and political network that guarantees you the valuable insights and sound predictions you need;

- solid tips on what works and what doesn't – and most importantly why;

- plus a Special on China – every week.

Act within 10 days and you will get a free gift of your choice plus an exceptional 80% discount!

Sincerely

Jonathan Watson

Jonathan Watson
Marketing Manager

3.3.4　Order Letter

An order letter is written by the person/company to place the request of purchase from another company. This letter confirms with the seller that the customer requires a certain number of products within a specified time. This letter comes into action when the desired product or service has been studied in the market and a decision for a purchase has been made according to the service, quality and price of the product agreed on. Order letters are important in the business world as they initiate the purchase and encourage sales. The order letter is comprised of the products purchased, the quality of the delivery, and after sale service information.

How to write an order letter:

Before drafting the letter, be sure that it writes out all the terms and conditions of the purchase for the benefit of both the seller and the customer. It should include details about the product like the specification, quantity, and the promised price.

Clearly state the exact name of the merchandise and the amount of payment being sent. In addition, the delivery date and the late delivery clauses should be clearly stated.

For convenience of both parties, write down the address and if possible, any landmark that is close to your address that would help the supplier locate your address and deliver your products promptly.

An incomplete order letter or one with error may complicate billing and even cause the loss of business. Thus, be extra careful when writing it and always proofread before sending it.

In an order letter, the personal signature of the person who places the order should be given. Meanwhile, the letter should be addressed to the person who is responsible for carrying out the execution of the order and also copied to the head of the department.

Below is a template and a sample for an order letter.

Template

Dear Sir or Madam,

As per our discussion on _____ (date of meeting) we are pleased to place an order for 100 copies of Mastering Mathematics book by _____ (writer) for Class VII for the ICSE Board on the following terms and conditions:

1. The cost of each book will be Rs._____ (inclusive of all taxes).
2. Payment terms will be a post-dated cheque for 50% advance with the order. This cheque will be cleared on the day of the deliver. The balance payment of 50% will be cleared 7 days after delivery and after random inspection.
3. Delivery will be done within 7 days from the order date.
4. Delivery will be done at _____ (address of organization).
5. If the order is not delivered as per the above terms and conditions, the order stands cancelled.

Please find enclosed cheque number _____ dated _____ for Rs._____ towards advance for the order.

Hoping to have a long business relationship with you,

Best regards

(Name of signing authority)

Sample

---

154 Green Avenue

New York, USA

January 5, 2010

Ms. K. Hutchinson

Beller Company, Inc.

424 Park Avenue
New York, New York 10021

Dear Ms. Hutchinson,

Thank you for sending your catalog so promptly. It arrived within a few days of my request. Please send me the following items by parcel post:

1 copy Emmet and Mullen,
High School Algebra @ $7.50 $ 7.50

25 copies Pinehurst,
Plane Geometry @ $8.75 $ 218.75

Total $ 226.25

Please mail the books to the address given above within a week. I have enclosed a money order for $226.25. If there are additional charges, please let me know.

Very truly yours,

Brandon Michael

3.3.5 Letter of Urging Payment

In business and trade, the so-called Cash on Delivery (COD) does not mean that the supplier immediately receives the payment once the goods are successfully delivered. Deferring payment is rather common. No matter how dissatisfied you are with the deferment, your wording in the letter of urging payment should be appropriate in case of possible partnership in the future. Sometimes the involved party may have difficulties making payments and your letter of urging payment should show your integrity and be reasonable and properly documented.

1. The First-round Reminder

In the first urging payment letter, be courteous and give the necessary details of the payment: (a) the amount owed by the opposite party; (b) the length of time the payment has been overdue; (c) what specific action the customer should take in order to make the payment. Write the first-round letter in a persuasive tone rather than threatening and do not forget to encourage prompt response and contact.

There are four steps to construct your first urging payment letter.

· Step 1 : How to start the letter.

I would like to remind you that you have not settled our invoice #C-O8524 for $ 87,605.00.

I am writing to remind you that the payment of your account at TRANSIT is overdue.

We would like to draw your attention to the following dental bills that are unpaid beyond the credit period permitted by our agreement.

It has been two weeks now since we delivered your desks, and we have not yet to receive your payment for $ 2,530.00.

May we call your attention to your payment for the desks we delivered to you two weeks ago?

· Step 2 : How to add more details.

Enclosed is a copy of our bill for $ 2,530.00 along with an envelope for your convenience.

We have enclosed a copy of the items listed below which remain open on your account: xxx.

This amount should have been paid by January 31, 2017 [date] , so you can see it has been overdue for quite a long time.

· Step 3 : How to specify your request.

Please let us know when the payment will be settled or if we can assist you to set up a payment plan.

Please send your check for $ 2,530.00 with the enclosed envelope.

If your check is in the mail, we appreciate your timeliness. If not, would you please give this your prompt attention?

If you are unable to clear the balance in full at this time, please let us know and we will be glad to arrange an installment plan with you.

It is to your advantage as well as ours to keep your credit accounts current.

· Step 4 : How to end the letter.

Your prompt payment would be highly appreciated.

We greatly appreciate your prompt payment of this sum.

Thank you for your attention on this matter.

Please let me know if I can be of assistance.

If you have already sent your check, please accept our thanks.

If you have already settled your payment, please ignore this notice and accept our appreciation.

Below is a template and sample for explaining how to write the first-round letter of urging payment.

Template

Dear _____,

We have not received your payment for $_____ which is overdue for _____ days. Please check your records.

If you have already sent your payment, please disregard this notice and accept our thanks for your payment.

Sincerely yours,

_____[name]

_____[title]

Sample

Dear Sirs,

We would like to inform you that the invoices detailed above and payable upon receipt are still outstanding to date.

We would be grateful if you could check whether these invoices have already been processed and if you could ensure that payment reaches us as soon as possible.

If you have organized the payment, please ignore this reminder and accept our sincere apologies.

Yours sincerely,

Gordon Ma

Gordon Ma

Assistant Accountant

If the involved party neither processes the payment nor gives a response after your first urging payment letter, then another reminder may be needed, and the tone of writing should be adjusted accordingly.

2. The Second-round Reminder

In the second urging payment letter, press for payment in a tone stronger than your first letter and remind the customer of the previous urging payment letter you sent. The necessary details of the payment should also be included: (a) the amount owed by the customer; (b) the length of time the payment has been overdue; (c) the additional late charge if any. You may tell the customer that further delay is harmful to his/her credit status. Four steps to compose the second-round urging payment letter are elaborated below.

· Step 1 : How to start the letter.

Once again, we draw your attention to the payment due May 31, 2017.

We are writing again to call your attention to the following bills according to our records are unpaid well beyond our normal terms.

We have not received any response from you concerning the previous reminder we sent you on March 15 about your overdue account.

Again, we are requesting your cooperation in paying your bill which is now more than three months past due.

You did not respond to our previous reminder of your overdue balance of $1,879.00.

You have not answered my recent letter requesting the payment on your $1,879.00 purchase.

· Step 2 : How to ask for an explanation.

Would you please give us an explanation of why the invoice is still outstanding?

We would like to know the reason for your delay in paying your long overdue account, if possible.

Please let us know why the balance has not been cleared.

· Step 3 : How to press for payment in a milder tone.

I am sure that you are not intentionally disregarding these reminders of your overdue payment at the expense of your credit standing.

I believe it is not your intention to make our work difficult, but that's what it amounts to.

We understand that your company's financial conditions have not been good recently. By now, however, we think you should be able to start paying again.

To avoid an unfavorable report of your credit records, we suggest a prompt payment of the amount due.

· Step 4 : How to end the letter.

We would greatly appreciate your immediate payment.

We are counting on your cooperation in making a prompt payment.

Please settle the balance today, or at least let us know your reason for the delay.

Please restore our confidence in you and maintain your good credit rating by sending us your payment immediately.

Sample

Dear Mr. Smith,

We still haven't received your $1200 payment for the garments you purchased on February 20. Would you please give us an explanation of why the invoice is still outstanding?

If you have difficulty in paying the full amount now, please call me as soon as you have received this letter to arrange a payment schedule. Further delay would be harmful to your credit status.

Yours sincerely,

Gordon Ma

Gordon Ma

Assistant Accountant

3. The Third-round Reminder

In your third urging payment letter, you have to choose a firm tone and remind the customer of your previous letters. Again, remind the customer of all the necessary details of the payment: (a) the amount owed; (b) the length of time the payment has been overdue; and (c) the additional late charge if any. Inform the recipient of the legal action you will have to take if the final collection effort fails. The five steps below can be followed to compose the third-round urging payment letter.

· Step 1: How to start the letter.

You did not give any response to our previous letters about your past due payment.

We remind you once more of your open account that is now 92 days beyond our 30-day terms.

Your invoice is still outstanding despite our continual reminders requesting your payment or at least an explanation for your delay.

We urgently request that you immediately pay your balance of $ 1,879. 00, which has been outstanding since May 31, 2017 in spite of several notices from us.

· Step 2: How to press for your payment in a firm tone.

This account is no longer allowed to continue to be unpaid.

To avoid any problem with your credit standing, it is essential to settle this account at once.

To continue to keep your accounts open, it is essential that the overdue balance to be paid within 10 days as agreed when they were opened.

The delinquent status of your account will leave us no choice but to remove your company from our credit customer list.

In this case, we have no alternative but to withdraw credit privilege of your company.

· Step 3 : How to warn the recipient against further delay.

Any further delay in paying your balance due cannot be accepted.

You must realize that we cannot afford to carry this debt on our books any longer.

You can no longer delay payment if you wish to keep your account open.

This is unpleasant for both parties and damaging your credit rating.

Our next step is to take legal action to collect the money due to us.

· Step 4 : How to specify your deadline or demand immediate payment.

We must now insist that you pay your account within the next five days.

If we do not receive remittance within five days from the above date, we will have no alternative but to pursue other collection procedures.

Our attorney will be instructed to start proceedings to recover the debt unless I receive your remittance within the next three days.

After June 30, we will have no choice but to cancel your credit privilege and turn your account over to a collection agency.

· Step 5 : How to end your letter.

We look forward to your immediate payment.

Your prompt response is necessary.

Please make every effort to ensure that we are not forced to take this drastic measure.

Whether or not we take legal action is now your decision.

We must hear from you at once to avoid further action.

Sample

Dear Mr. Smith,

You have not responded in any way to our recent letters about your past due account.

I am afraid your failure to settle your account which is overdue for more than two months will leave us with no alternative but resort tolegal proceedings. To avoid this unfortunate situation, please send us your remittance within three days.

I look forward to receiving your cheque by this Wednesday.

Yours sincerely,

Gordon Ma

Gordon Ma

Assistant Accountant

The following presents an example for three rounds of urging payment letters.

First-round

As you are usually very prompted settling your accounts, we wonder whether there is any special reason why we have not received payment of the above account, already a month overdue.

We think you may not have received the statement of account we sent you on 30th August showing the balance of US$ 80,000 you owe. We send you a copy and hope it may have your early attention.

Second-round

Not having received any reply to our E-mail of September 8 requesting settlement of the above account, we are writing again to remind you that the amount still owing is US $80,000. No doubt there is some special reason for delay in payment and we should welcome an explanation and also your remittance.

Third-round

It is very difficult to understand why we have not heard from you in reply to our two E-mail of 8th and 18th September for payment of the sum US$ 80,000 you are still owing. We had hoped that you would at least explain why the account continues to remain unpaid.

I am sure you will agree that we have shown every consideration and now you fail to reply to our earlier requests for payment, I am afraid you leave us no choice but to take other steps to recover the amount due.

We are most reluctant to do anything from which your credit and reputation might suffer and even now we prepare to give you a further opportunity to put the matter right. We therefore propose to give you 15 days to clear your account.

3.3.6   Letter of Payment Confirmation

Upon your remittance to the recipient, a confirmation is usually needed to ensure whether your remittance has been successfully received. The letter of payment confirmation should be brief, and the remittance information is clearly provided. The amount of payment, the invoice number, the date of remittance, and more are usually included in this letter. Usually a copy of the remittance slip is enclosed in the letter.

First, inform the opposite party that you have made the remittance. Then indicate the exact date and the amount of your remittance; the invoice number is necessary here. At the end of the letter, ask for his/her acknowledgement of receipt and show your appreciation. For informative messages, be concise rather than redundant.

The following are samples of payment confirmation.

Sample 1

> Dear Ms. Lewinsky,
>
> On May 28th 2018, we transferred to you for the amount of US $60,780.00 as payment for your invoiceNO. CA 1234567. Please kindly check.
>
> I have also faxed a copy of the remittance slip for your reference. Your prompt reply would be highly appreciated when you receive the remittance.
>
> Yours sincerely,
>
> Lily Clair

Sample 2

> Dear Sir,
>
> On August 15th, 2015, we transferred the amount of 800,000 US dollars as payment for your invoice No. 9399 into your account. Please verify it.
>
> Please find the enclosed copy of the remittance slip for your reference.
>
> We will appreciate it if an acknowledgement is given us in response.
>
> Sincerely yours,
>
> James Smith

3.3.7　Letter of Complaint

A letter of complaint usually includes the following stages:

(a) Background;

(b) Problem-cause and effect;

(c) Solution;

(d) Warning (optional);

(e) Closing.

1. Background

The general situation is described in this section, for example:

I am writing to inform you of my bad experience with the room service at the Angel Hotel on 10 February this year.

I am writing to inform you that the goods we ordered from your company have not been supplied correctly.

I attended your exhibition Automobile 2017 at the Qujiang Exhibition Center (3—6March) and found it informative and interesting.Unfortunately, my enjoyment of the event was spoiled by a number of organizational problems.

2. Problem

· Cause:

On 17 November 2015 we placed an order for 12,000 tents from your company. The consignment arrived yesterday but contained only 1,200 tents.

You sent us an invoice for $20,200, but did not deduct our 5% discount as agreed.

We have found 15 spelling errors and 3 mislabeled diagrams in the sample book.

Firstly, I had difficulty in registering to attend the conference. You set up an on-line registration system that seems unworkable.

· Effect:

This error put our company in a difficult situation, as we have had to make emergency purchases to fulfill our commitments to all our customers. This caused us considerable inconvenience.

I am therefore returning the invoice to you for correction.

This large number of errors is unacceptable to our customers, and we are therefore unable to sell these books.

Even after spending several wasted hours trying to register following prompted instruction, the system would not accept my application.

3. Solution

I am writing to request you please make up the shortfall as soon as possible and ensure that such errors would not happen again.

Please send us a corrected invoice for $19,190.

Enclosed is a copy of the book with these errors highlighted. Please re-print the book and send it to us by next Monday.

May I call your attention to these matters?

4. Warning (optional)

Otherwise, we may have no alternative but to look elsewhere for our supplies.

If the outstanding accounts are still not cleared by Friday, 1 June 2018, you will be charged a 10% late payment fee.

I'm afraid that if these conditions are not met, we may be forced to take legal action.

5. Closing

I am looking forward to your explanation of these matters.

I look forward to receiving your prompt payment.

I look forward to hearing from you shortly.

Make the tone of your complaint letters polite rather than aggressive or insulting, this would annoy the reader and not encourage them to provide the solution. In addition, do not write in a reproachful way and ask questions such as, "Why can't you get this right?"

The content should provide enough details about the problem so that the recipient does not have to write back requesting more information. Unless the situation is very serious, legal action is normally not threatened in the first letter of complaint.

Sample 1

Well Goods
317 Pok Fulam Road
Hong Kong

24 November 2017

Attn: Mr. David Choi
Sales Manager
Everlong Batteries
171 Choi Hung Road
Hung Hom
Hong Kong

Dear Mr. Choi,

Re. Order No. 768197

I am writing to inform you that the goods we ordered from your company have not been supplied correctly. On 17 November 2017 we placed an order with your firm for 12,000 ultra-super long-life batteries. The consignment arrived yesterday but contained only 1,200 batteries.

This error put our firm in a difficult position, as we had to make some emergency purchases to fulfill our commitments to all our customers. This caused us considerable inconvenience.

I am writing to ask you to please make up the shortfall immediately and to ensure that such errors do not happen again. Otherwise, we may have to look elsewhere for our supplies.

I look forward to hearing from you by return.

Yours sincerely

Q. Chang

Q. Chang
Purchasing Officer

Sample 2

Flat 303 Lucky Mansions
856 Cheung Sha Wan Road
Cheung Sha Wan
Kowloon

23 November 2015

The Administrative Officer
Exhibition Services
Exhibitions International
33 Kadoorie Avenue
Kowloon

Dear Sir/Madam,

I attended your exhibition Sound Systems 2015 at the Fortune Hotel from 13-16 November and found it informative and interesting. Unfortunately, my enjoyment of the event was spoiled by a number of organizational problems. I explain each of the problems below.

Firstly, I had difficulty in registering to attend the event. You set up an on-line registration facility, but I found the facility totally unworkable. Even after spending several wasted hours trying to register in this way, the computer would not accept my application. I eventually succeeded in registering by faxing you.

Secondly, the exhibition was held at one of Hong Kong's most prestigious hotels, but frankly the venue was better suited to a medium-sized business conference than to a large exhibition open by registration to the public. The lack of space led to serious overcrowding in the venue, particularly at peak visiting times (i.e. lunch times and early evening). On one or two occasions I was also seriously concerned about the physical safety of attendees.

The final point I want to make concerns is the product information. It is very enjoyable to see and test a range of excellent sound systems, but it is also important to be able to take away leaflets on interesting products, so that more research can be done before deciding which system to buy. However, by the time I attended the exhibition all the leaflets had been taken.

Could I please ask you to look into these matters-not only on my behalf but also on behalf of other attendees, and in fact on behalf of your company, too.

I look forward to hearing from you.

Yours faithfully,

Michael Leung

Michael Leung

3.3.8 Letter of Reply to Complaint

If you operate a business or have clients of any sort, you may at some point receive a complaint letter. In some professions like a customer service representative, you may deal with complaint letters on a regular basis. Some of these complaints are justifiable while some are simply outrageous. The response that you offer to the complaint letter will partially depend on what you think of the complaint and whether you plan to do anything about it. The important thing is to offer some kinds of replies to the letter.

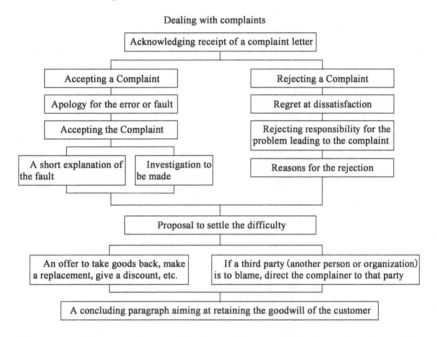

Dealing with complaints

Figure out what you plan to do about the complaint (see the above figure). Doing nothing about the complaint is not an option. You can accept the complaint, or you can reject the complaint.

If you are accepting the complaint, offer an apology. Let the person know that you will be investigating the issue or give him an explanation of what happened. (Choose one depending on the situation.)

If you are rejecting the complaint, explain to the person as politely and professionally as possible why the complaint is not valid. You may also wish to explain why you are not at fault or why you are not responsible for the issue he is complaining about.

State what you plan to do about the complaint. If you are doing nothing, state that there is nothing you can do at this time. If you accept the complaint, tell the person what it is in your power that can be done. If you reject the complaint, you can choose to do nothing. You can refer the person to someone else who might do something, or you can offer the person something as amends for his unhappiness.

Let the person know how he/she can contact you with further questions.

Include your typed name, signature, and title at the bottom of the letter.

Useful Expressions:

· Acknowledging the receipt of a complaint letter: State that you have received the complaint letter and thank him for taking the time to write.

Thank you for writing us ... regarding/concerning/in connection with...

I refer to your letter ... relating to/about ...

· Apology for the error or fault

Please accept our sincere apologies for ...

I extend my apologies for the inconvenience this problem has caused you.

We sincerely apologize for ...

I would like to apologize for the error made by our company in ...

· Accepting the Complaint:

We agree that the usual high standards of our products/services were not met in this instance.

· A short explanation of the error or fault:

As a result of our investigation, we found that...

· Causes:

The error was due to/was caused by ...

The cause of/reason for the mistake was ...

Apparently, the problem was the result of/resulted from ...

· Effects:

As a result/consequence ...

Consequently, ...

This led to ...

· Solutions:

We have changed/modified/replaced ...

To avoid/prevent re-occurrences we have set up ...

· Assurances:

We ensure/assure you that this will not happen again.

We will make every effort to assure this never happens again.

· Investigation to be made:

We are currently investigating the cause of ...

We are conducting a full investigation on the matter.

· Proposal to settle the difficulty:

To show our sincere regret/good will, we would like to .../we are willing to .../we are prepared to ...

· An offer to receive returns, make a replacement, or give a discount, etc. :

To show our goodwill, we would like to offer you a 5% discount on your next order with us.

We have dispatched the new items by SFExpress. They are supposed to arrive by Thursday, 30 November 2017.

· Regret at dissatisfaction:

We regret any inconvenience you have experienced.

We understand how disappointed you were when…

I certainly understand your frustration at…

· Rejecting responsibility for the problem leading to the complaint:

I am afraid that …

I regret to inform you that …

Unfortunately, I have to point out that …

· Reasons for the rejection:

This is because the guarantee period has expired.

This is due to the fact that the guarantee period has expired.

· If a third party (another person or organization) is to blame, direct the complainer to that party:

We therefore suggest that you contact…

· A concluding paragraph aiming at retaining the goodwill of the customer:

We look forward to continuing to serve you and assure you that this will never happen again.

We look forward to receiving further orders from you, and assure you that they will be filled correctly/promptly.

Sample 1

Everlong Batteries
171 Choi Hung Road
Hung Hon, Hong Kong
Tel/Fax 2235 2449
26 Nov 2015

Mr. J Wong
Purchasing Officer
Fortune Goods
317 Orchard Road
Singapore

Dear Mr. Wong,

Order No. 2639/L

Please accept our apologies for the error made by our company in filling your order No. 2639/L dated Monday, 23 November 2015.

You ordered 12,000 size Ultra super-long-life premium batteries, but our dispatch office sent 1,200. This was due to a typing error.

The balance of 10,800 batteries was dispatched by express courier to your store this morning and will arrive by Friday, 4 December 2015.

Since we value your business, we would like to offer you a 10% discount off your next order with us.

We look forward to receiving your further orders and assure you that they will be filled correctly.

Yours sincerely,

David Choi

David Choi

Distributions Manager

Sample 2

Everlong Batteries

171 Choi Hung Road

Hung Hon, Hong Kong

Tel/Fax 2235 2449

26 Nov 2015

Mr. J Wong

Purchasing Officer

Fortune Goods

317 Orchard Road

Singapore

Dear Mr. Wong,

Order No. 2639/L

Thank you for your letter of Monday, 23 November 2015 regarding your order No. 2639/L. We understand that this is a difficult situation for you.

We have investigated the situation, and found that you ordered 12,00 size Ultra super-long-life premium batteries. Please see the enclosed copy of your order form. Our dispatch office therefore sent 1,200.

If you need the remaining batteries urgently, the balance of 10,800 batteries can be dispatched today by express courier to your store and would arrive by Friday, 4 December 2015.

Please phone me at the number given above if you would like to order these batteries.

We look forward to receiving your further orders.

Yours sincerely,

David Choi

David Choi
Distributions Manager

Encl:
- Order Form No. 2639/L

3.3.9 Letter of Recommendation

Recommendation letters are letters of references written to the concerned authority to provide relevant information and present a candidate truthfully and positively to indicate his/her merit in a respective field. It is advisable to request someone responsible, reliable, and trustworthy to write the recommendation letters as they are of great importance when applying for jobs and academic courses.

Concerning recommendation letters, the person writing the letter should know the candidate personally so that he or she is a credible source to rate and comment on the qualities of the candidate and the relationship between the writer and the candidate should in no way bias judgments.

The recommendation letters should be detailed and complete so that the reader gets a wholesome understanding of the candidate's potentials.

Here are some main points for writing a recommendation letter.

· Present the person truthfully but positively. Neither paint an unrealistic picture of a candidate nor focus on his/her negative qualities.

· Tailor the recommendation to the position. A letter recommending a candidate for a job as a salesman should contain different information from that in a letter recommending the same candidate for a job as an accountant.

· At the beginning of the letter, briefly describe how you know the candidate you are recommending and the specific context your evaluation is based on. Consider questions like, "In what situations and for how long have you known the candidate? How close are you?"

· Present the general qualities that are relevant to the position and give one or two detailed examples. It is much more effective to include vivid details in the recommendation letter.

· The letter normally comprises of three or four paragraphs and does not exceed one page in length.

Sample letter of recommendation

Dear Mrs. Wang,

It's my great pleasure to recommend Miss Yan Wang for the Sales Manager position with The Sales Company.

As Yan's direct manager at Chang'an Sales Company, I've worked closely with her during the past three years.

I thoroughly enjoyed my time working with Yan who is a truly valuable asset to any team. She showed excellent communication skills and consistently exceeded company quotas. On a personal level, she is honest, reliable, and incredibly hard-working. Beyond that, she is an impressive problem solver who is always able to address complex issues with strategy and confidence. Yan is inspired by challenges, and never intimidated by them.

Her knowledge of sales etiquette and expertise in cold calling was a huge advantage to our entire office. She put this skill set to work in order to increase our total sales by over 21% in just one quarter. I know that Yan was a huge piece of our success.

Along with her undeniable talent, Yan has always been an absolute joy to work with. She is a true team player, and always manages to foster positive discussions and bring the best out of other employees.

In closing, I'd like to restate my strong support for Yan's application to join your team at The Sales Company. I'm confident that she will surpass your expectations in this new role. Please feel free to contact me at 029-1234-5678or abcdef@chs.com with any other questions. Thank you for your time.

Best wishes,

Yifan Liu

Yifan Liu

Director of Sales

The Sales Company

3.3.10   Letter of Invitation

A letter of invitation is designed to serve as a formal request for an individual or an organization's presence or attendance to a conference, celebration, or formal event. It is used for both personal as well as business purposes such as birthday parties, weddings, graduation celebrations, anniversary parties, retirement ceremonies, and formal galas in the community.

When beginning an invitation letter, mention what the recipient is being invited to. The letter should contain basic information including the type/name of the event, the host, time, date, and location. The expected dress code can also be mentioned in the letter. Details about the event like a person's age for a birthday celebration or whether lunch/dinner is provided can help the readers to come better prepared for the occasion.

A sample invitation to a conference

Dear Mr. Yang,

This letter is to formally invite you, on behalf of the Board of Directors, to be the Closing Keynote Speaker at the upcoming 2008 NEERI Conference.

The theme of this conference is "Solar Energy: A New Clear Sustainable Resource." The conference will be held Mountain-view Conference Facility, in Birmingham, Derby from December 3 to 5, 2008.

For your information, Susan McLeen will be the opening Keynote Speaker. The provisional title of her presentation is "Applications of Solar Energy." We will forward a complete draft of the program to you in a couple of weeks so that you can know what specific subjects will be covered by the other speakers.

We expect attendance this year to higher than it has ever been – approximately 2,000 delegates and 150 speakers. This includes a large contingent from our new European chapter, which is based in Geneva.

We would be pleased and honored if you would be our closing speaker at the 2008 NEERI Conference.

I will call you in a week or so to follow up on this.

Thank you for your consideration.

Yours sincerely,

Lily Lam

Lily Lam

3.3.11　Follow-up Letter

The follow-up letter is served as a summary description or reminder of a specific proposal, application, or document presented before a certain individual, or company after a business meeting, job interview, etc. It can be of great significance for you to consolidate the relationship between you and the recipient. Follow-up letters are normally written for various situations, but they are most often written for one of these four main purposes:

· Provide further information as well as show continued interest after an interview.

· Recap important points, agreements, or decisions made at a seminar, meeting, workshop, etc.

· Reiterate the unique features, benefits, or advantages of a product or service, or show continued interest in a potential customer by providing a special offer.

· Remind recipients of an upcoming conference or other important event.

The basic content of a follow-up letter is similar to the previous letter or the earlier document but should be presented in a brief professional manner. A sample follow-up letter for a job application is as follows:

Mr. John Smith
Senior Manager
Goodluck Pvt. Ltd.
10th South Building
87 Delaware Road
Hatfield, CA 08065
13th October 2016

Dear Mr. Smith,

I submitted a letter of application and a resume earlier this month for the programmer position advertised in *The Wall Street Journal*. To date, I have not heard from your office. I would like to confirm receipt of my application and reiterate my interest in the job.

I hold a master's degree in Computer Applications and also have an experience of more than three years working as a software engineer. I am confident that my skills and experience would be an ideal match for this position in your company.

Please let me know if you need any further materials from me.
I can be reached at (555) 555-5555 or jdoe@abcd.com. I look forward to hearing from you.
Thank you for your consideration.

Regards,

Jane Doe

3.3.12　Letter of Appreciation or Thanks

A letter of appreciation or thanks, sometimes referred to as letter of gratitude, is a way for you to appreciate the recipient for good work she/he has done. An appreciation letter written in professional and business situations does not exceed one page. Typical situations include: thanks to employees for exceptional service or performance, appreciation for special consideration extended by another organization, appreciation to volunteer service workers for their personal contributions to a public service campaign, appreciation to an individual or organization for a customer referral, thanks to a speaker for a presentation at a board meeting, etc.

In some cases, if you want to acknowledge a team, addressing your appreciation letter to one individual is more effective. For example, you can address the appreciation letter to the team leader and request that the appreciation be passed on to other team members. The letter should be composed in a sincere and genuine manner with a warm and personal tone.

Sample Business Appreciation Letter

Mr. Hennery Smith
Chief Executive Officer
Fortess Group & Companies Ltd.

Dear Mr. Smith,

I, Daniel Brown, Minister for Infrastructure Development, United States, am writing this letter on behalf of the ministry to express appreciation for the completion of the No.104 Highway project by your firm. Your firm has been assigned a project from the ministry for the first time and you have performed exceedingly well. The project has been completed well before the deadline which was awarded to you. The inspection report of the project has elucidated the fact that the project has been completed as per the standards desired by the ministry.

I appreciate you and your firm for such an excellent work on the No.104 Highway project. The ministry would be more than willing to share responsibility for work with your firm in the coming future. We hope that the satisfaction for the completion of the work is same on your part. We are looking forward to further work relations between two sides.

Thanks & Regards,

Daniel Brown

3.3.13 Letter of Apology

Letter of apology is written when you need to apologize and make amends for wrong things. Writing an apology letter conveys more integrity than a verbal apology. Here are some guidelines for writing a business apology letter.

· An apology letter is most effective when it is specifically addressed to a recipient. Avoid impersonal and overused greetings like, "Dear Sir" or "To whom it may concern." Such greetings make your letter ordinary rather than earnest.

· At the beginning of the letter, state why you are writing the letter and let the recipient know that the letter is an apology, this will prepare the recipient emotionally for every word that comes after.

· State what you are apologizing for as well as the reason for it. By doing this you are not only openly acknowledging the mistake, but ready to take the responsibility for it.

· Offer a solution you are taking to make amends. What really makes your apology effective is finding a way to solve the problem and make sure such a mistake will not be repeated in the future.

· State your desire to continue the relationship with the recipient. An apology is not just for seeking the recipient's forgiveness; it is ultimately meant to mend the fault in your relationship and keep the relationship going smoothly once again. Express your expectation of a continued business relationship.

· Keep the letter simple, straightforward, and sincere. At the end of the letter you may repeat your apology once again.

Sample

Dear Miss Dong,

On behalf of Fortress Company, I extend our sincerest apologies for the bad experience you had with our sales associate, James. I understand that James provided improper service when you visited our storefront to inquire about a new laptop. You came to us in search of information, and instead were subjected to a pushy salesperson.

At Fortress, it's our goal to help you make an informed purchase decision without having to deal with aggressive sales tactics. James is a fresh employee that I've been training. I take full responsibility for his unprofessional behavior. He has received a written reprimand and will be shadowing one of our senior sales associates until he has a better understanding of the Fortress's mission to customer service.

I'm grateful that you brought this issue to my attention and I ask your forgiveness. We assure you that such a disturbing situation would not arise and hence we request you to kindly continue patronizing our store. I've included a voucher for 20 percent off your next purchase in our store as a thank-you, should you decide to give us a second chance. We hope to see you again soon!

Kind regards,

Jennifer Smith
Sales Manager
Fortress Company

3.3.14   Letter of Intent

A letter of intent (LOI), also known as Memorandum of Understanding (MOU) or Memorandum of Agreement (MOA), is a document to indicate your intention or agreement on a specific matter. A letter of intent in business is a document outlining the agreements achieved between involved parties before legal agreements are finalized. The outlined agreements can be, for example, property lease agreements, merger and acquisition transaction agreements, joint venture agreements, etc. It is similar to a term sheet, heads of agreement, or memorandum of understanding.

A letter of intent may be presented by one party to another party and subsequently negotiated before execution (or signature). First, one party may present an LOI and then the other party can counter with edits or an entirely different LOI. Ideally, the end product will protect both parties in their subsequent negotiation and fulfillment of the contract that the LOI posits they will attempt to agree on.

Sample

June 20, 2013
Kate Anderson
Organic Vegetable Growers Association
Company, Address

Dear Ms. Anderson,

We welcome the opportunity to submit a proposal to acquire the business of Organic Vegetable Growers Association operating approximately 15 retail stores in Washington (the "Business"). We understand the desire to proceed expeditiously with a sale of the Business. We are prepared to move quickly on the transaction and believe we are well suited to do so. This letter summarizes our proposal.

1. Purchase Price

An entity newly formed by Cadeson, LLC ("Buyer") would purchase substantially all of the operating assets, including all tangible and intangible assets, equipment, leases, contract rights, and intellectual property used in the Business for a purchase price of one million seven hundred thousand dollars ($1,700,000). Buyer will not assume any liabilities of the Business of the Company other than liabilities accruing after the closing under contracts or leases assumed by Buyer.

2. Definitive Agreement

The closing will be subject to the negotiation and execution of definitive transaction documents that will include, among other things, customary representations, warranties, covenants, and indemnities by the Seller and their principals regarding the business, operations, and financial condition of the Business.

3. Closing Date

The parties acknowledge that time is of importance and that they will work towards closing the transaction as quickly as possible.

4. Conditions to Closing

The consummation of the Transaction will be subject to the satisfaction of customary conditions, including, without limitation, the following:

a) The negotiation, execution, and delivery of definitive agreements satisfactory to each of the parties, including retail leases, and securing of any required governmental or third-party approvals, waivers, or consents.

b) Maintenance of the Company's business in the ordinary course, and the absence of any material adverse change in the Company's business of financial condition or material changed in the conduct of its business as of the date of this Letter of Intent.

c) The Company not seeking or requesting any type of bankruptcy protection or bankruptcy procedure.

5. Binding Agreement

Other than this Paragraph 5, which is intended to be and is legally binding, this letter is nonbinding and constitutes an indication of intent only and creates no liability or obligation of any nature whatsoever among the parties hereto with respect to any contemplated transaction or any other matter or action described or referred to herein. Legally binding obligations with respect to the contemplated transaction will only arise upon execution of a definitive agreement and related agreements with respect to the transaction.

> If the foregoing is satisfactory, please indicate your agreement with the foregoing by countersigning a copy of this letter and returning it to our attention. We look forward to proceeding together on this transaction.
>
> Regards,
>
> Derek D. Kepner
> Managing Director
> ddkepner@cadeson.com

3.4 EXERCISES

1. Write a formal letter to the head of your department telling him or her about your difficulties in the coursework and ask for help.

2. Suppose you have a six-year work experience for an information technology company after graduation. You have rich experiences as an engineer with multi-cultural background. You are absolutely qualified for the job opening. Please email the HR to apply for the position.

3. Leave a note to your friend to apologize for keeping him or her waiting for you for one hour.

4. Suppose you have developed an/a interesting/useful/creative product or service. Please write a sales letter to a potential customer.

5. Suppose you are the potential customer mentioned in the case above. Please write an order letter to place your order.

6. Please write a letter to remind the customer of his overdue payment.

7. Please try to write a complaint letter on a supposed matter and give the corresponding replies.

8. Suppose there is a seminar host in your class and you would like to invite one of your teachers as the opening speaker, write him a letter of invitation.

9. For the situation in the case above, write a letter of appreciation to the invited teacher for his/her attendance.

10. Suppose you are a senior undergraduate student majoring in civil engineering, transportation planning and management, and have a minor in computer science at Chang'an University. You are seeking a summer internship position in a transportation-consulting corporation TCC. You need to contact with HR Mr. Zhang in TCC.

a) Please write one-page cover letter for seeking the summer internship position in TCC.

b) Please compose a brief autobiography including your background of childhood, education, and culture.

c) Please create your own resume. If you do not have the relevant experiences to support your objective, you can create virtual ones and annotate them with "expected in month/year".

3.5 BIBLIOGRAPHY

1. LANG S. Business & Technical Writing for International Projects [M]. 1st ed. Beijing: China Architecture & Building Press, 2010.

2.HAROLD J. Writing and Communicating in Business. 2nd ed. New York: MAC-Millan Publishing Co. , INC, 1973.

3.Centre for Independent Language Learning. Workplace Correspondence [OL]. [2018-03-08]. http://www2. elc. polyu. edu. hk/cill/topics/correspondence. htm.

4. Wikipedia. Autobiography [OL]. [2018-03-08]. https://en. wikipedia. org/wiki/Autobiography.

5. XFLEMING G. How to Write Your Autobiography [OL]. [2018-04-15]. https://www. thoughtco. com/how-to-write-your-autobiography-1857256.

6. SCHALL J. Describing Interesting Personal or Educational Experiences [OL]. [2018- 04-18]. https://www. e-education. psu. edu/writingpersonalstatementsonline/p2_ p9. html.

CHAPTER 4. WRITING FOR SPEECHES AND PRESENTATIONS

Speeches and presentations are useful mechanisms to deliver your ideas, claims, and findings to public. These are usually comprised of what is referred to as "public speaking." You may ask what the differences between public speaking and our daily conversation are. The differences between these two are listed below:

1) Public speaking is highly structured,
2) Public speaking requires formal language, and
3) Public speaking requires a different method of delivery.

This chapter teaches students two major components when preparing a speech or a presentation: writing for public speaking and how to prepare for visual aids effectively.

Speech and presentation are sometimes used interchangeably because the boundary between these two is blurry. According to *the Merriam-Webster Dictionary*, the definitions of the two words are different.

· Speech is "*a spoken expression of ideas, opinions, etc., that is made by someone who is speaking in front of a group of people.*"

· Presentation is "*an activity in which someone shows, describes, or explains something to a group of people.*"

Based on the definitions, speeches are focused on talking while presentations are activities focused on describing and explaining using visual or illustrative materials. It does not mean that you cannot use visual aids in your speeches, but it is important to remember that visual aids should only be used to support or enhance your speeches. Too many visual aids may generate negative effects to your speeches by distracting your audience.

Most western universities pay significant attentions and efforts to improve students' public speaking and communication skills. If you look at job advertisements posted on markets or job searching websites like Linkedin or Monster, good communication skills are required for almost every position. Because of this requirement, universities have long recognized that students must learn fundamental knowledge and skills of speech and presentation, so they encourage sudents practice as much as possible. In western universities, undergraduate students are required to take at least one speech course during the freshmen or sophomore year of college. Almost all the major courses require students to give a speech or an oral presentation at the end of the semester to explain how they solve real problems using knowledge they learned from this course. For graduate students, oral presentations play a more important role. Graduate students need to make presentations to introduce their research topics and the problems to be solved, to explain the methodologies they use, and to defend their final conclusions.

When you make a speech, you will need to know your proposed topic and specific purpose of your speech. In addition, you want to ask the following questions:

1) What special ideas, experiences, or passions do I bring to this topic?

2) How will I connect this topic to my audience?

3) How will I make them care about the problem or be motivated to adopt the solution?

4) What pattern of organization might best fit this topic? Why?

4.1 SPEECH

The following sections introduce different types of speeches and their corresponding purposes, a general step-by-step procedure for writing a speech, some commonly used organizational patterns of speech, tips for writing a speech, and tools for preparing a speech.

4.1.1 Types of Speeches

Speeches can be categorized into many different types depending on the purposes. The following three types are the most commonly used:

1. Informative

The basic theme of an informative speech is the information. It aims at providing useful information to audiences. For example, a computer programmer tells people what Alpha Go is. The speaker needs to be responsible for presenting detailed information in a very clear and concise manner.

2. Persuasive

The goal of a persuasive speech is to convince the audience to accept a point of view or a perspective. For example, eating vegetables can help people live longer or automobile exhaust is the main cause of the air pollution in big cities. Persuasive speech is the type of speech that most people likely engage in during daily living.

3. Special occasion

A special occasion speech is a speech given at ceremony, commemoration, or wedding, etc., usually praising an institution, event, or a person.

4.1.2 General Steps for Writing a Speech

The different types of speeches usually have the same goal to clearly and effectively deliver a message or claim to your audience. When you write a speech, imagine yourself as a salesman and the message is the product you are trying to sell to your audience. Therefore, the thinking and writing processes are always audience-centered. Below is a general step-by-step procedure for writing a good speech.

1. Know your audience

The first step is the most important step for writing a speech, understanding your audience, including their knowledge, and their interests. For example, if you are speaking in front of a group of kindergarten students explaining why artificial intelligence technology is very powerful, using professional words like Artificial Neural Network (ANN) or Convolutional Neural Network (CNN), will not keep their attentions. When you prepare for your speech, the first step is to analyze your audience and understand the goal or specific purpose you want to achieve. Things you should know about your audience are:

1) They want you to succeed!

2) They feel empathy for your anxiety.

3) They are eager to listen and learn.

4) They hope to be taken away by your enthusiasm and excitement about the topic.

2. Set your topic

A good speech usually focuses on one thing or one claim only, and everything you say should support it. People usually call the claim as a central idea. It takes time for people to understand and accept a new idea or perspective so do not try to include several different claims in your speech. Without enough evidences or supporting information, your speech may generate a negative influence.

3. Write an outline

An outline is the backbone of your speech. The most basic outline consists of three main parts: introduction, body, and conclusion. For different types of speeches, there are different organizational patterns that can be used depending on the purpose of your speech. We will get into details and see some examples in the next section.

The introduction of a speech is to inform your audience of what you are going to say, to make a claim or to send out the core message of your speech. Remember that your introduction must grab the attention of your audience. You can begin your speech with an interesting story, a joke, or ask a question to bring out your claim. Below is an example structure of an introduction.

1) Draw attention.

2) Reveal topic.

3) Relate to the audience.

4) Provide background/ explain the importance.

5) Preview your speech.

4. Collect evidences

For a successful speech, you need evidences to support your claims. Examples from history, current events, or daily life can be easily accepted. Quotations from experts in the field and government sources for statistics are also good evidences due to their credibility. As a speaker, you are responsible for validating the evidence you collect. Searching on the Internet is an easy and quick way to find information, but the accuracy and validity of the information is not guaranteed. Fake or incorrect information can damage your entire speech and credibility, which are very difficult to be remedied.

5. Make a conclusion

Most audiences can absorb only a small portion of what they hear, so repetition is a powerful tool. Do not think that making your point several times is too wordy but you need keep your point short and memorable. For example, in the 1990s, a Chinese TV commercial of a company of wool products used very simply advertising commentary: "sheep, sheep, sheep and then the company's name". Now most people who watched the commercial 30 years ago still remember the company's name because of the simple and memorable advertising commentary. At the end of your conclusion, finish with a concrete and vivid image that emphasizes your topic or ask people to take actions. This is usually called the take-home message.

4.1.3 Organizational Patterns of Speech

The pattern or structure of your speech is determined by your purpose. If you want to inform your audience, you may want to use a chronological organization. If you want to convince your audience to take a stand, you may want to introduce the problem and then propose a solution. Below lists out five commonly used organizational patterns: chronological/sequential, spatial, causal, problem/cause/solution, and topical/categorical.

1. Chronological/Sequential

A chronological speech organizes the main ideas of your speech in chronological order. For example, a speech on the development of the Internet would be written in chronological order. The first main point is to introduce when the Internet was first conceived in 1962 as the ARPANET; the second main point talks about the TCP/IP created in the 1980s; the third point focuses on explaining why the ARPANET decommissioned and the WWW was born.

2. Spatial

A speech organized spatially is in space or a directional pattern. For example, if you make a speech about how trees can produce fruits or food, you may want to use the spatial pattern. First, explain how the roots get water and mineral nutrients from the soil. Second, explain how the trunk of the tree transports water and nutrients to leaves and branches. Last, explain how the branch and leaf system provides food through photosynthesis.

3. Causal

A speech organized causally is based on cause and effect. For example, many people in the U. S. think the commercial beers are unsatisfying. Because of this (cause), the home brewing beers have become more and more popular (effect).

4. Problem/Cause/Solution

The Problem/Cause/Solution pattern is straightforward and the most commonly used pattern by researchers and government officials for persuasive speech. One thing that needs to be mentioned here is that you must fully understand the problem and its cause before you attempt this speech. You need to do a lot of research on the problem, and the solution you proposed must be carefully evaluated.

5. Topical/Categorical

A speech organized topically consists of several sub-topics. In this pattern, discuss several main points in a more random order that labels specific aspects of the topic and addresses them in separate categories. For example, if you are the mayor of a city and try to introduce the city to foreign companies to invest, you can talk about the solid economic stability, enormous array of cultural activities, extremely accessible public transportation system of the city.

4.1.4 Tips for Writing a Speech

1. Write for the ear not for the eye

Keep in mind that your audience is going to listen to your speech rather than read your speech. Do your best to write your speech for the ear but not the eye. That means you need to use simple words instead of jargon. Although speakers want to make their audience think they are very knowledgeable on the topic, remember that the process of preparing a speech should be audience-centered. Not all your audience are experts in your field, so when you must use jargon, use simple words to explain what the jargon means.

2. Keep it short

Your audience will lose attention to your speech after few minutes. The audience may feel bored and lost when listening to a long speech, and this will generate negative effects. You want to use short words, as Winston Churchill said: "Short words are the best, and old words when short are the best of all." Short sentences are good for speeches and are more effective than longer ones. Most memorable lines from famous speeches are typically less than twenty words. Making your grammar simple is very important; remember your purpose is for your audience to remember your key points.

3. Use strong words and quotes

Clarity, beauty, and power are three important factors for selecting words for your speech. Among these three factors, clarity is the most important. You can use very beautiful and powerful words, but if your audience cannot understand what you are trying to say, these words do not help make your point. Some international students or foreign speakers may think that using simple words in a speech in front of native English speakers will make them sound silly, which is completely wrong. Yes, most native English speakers know many more words than international students, but people still tend to use the same limited pool of words. Below are some general tips for selecting words for a speech.

1) Use "we" to create a sense of unity, "them" for a common enemy, "you" if you're reaching out to your audience, and "I" / "me" if you want to take control.

2) "Every", "improved", "natural", "pure", "tested" and "recommended" will get a positive response from your listeners.

3) Poetry: Repetition, rhyme, and alliteration are sound effects, used by poets and orators alike that make a speech more memorable.

4) Use quotes of famous people. Quotes can help your audience accept your claims more readily because of the credibility of well-known people. However, you need to make sure you select quotes from the right people in light of your audience.

4. Use transitions

Sometimes your audience cannot predict what you are going to say next and will be unable to recognize what is important. In your speech, use transitional words or phrases to give them a signal. For example, "What does it matter?" and then wait for a couple of seconds to let your audiences think about your question and draw their attentions. Similarly, a phrase like "So here's what I learned from the lesson" also grabs their interests because you have alerted them that something important is about to be shared.

5. Read it out loud

Practice reading your speech draft out loud. You may hear something that sounds awkward in your first draft, and you will want to use daily life language to make it sound natural, no matter what the occasion is. You may want to find family members or friends as audience to practice, set a timer, give your speech, and ask for comments and suggestions.

6. Use visual aids if needed

Visual aids such as charts, tables, and photos can quickly convey data or provide compelling supports. Consider using visual aids in your speech if some of your evidences need to be supported by data and are difficult to describe by words. In such cases, visual aids can make it more powerful and easily accepted.

4.1.5 Sample Speech Preparation Form

When you prepare a speech, write down your ideas and the outline of your speech. Below is a sample speech preparation form prepared by an international student who is going to give an informative speech about reinforced concrete material. You can follow the structure of this form when preparing your own speech.

Sample Speech Preparation Form

Title: Introduction of Reinforced Concrete

Specific Purpose: To provide the audience general information about reinforced concrete.

Central Idea: Reinforced concrete is the most commonly used construction material that has many advantages. However, the failure in reinforced concrete can bring serious consequences.

Pattern of Organization: Topical

Introduction:

[Draw attention] Is there someone who can tell me the name of this in my hand and what it is used for? (Visual aid: A piece of reinforced concrete)

[Relate to my audiences] Reinforced concrete is a kind of construction material widely used all over the world. We can see it everywhere. This building and this classroom are made of the reinforced concrete.

[Reveal topic] Today, I want to give you a brief introduction of this material: reinforced concrete.

[Credibility] I am a junior student in civil engineering; I took the reinforced concrete design class last semester.

[Preview] Today, I will talk about the reinforced concrete from three aspects: first, the wide range of applications of the material; second, the advantages of using reinforced concrete as a construction material; third, some serious failures of structures constructed using the reinforced concrete.

[Signpost] Let's get started by looking at the applications of the material.

Body:

Reinforced concrete has a wide range of applications.

Most designers and engineers select reinforced concrete as the major construction material. Pier Luigi Nervi, one of the greatest designers in the world, has described reinforced concrete as "the most fruitful and generous of all building materials". [Quote]

Reinforced concrete can be used in almost every part of a structure.

Reinforced concrete is used for buildings.

Reinforced concrete is used for roadways.

Reinforced concrete is used for bridges.

Reinforced concrete is used for foundations. [Visual Aid]

[Transition] As we know that the reinforced concrete has a wide range of applications, you may ask why it is so popular as a construction material? Next, I will tell you what I learned from the reinforced concrete design class I took last semester.

According to our textbook *Design Reinforced Concrete* written by Jack C. McCormac and Russell H. Brown, there are several advantages of reinforced concrete used as a construction material.

Reinforced concrete is cost efficient and safe.

It is very strong compared to most other materials.

It is very durable and does not need much maintenance.

It is very easy to get the raw materials to make the reinforced concrete.

It has great resistance to fire and water.

[Transition] Nothing is perfect in the world; failures of reinforced concrete structures can cause very serious consequences.

Its damage can affect the quality of a project. [Visual Aid]

It endangers peoples' lives and property.

Conclusion:

[Sign the end of the speech] As we have learned so far, the reinforced concrete is a very important construction material.

[Reinforce the central idea] It has a wide range of applications because of the advantages as a construction material. However, the misapplication of reinforced concrete may cause serious consequences.

[Closing] Hopefully, my speech gives you some general information about reinforced concrete.

4.1.6 Speech Analysis Form

As a speaker, you should also learn how to analyze a speech manuscript to find out what make a speech famous and influential or what make a speech fail. Below is a sample speech evaluation form that you can use to analyze the manuscript of an example speech or your own speech.

Aspects	Strengths	Recommendations
What is the speech type?		
Does the opening give a clear intent?		
Is the organizational pattern of the speech proper?		
Can the evidences support the main topic?		
Is the closing concise and memorable?		
Are the words, grammar, and rhetoric used properly?		

The following table summarizes ten great speeches in history. Students are highly recommended to study and analyze these speeches using the form provided above.

NO.	SPEECH NAME	SPEAKER	DATE
1	GETTYSBURG ADDRESS	ABRAHAM LINCOLN	NOVEMBER 19, 1863
2	I HAVE A DREAM	MARTIN LUTHER KING, JR.	AUGUST 28, 1963
3	I AM PREPARED TO DIE	NELSON MANDELA	APRIL 20, 1964
4	WE SHALL FIGHT ON THE BEACHES	WINSTON CHURCHILL	JUNE 4, 1940
5	FAREWELL TO BASEBALL ADDRESS	LOU GEHRIG	JULY 4, 1939
6	QUIT INDIA	MAHATMA GANDHI	AUGUST 18, 1942
7	SURRENDER SPEECH	CHIEF JOSEPH	OCTOBER 5, 1877
8	FREEDOM OR DEATH	EMMELINE PANKHURST	NOVEMBER 13, 1913
9	INFAMY SPEECH	FRANKLIN D. ROOSEVELT	DECEMBER 8, 1941
10	APPEAL OF 18 JUNE	CHARLES DE GAULLE	JUNE 18, 1940

4.2 POWERPOINT PRESENTATIONS

PowerPoint is a presentation program widely used to help attract audience's attention and explain ideas. It was created by Robert Gaskins and Dennis Austin and released in 1987. In the previous software versions, PowerPoint saves its file as "∗. ppt" file format/extension. Hence, its file is also called PPT.

PowerPoint is a slideshow presentation that can be used to create, collaborate, and present your ideas in a dynamic and visually compelling way. PowerPoint has become the most commonly used assistance for all presenters in the world. This section introduces how to create a well-designed PowerPoint and how to use the PowerPoint for your presentation.

4.2.1 Audience and Context

Similarly with other types of presentation, preparation is needed before jumping into the PowerPoint. The most important part of preparation is to know your audience and bridge the gap between the audience and the content you are presenting. More specifically, the goal of presentations is to deliver your context to your audience. It is important to make sure that the audience is able to understand your presentation and has the interest to listen to your presentation. Therefore, knowing your audience is as important as the presentation itself.

The presenters should know the audience by knowing their backgrounds, professional characteristics, and interests, some of which include:

1) Audience focus: The key of a good presentation is that the delivered information can match the audience's focus. For example if you are introducing your bridge design to the general public, you probably want to talk about the traffic improvement the bridge will offer rather than the reinforcement system of the bridge.

2) Audience educational background: Understanding the audiences' educational background can guide you to use the right words and sentences that the audiences are able to understand clearly. For example, if you are presenting to a group of freshmen, you probably do NOT want to use professional terminologies, as they may not understand.

3) Other helpful information about the audiences includes their age group, gender, cultural background, position in organizations, likes and dislikes, etc. The information can help you know your audiences and prepare a focused presentation that will attract your audiences' attentions and arouse their interests. This is the first step of a successful presentation.

Beside the audiences, you need to know your presentation purpose and understand the situation surrounding it. It will help you understand the main focus of your presentation and improve the speech.

First, the motivation of the presentation must be addressed. Why are you giving this presentation and what do you want to achieve through the presentation? It is critical to remember your motivation throughout the whole presentation process and prepare accordingly.

Second, the target of the presentation must be clear. What do the audiences expect to do or be able to do after the presentation? This is related to the motivation as it focuses on the audiences. Think about the results the audiences can obtain after the presentation.

Third, introduce the topic. How is your presentation related to the audiences or current issues? To arouse the audiences' interests, your information must be presented in a proper way. A good beginning can attract audiences' attentions and improve your presentation.

Fourth, knowing your audiences' knowledge background will prove helpful in preparation. How much do the audiences already know of the topic? If your audiences do not have any background knowledge, you will probably need to arrange a background-introduction section in the beginning of your speech. If the audiences have previous knowledge of your topic, they may be bored with a tedious background introduction.

Finally, the available assistance and plan B should be assessed. Often the host will provide multimedia tools or speakers to assist with the presentation. Check out the presentation room and make sure you know how to use them. Occasionally, the electronic devices may malfunction, for example, the computer may not read your flash drive. Plan B is always needed in case the electronic devices do not work well.

4.2.2　Choosing Format

Presentations can be delivered in various formats. It is important to choose the right format that improves the presentation and enhances the information. The format of presentation may be on-stage presentation, poster session, round-table session, workshop, 5-minute expose, and others.

1. On-stage presentation

This type of presentation is commonly used in academic conferences. For on-stage presentations, the presenter stands on stage in front of the audiences and presents his/her research directly to the audiences. Depending on the type of presentation, presenting time ranges from 15 ~ 20 minutes for a normal presentation to 20 ~ 30 minutes for keynote presentations.

Often the presenting is unidirectional and at the end of the presentation, the audiences can ask questions and interact with the presenter. This chapter mainly introduces the on-stage presentation, but the techniques and skills can be used with other types of presentations.

2. Poster session

In some conferences a poster session is held where presenters display their posters and talk to the audiences directly. These posters often include an introduction and background, methodology, main outcomes, discussion, and conclusion. Visual elements such as photos, figures, and tables are commonly used on posters for a clear and simple illustration. During poster sessions, presenters must stay beside their posters, introduce the information to any audience, and answer questions.

3. Round-table session

Round-table session is also a type of presentation format where a group of people sit around a table to discuss an important theme or issue. These round-table sessions are held by a conference organizer and the detailed information, including time and location, will be announced on the conference program. This type of presentation provides a great opportunity for all the presenters to directly discuss the theme or issue they are interested in.

4. Workshop

A workshop is a longer version of an on-stage presentation that can be as long as 90 minutes. With all that time, presenters can introduce their outcomes, discuss their skills and techniques, or share their experiences with the audiences. Workshops often have specific objectives or focus points on a particular topic or subject. Different from on-stage presentation, the interaction of audiences is more important for workshops as it can increase the competence of the audiences and therefore achieve the goals of the workshops. Feedbacks, games, practices, and tests can be included during workshops depending on the theme. Because workshops have specific objectives and require more time, it is important to clearly state the objectives, agenda, and participation process in the workshop proposal.

5. 5-minute expose

The 5-minute expose is a way to show different ideas and innovations from different presenters on a similar topic or subject. The challenges of this type of presentation are to clearly and concisely introduce the presenters' expose in only five minutes. This type of presentation is an active and exciting part of a conference as a group of young presenters inspire their research together and create sparks.

Based on the content, the information may be presented by an individual person or a group of people. When the presentation content is well known by an individual person, this person will be the presenter during the presentation. However, when more than one person knows the presentation topic, then a group of presenters may be needed while each person introduces his/her contribution.

When presenting with more than one person, everyone will introduce different sections of the presentation, so it is critical to maintain the consistency of the entire presentation. For example, everyone is recommended to use the same PowerPoint with the exact same template. Every presenter needs to clearly state their contributions for the topic and their introductions during the presentation. The transitions between different presenters are also important. Often the former presenter should introduce the later presenter at the end of his/her presentation and tell the audiences that "my part is done and the following part will be explained by the following." After standing on the stage, the later presenter should thank the former presenter, and tell the audiences that "the former presenter has done his/her part, and now it is my time." Because of time limitation, the transitions between different presenters should be quick, simple, and clear.

4.2.3   Structuring the Context with PowerPoint

PowerPoint is a widely used graphics software that can help demonstrate your context in a vivid and visualized manner. When creating a PowerPoint for a presentation, the following sections should be considered.

4.2.3.1　*Templates*

A template is a master layout for all the slides in your PowerPoint file. Once you apply a template, all the slides will have a similar layout, which provides a more uniformed and professional look. However, you can also choose different templates for different slides. PowerPoint offers a variation of templates to suit different needs, and more templates can be downloaded from the Internet.

A template is often designed with a certain type of font, color, size, and position for different types of texts, and users can directly apply its design or adjust the design to suit their own preferences.

4.2.3.2　*Title Page*

A title page is the first slide of your presentation. It shows the basic information about your presentation, including:

1) Title of the presentation;

2) Presenter's name and affiliation;

3) Logo of the affiliation;

4) Date and location of the presentation.

A typical example of the title page is shown in Figure 4.1. The title of the presentation, which is the most important, is shown in the middle of the slide with bold and large font. The presenter's name and presenting date are shown in the middle under the title. The logo and affiliation name can stay in the upper left corner of the slide.

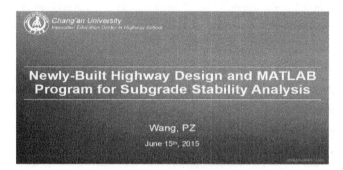

Figure 4.1　Example of Title Page

By showing the title page, the presenter introduces his/her name, affiliation, topic, etc. Sometimes the presenter's background and research interest are also introduced here.

4.2.3.3　*Table of Contents*

The table of contents covers the main points that will be presented. It gives the audiences an outline of your presentation, which can help the audiences better understand your presentation. Often in the slides of content, short and clear phrases are used rather than complete sentences. Bullet points are commonly used for easy and fast reading, such as:

- *Introduction*
- *Methodology*
- *Case study*
- *Result and discussion*

This section gives only the outline of the presentation, showing the audiences what you are going to tell them. A brief introduction is expected here, and the details should be saved for later sections. The beginning could be like:

- *In this presentation, I would like to discuss...*
- *I will show you the presentation in the following areas...*
- *I will claim the changes that can be made in these areas...*
- *I will demonstrate to you...*

4.2.3.4   *Introduction*

Introduction is one of the most important parts for a presentation. Good introductions can capture your audiences' attentions and increase their interests.

In the section of introduction, the presenter should:

1. Grab audiences' attentions

It is important to grab the attentions of your audiences for the purposes of your presentation. Once the audiences are interested in your topic, they will follow your presentation more eagerly. Different strategies can be used to begin your introduction. Commonly used introduction strategies include:

1) Sharing life experience,

2) Discussing recent news,

3) Stating powerful quotes,

4) Interesting demonstration, and

5) Engaging activities.

Other introduction strategies can also be used to get a more dramatic reaction from the audiences, such as:

1) Provocative or challenging questions,

2) Quick survey,

3) Startling statement,

4) Unusual analogue,

5) Striking example, and

6) Dramatic contrast.

2. State your purpose

The audiences must know why they should listen to your presentation; otherwise you may lose the audiences even if they are still sitting in the presentation room. It is important to show them the purpose of your presentation and to link the purpose to your audiences based on your knowledge of their background. Often the presentation time is limited so state the presentation purpose clearly and concisely, for example, one sentence in the slide. You can also emphasize your purpose by using a statement "I am here to prove that..." or "Today, I want to solve...".

3. Forecast the message

After a brief introduction of the presentation purpose, show the audiences what they will hear from you throughout the presentation. It can largely keep attracting the audience's attention. In this section, you can use different phrases to describe the message that will be delivered. For example, "In my presentation, I will discuss the design of a road from three aspects: first ...; second ...; and third ...".

4.2.3.5 *Body*

The body is the main part of a presentation. In this section, the presenter should clearly introduce the content and deliver the information to the audiences. It is based on the information provided in the introduction, but it gives all the details. It often consists of a series of slides telling your audiences what you want them to know and achieve the purpose of your presentation.

The body often contains a series of slides; each contains a key point of your presentation. These slides can be organized in different orders according to your content. The commonly used orders are:

1) Importance: The important content is introduced earlier and followed by the less important content later.

2) Time: The introduction follows the time stream of the activities, procedures, or products.

3) Components: The components of a large object are introduced one by one.

4) Criteria: The criteria of a consideration or evaluation are introduced one by one.

5) Cause and effect: The cause of a result is introduced followed by its corresponding effect.

6) Problem and solution/troubleshooting: A problem is introduced followed by its corresponding solution or troubleshooting.

In this section, various techniques can be used to support your statement and attract the audiences' attentions. These techniques include:

1) Examples, analogies, and quotations that can help the audiences understand your statement.

2) Visual elements: Visual elements including graphs, charts, photos, and videos make your presentation interesting and vivid. They can increase the interest of your presentation and help the audiences understand better.

3) Samples: These can help the audiences intuitively understand the problems you are handling.

4) Comparison: It can easily and directly show the strengths and weaknesses of different objects, considerations, or solutions.

The section of the body must correspond to the introduction section and with more details. All the information you want to deliver in your presentation should be clearly and completely stated in this section.

4.2.3.6   *Conclusion*

Similar to the introduction, the conclusion is one of the important sections of your presentation. Good conclusions can effectively increase the impression of your information to the audiences. Often the conclusion is to summarize and emphasize the key points of your presentation rather than to present any new information. A classic conclusion should contain:

1) A summary of all the key information of the presentation:

In your presentation, a range of ideas and points may be introduced and discussed. In your conclusion section, it is important to recap and summarize these items.

2) Significance of the key information:

The conclusion is a good place to emphasize the significance of your presentation and enhance the impact on the audiences.

In this section, bullet points are widely used, while long sentences should be avoided, so the audiences can easily get the key points.

4.2.3.7   *Question and Answer (Q&A)*

A formal presentation often has a slide titled, "Question and Answer (Q&A)." When this slide comes out, it means the presenter is done presenting and is ready to answer questions from the audiences. If the audiences have any questions, they can ask and get the answer immediately while the presenter is still on the stage. The signal of ending the presentation can include phrases such as "Thank you," and these can be added to the slide to thank the attentions of your audiences.

Sometimes asking questions is not allowed after the presentation. In this case, the presenter does not need to add a "Question and Answer" slide but should only add a "Thank you" as the final slide for the presentation.

4.2.3.8   *Skills of making slides*

1) Do NOT write long sentences or paragraphs; they will not be read.

2) Use bullet points to present main ideas and using a phrase of keywords.

3) Keep to a maximum of seven words per line, and two lines per bullet point. This will not only encourage the audiences to read your slides but also encourage you to make your information concise.

4) Keep to a maximum of five or six bullet points per slide, or six lines of text per slide. Otherwise the slides look crowded, and the audiences may lose their desires to read them.

5) Choose the right font size. The font size should be large enough, so the entire audience can clearly read the words. It should not be too large, too attractive, or too towering as to distract. Often the font size for bullet items should be at least 22 points and the titles should be at least 28 points.

6) Do not use too many different typefaces, because it can make a slide look untidy and messy. Limit the typefaces to three per slide.

7) Use the same typeface with the same style and size for the same elements throughout all the slides. The consistency in the presentation will improve the professionalism and help your audiences understand the organization of your ideas.

8) Improve the color blending in the slides. Colors can be used for emphasis; however, overusing colors can have a negative effect. Do not use more than four colors per slide. Too many colors may cause confusion and distract the audiences' attentions. For emphasis, the selection of colors depends on the background color of the slides. If the background is light color, use red for the text you want to emphasize because yellow may be hard to be read.

9) Do not capitalize all the words in a sentence. Capitalized words are difficult to read even for English-speaking audiences. All caps can be used for emphasis but be careful not to overuse.

10) Use speaker's notes wisely. Software PPT has a function named "speaker's notes." You can add notes to remind yourself of certain things when delivering the message.

11) Use multimedia elements to improve the presentation. It will be introduced in the following sections.

4.2.4　Visual Effects

Visual effects are an important element of a presentation that can largely enhance the understanding and attraction of what you are trying to communicate. They are able to:

1) Make, explain, or identify a point;

2) Emphasize, clarify, or reinforce a point;

3) Remind, summarize, or review a point.

When attending a presentation, we only receive 10% of what we read, 20% of what we hear, 30% of what we see, and 50% of what we see and hear. Hence the visual elements can deliver the information in an effective and direct manner that just speaking alone cannot do. Therefore, visual elements are commonly used in presentations.

Visual elements include different types of figures and tables. In the following sections, we will introduce how to use figures and tables in a presentation.

4.2.4.1 *When and Why Do You Need a Figure/Table?*

First of all, it is important to think about how to inform the audiences of the information you want to deliver. This is especially true when you use texts, numbers, or images to help build and support your arguments. Texts, tables, and images are taken as data summaries. Most writers are familiar with using words to summarize data, which is usually the best way to convey results directly, and a table or figure is probably unnecessary in this case. However, if the data is too large or too complex to describe in a small space, tables or figures would be more effective in communicating the information. Moreover, tables and figures provide your readers with a quick reference that can make the trends, models, or relationships easier to understand.

4.2.4.2 *Differences between Tables and Figures*

Tables can be used to:

1) Present numbers or texts in columns.

2) Summarize literature, explain variables, etc.

3) Show raw data to present a relationship between variables.

Figures can be used to:

1) Show results visually (in forms of chart, graph, drawing, photo, map, etc.).

2) Present primary findings effectively.

3) Display trends, patterns of relationship, and communicating processes simply.

Note: The content in figures and tables should not display the same information.

4.2.4.3 *Using Tables*

Organization of tables is as important as paragraphs in a paper. A well-organized table allows readers to grasp the meaning of the data presented, while a disorganized one will leave the readers confused about the data and its significance.

Basic elements in a table:

1) The Legend/Title of the table,

2) Headings for each column,

3) Quantitative/qualitative data,

4) Subheadings and footnotes (optional).

Title: Tables are titled with a number followed by a clear and descriptive title or caption. Titles should be concise and further explanation of the data should appear in the text.

Column headings: The aim for each heading is to make the table simple and logical for the audiences to understand.

Quantitative/qualitative data: the data should be well organized in order to highlight the significance. The important thing is to guide your viewers to follow what you want them to compare and know.

4.2.4.4 *Other Elements*

Each table should have a number (in order) before the table title. Tables may or may not have subheadings or footnotes. such as table 4.1 and table 4.2.

A Check list for Preparing Tables:

1) Numbered and referenced in the order as they appear.

2) Title should be descriptive and concise.

3) Column heading should describe the data.

4) Don't forget to label the units of measurement.

5) Give some space between the table and text.

Table 4.1   Physical Characteristics of Teachers

	Gender	Height (cm)	Age (yrs.)
Dr. Li	male	169	45
Dr. Wang	female	174	34
Dr. Ma	male	180	28

Table 4.2   Physical Characteristics of Teachers

	Appearance	Outfits
Dr. Li	Bobbed hair	Black trench coat
	Brown eyes	White shirt
	Medium build	Black boots
Dr. Wang	Long hair	Brown leather jacket
	Brown eyes	Skinny Jeans
	Slim build	Platform shoes
Dr. Ma	Short hair	Denim jacket
	Grey eyes	Basic V-neck shirt
	Strong build	Brown Boots

4.2.4.5 *Using Figures*

· There are several types of figures such as graphs, diagrams, photos, drawings, or maps; choose one that reveals your data best.

· Choose the most effective figure that will convey your main point.

· A map or photograph may be more practical when showing spatial relationships.

· A pie chart or bar chart can be used to illustrate proportions or an experiment.

· A line graph or scatter plot can be used to illustrate the relationship between two variables.

Basic elements in a figure:

1) Caption/title: Captions or titles should describe the data and be comprehensive. They should draw the viewers' attentions to the main point of the figure and the words should be concise.

2) Image: Images should be self-explanatory to the readers who can grasp the important features clearly and quickly. Figures should be large enough to contain all the details and elements and can be easily seen by the viewers. Color can be used to highlight information that needs attention. This may be a good idea for PowerPoint presentations or papers that will be published online.

Additional Information:

1) Tables and figures are numbered independently.

2) Labels, symbol explanations, or marks may be needed for graphs.

3) A scale or an orientation arrow may be needed for maps.

A Check list for Preparing Figures:

1) Labeled with the figure number and appropriate descriptive title as ["Figure 1. "] or ["Fig. 1. "] under the figure.

2) Numbered and referenced in the order they appear in the text.

3) Leave space between the figure and text; figures should not be surrounded by text.

Every graph is a figure but not every figure is a graph. Each kind of graph displays quantitative relationships or trends differently. Common forms of graphs are bar charts, histograms, pie charts, scatter plots, and line graphs. Carefully choose the type of graph to show the relationship of your data, and keep it simple. Communication is your main objective for using graphs so if your viewers are unable to understand it, then the mission has failed.

1. Pie Charts show relative proportions, particularly the relationship between parts and whole. Below are some bad examples of pie charts. Problems in Fig. 4. 2 and 4. 3 are:

· The reader will not get all the information you want to communicate due to too many variables in Fig. 4. 2.

· In Fig. 4. 3, the viewer cannot compare the difference due to the similar proportion of each slice without an accurate value listed; more details are needed there.

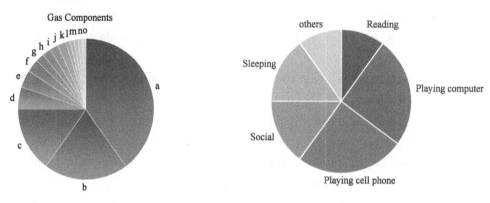

Figure 4. 2　Gas components　　　　**Figure 4. 3　Entertainments of Chinese teenagers**

2. Bar Graphs uses rectangular bars to display proportions, to show comparisons among discrete categories (examples: occupation, gender, and species). Data are plotted either vertically or horizontally. Below is an example of a bar graph.

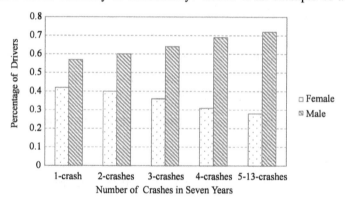

Figure 4. 4　Percentage of driverinvolved in seven years

3. Frequency Histograms/distributions: Frequency histograms are a special type of bar graph that show the relationship between independent and dependent variables. The independent variable is continuous, rather than discrete (the distribution of exam scores for students in a class or the age distribution of the people living in Xi'an).

4. Scatter plots: a scatter plot is another way to illustrate the relationship between two variables. In this case, data is displayed as points in an x-y coordinate system, and each point represents one observation along two axes of variation. Below is an example of a scatter plot:

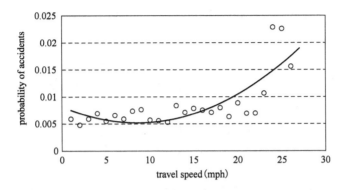

Figure 4.5   Relationship between travel speed and probability of accidents

5. Line graphs: Line graphs are similar to scatter plots and they also display data along two axes of variations. Line graphs, however, plot a series of related values that depict a change in one variable as a function of another. For example, the world population (dependent) and its change over time (independent) would be information well shown on a line graph. Below is example of an X-Y line graph:

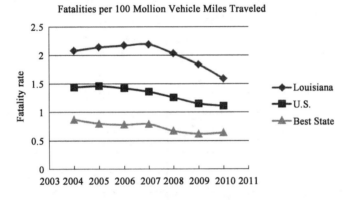

Figure 4.6   Fatality rate between different states

Tips for Preparing Figures:

· Simplicity: Remember that figures are used to convey the most significant things about your data.

· Clarity: Figures play a role in making the data visually clear so be sure every detail of the figure is explained clearly.

· Always think about the reader: Can they understand or not? You do not want the viewer to put too much effort in figuring out what you mean by the figure.

· Accuracy: Double check if there is any error that would cause misunderstanding of the data.

4.2.4.6 *How should tables and figures interact with text?*

Use text to guide the reader in interpreting the information included in a figure, table, or graph—tell the reader what the figure or table conveys and why it was important to include it. When referring to tables and graphs from the text, you can use:

· Clauses beginning with "as": "As shown in Table 1, ..."
· Passive voice: "Results are shown in Table 1."
· Active voice: "Table 1 shows that ..."
· Parentheses: "Each sample tested positive for three nutrients (Table 1)."

4.2.4.7 *How to describe tables and figures*

Below is an example for describing a table in text.

Example A:

Read the table below, summarize the information and make comparisons where relevant.

	From 30 - 50 years old						
	TV	Sport	Reading	Hobbies	Music	Beach	Sleep
Canada	60	22	15	40	3	0	2
France	/	/	30	20	4	/	/
England	/	/	30	21	4	/	20
Australia	65	30	15	45	5	30	4
Korea	22	21	60	45	2	2	4
China	15	25	60	50	0	5	5
USA	60	23	15	42	23	30	2
Japan	/	/	62	/	/	/	/

Tips: take a few seconds to think about the following questions before writing.

· First, pay attention to the value in each cell; is it a number or a percentage? (We value here as percentage of people)

· Second, consider why there are blanks in the table; how does the value zero exist? Notice the special values circled in red as an example.

· Last but not least, how do you want to compare the data shown in the table?

Model Answer:

This table reveals and compares favorable leisure-time activities in eight different countries. People from age 30 to 50 chose their favorite entertainment from eight categories such as TV, sports, reading, etc.

Clearly, more than two thirds of Canadians, Australians, and Americans prefer watching TV. While only 15% of people like to watch TV in China. Surprisingly, there about 23% of Americans like listening to music while no more than 5% of people in the other countries feel the same way. In England, 20% of people regard sleeping as their leisure-time favorite; however, only 2% to 5 % of people choose that in other countries. Chinese people like hobbies the most at 50% and more than 60% people from Asia countries including Japan, China, and Korea like reading. Australians and Americans have the highest proportion at 30% on beach. Surprisingly, no one in Canada choose the beach as a pastime. Maybe the weather is too cold there. Similarly, it is odd that no one in China chose music; this may due to insufficient sample size.

In general, because of the cultural differences, people of different nationalities prefer various leisure-time activities. This can all depend on social environment, economic status, cultural background, climate, and so on.

Below is a general step-by-step procedure to describe a table or figure in text.

1. Step 1: Give a simple introduction of the figure

The first paragraph usually begins with a simple introduction in one or two sentences describing what the figure shows and paraphrasing the title.

2. Step 2: Describe the main features of the figure

Give an overview of the figure and state what the main trend/s are. Let the reader know what is happening overall.

3. Step 3: Give the Details

Give more specific details in the following paragraphs. The key to organizing your body paragraphs is to pick a special value (peak or bottom value, zero point, negative point, sharp increase or decrease) and categorize the data with similarities or differences that can be compared. Summarize the data and analyze the reasoning. Remember that you should not overread the background or exaggerate the fact.

4. Step 4: Conclusion (optional)

Sometimes an overview is enough here. You may need a separate part if the figure is too complicated.

Below are some examples for describing figures in text.

Example A

The pie charts below give information concerning the world population in 1955 and 2015. Summarize the information and make comparisons where relevant.

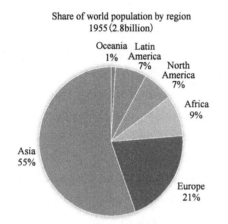
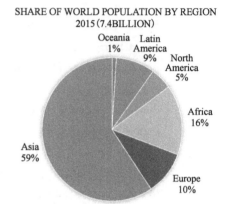

Figure 4.7   Share of world population by region, 1955 and 2015

Model answer

The pie charts illustrate changes in the population of different areas of the world between 1955 and 2015. The major regions are represented by percentages of the total world population. From 1955 to 2015, the percentage of people living in Africa almost doubled from 9% to 16%, while Asia's proportion increased from 55% to 59% which was already near three-fifths of the world's population. On the other hand, the percentage of population in Europe and North America decreased over the past 40 years. Europe's percentage dropped from 21% to 10%, while North America declined from 7% to 5%. Oceania's percentage however, remained constant at 1% in 1955 and 2015, while Latin America's proportion slightly rose from 7% to 9%.

Overall, these charts illustrate a huge increase in terms of population on the planet, from 2.8 billion to 7.4 billion in no more than half century. Most of this population growth has occurred in developing countries.

Example B

The bar chart below shows shares of U. S. household consumer expenditures by major categories in the years 2009 and 2016. Describing the information below.

Note: 'Other'includes insurance, entertainment, alcoholic beverages, savings, apparel, and personal care products. (Source from U. S. Bureau of Labor Statistics)

Model Answer

The bar chart compares the average spending of several household categories such as housing, transportation, food, health care, and education in 1950 and 2016. As observed from the bar graph, more than half expenditure was in housing whereas the average expenditure has been increased for health care, food, and transportation in 2016.

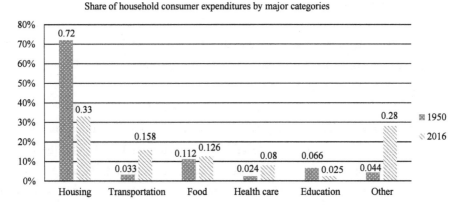

Figure 4.8   Share of U. S. household consumer expenditures by major categories in 1950 and 2016

The figure indicates that housing is the highest expenditure share of total expenditures in 1950. The second was for food; all the others were less than 20% in total. After six decades, expenditure on housing was still the highest. Transportation became the second highest expenditure share at 15.8%, which was five-fold than in 1950. Health care expenditure ratio was the lowest in 1950, whereas consumers spend much more money on health care with almost a 300% increase at 8% in share value after 66 years. However, the proportion of education expense has decreased over time from 6.6% to 2.5%. According to the figure, customers spend more money on insurance, entertainment, alcoholic beverages, savings, apparel, and personal care products, etc. than in 1950.

In summary, the trends of expenditure in this country have significantly changed in the past 66 years. Housing and food are still the major categories most households spend their money on.

Example C:

The line chart below shows the wheat exports in three countries from 2007 to 2017, summarize the information and make comparisons where relevant.

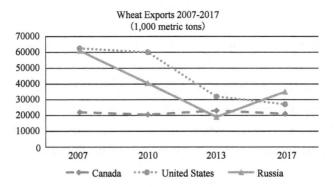

Figure 4.9   Wheat exports 2007-2017 (Source from: USDA data)

Model Answer

The three lines of wheat exports show quite a different pattern between 2007 and 2017. Exports from United States declined over the ten-year period, while the Russian market fluctuated considerably and the trend in the Canadian Community showed a stable export.

In 2007, the United States exported about 62 million tons of wheat and the following year the number gradually decreased from 60 million tons to 3 million. Then there was a sharp decline until 2013, and over this decline the US decreased about 27 million tons. Over the same period, the amount of Russian exports started at 61 million tons in 2007, almost the same as United States. After that, their exports dropped dramatically in 2013 to 19 million and then climbed back to 35 million in 2017. Twenty-one million tons were exported from Canada in 2007, which is the lowest among all three countries. And it was quite stable over 10 years at around 20 million. There was a slight increase to 23 million in 2013 and back to 21 million in 2017. All in all, the amount of wheat exports dropped significantly for United States and Russia between 2007 and 2017, while Canada seems very stable over the ten years.

4.2.5 Videos and Sounds

Besides figures and tables, videos and sounds can be used to support or enhance your presentation. Videos and sounds are more vivid and interactive than figures and tables and attract attention easily. Audience probably needs a longer time to watch videos and to listen to the sounds, the proper arrangement is needed when you want to use these in your presentation, especially when time is limited. Well-designed and organized videos and sounds can quickly attract audience attention and improve the variety of your presentation; while poorly designed and organized videos and sounds will distract the audience from your message. Also adding too many videos or sounds will confuse your audience and may have negative effects.

When playing a video or sound, the presenter can stand aside or he/she can explain it and tell the audience what they should focus on. When presenting videos and sounds in your slides, it is important to make sure that the place you will present has the equipment necessary to facilitate videos and sounds. The presenter should check the sound system to ensure its use. The sound should be loud enough so that the audience sitting in any location of the presenting room can clearly watch the video and hear the sound.

4.2.6   Delivering Effectively

Presentation is to deliver your ideas to the audience. The effectiveness of the delivery is critical. Effective delivery can largely enhance the presentation, while poor delivery may fail to deliver important information. This section introduces some strategies to effectively deliver information in your presentation.

4.2.6.1   *Handle the tension during the presentation*

When presenting in public, you may experience tension that can cause you to become nervous and upset; this is normal. Presenters should handle the tension to their advantage. First, you must accept that the tension exists when you are making a presentation in public. Do not feel ashamed or upset because of it. Second, relieve the tension. You can try simple exercises to release your mind and muscles. For example, some massage can release the tension of your muscles; and deep, slow breathing with closed eyes may help reduce the tension in your mind. Third, if you still feel tense during the presentation, slightly move your body; for example, walking several steps on the stage and gesturing your hands. The natural movement will not distract the attention from the audience, and it will help release tension.

4.2.6.2   *Before presentation*

Preparation is a critical step for an effective presentation. Preparation not only helps you becomefamiliar with the information, but it also helps to find errors and inappropriate sections in the PowerPoint. Good preparation can largely improve the fluency of the presentation and give youassurance while improving your confidence.

First, it is necessary to have an overview of the information and the support you want to use. It is suggested to practice the presentation with all your support such as slides, videos, etc. When you practice, you will likely find some errors and inappropriate parts that need to be corrected and improve your presentation.

You probably cannot identify all the errors or inappropriate parts of your presentation so invite friends, classmates, or family to listen to your presentation and help you improve your presentation.

In case you forget your information during the presentation, you can prepare brief notes for personal use. However, it is not acceptable to keep reading the notes or your slides.

4.2.6.3   *During the presentation*

To achieve an effective presentation, many strategies can be used during your presentation, as introduced below:

Introduction of yourself. Introducing yourself can help the audience get to know you. Often for a formal event, the presenter should introduce himself/herself to the audience even if some of the audience has already known the presenter. If the presentation is given by a group of presenters; often the first presenter will introduce the presenting group. Yet for a regular internal presentation where all the audience knows you very well, an introduction is not needed.

Eye Contact. Eye contact is a simple but powerful way to gain attention and agreement from the audience. It is important to remember that you are presenting to a group, not talking to yourself. Besides the oral information, eye contact can deliver information to the audience. Looking at the audience can assure whether your information is correctly and effectively delivered to the audience and make sure the audience's attention is always on your presentation. An experienced presenter will modify his/her presentation after reading the audience reaction. However, when you want to eye contact with your audience, do not stare at one person for a long time because you may frighten him/her.

Appreciation. At the end of the presentation, it is necessary to express your appreciation to the audience and this provides a verbal signal of the end of the presentation.

4.2.6.4 *After the presentation*

The "Question and Answer" section is usually immediately after the presentation. Some presenters are afraid of the "Question and Answer" section, as they are afraid the questions may be too difficultto answer with such a short time to think. This situation becomes worse when presenting in a foreign language. However, the presenters must understand that the audience asks questions because they are interested in the information, and they are not going to blame you.

Before answering the questions from the audience, make sure you have clearly understood the entire question. If you do not understand the question, it is fine to ask the audience to repeat or explain the question again. Before you answer the questions, organize your answer before speaking. If you need a few seconds to think about your answer, use an opener like "that's a good question ... "or "what you're asking is ... ".

The presenters need only to tell the audience what you thought and did. If the questions cannot be answered, the presenter can honestly and simply tell the audience that you do not know the answer and you will think about it later.

Also, before the presentation, presenters can think about the questions that may be asked during the Q & A and prepare answers for these questions.

4.3 EXERCISES

1. Please prepare an outline for an informative or a persuasive speech. The outline should include the title of your speech, specific purpose, central idea you want to deliver to your audience, the pattern of organization you want to use, and a detailed outline. Please see Section 4.1.5 for an example.

2. What are the criteria of a good presentation?

3. Please prepare a group presentation to introduce a Civil Engineering project, each student needs to presenta section of your chosen topic. The duration of the entire presentation is 15 minutes.

4. Match the following graphs and statements

A	1.There was a peak in customer numbers
B	2.Customer numbers were erratic
C	3.Numbers fell steadily
D	4.There was a steep rise in customer numbers
E	5.There was a slight dip in customer numbers
F	6.Customer numbers fluctuated wildly
G	7.Customer numbers plunged
H	8.Customer numbers fluctuated slightly

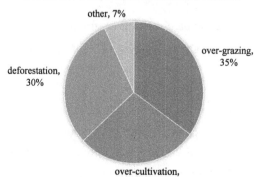

CAUSES OF WORLDWIDE LAND DEGRADATION

over-grazing, 35%
other, 7%
deforestation, 30%
over-cultivation, 28%

CAUSES OF LAND DEGRADATION BY REGION

Region	% land degraded by...			
	deforestation	over-cultivation	over-grazing	Total land degraded
North America	0.2	3.3	1.5	5%
Europe	9.8	7.7	5.5	23%
Oceania	1.7	0	11.3	13%

5. Writing task: Based on the given information in the following pie chart and table, describe the main features, and make comparisons where relevant. (At least 150 words)

6. Writing task: Based on the given information in the following table, describe the main features and make comparisons where relevant. (At least 150 words).

Fairtrade: a category of products for which farmers from developing countries have been paid an officially agreed fair price.

Sales of Fairtrade-labelled tea and pineapples(2010&2015)

Tea	2010(millions of euros)	2015(millions of euros)
Country A	2.5	21.0
Country B	4.0	8.0
Country C	2.8	3.0
Country D	2.0	2.7
Country E	1.8	2.0
Pineapples	2010(millions of euros)	2015(millions of euros)
Country B	16.0	48.0
Country A	2.0	6.5
Country D	1.6	5.0
Country E	2.8	2.0
Country C	3.0	1.9

7. Writing task: Based on the information given in the following bar chart, describe the main features and make comparisons where relevant. (At least 150 words)

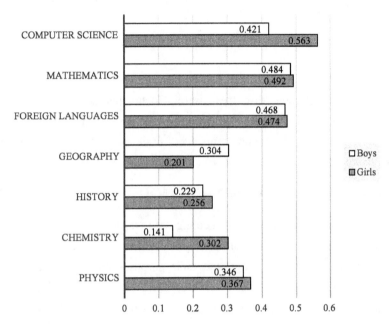

Note: students passing high school competency exams , by subject and gender, 2010—2011 * includes French , German, and Spanish(Source from: https://www. ielts-exam. netl)

4.4 IBLIOGRAPHY

1. Merriam-Webster. Speech [OL]. [2018-06-04]. https:// www. merriam-webster. com/dictionary/speech.

2. Merriam-Webster. Presentation[OL]. [2018-06-04]. https:// www. merriam-webster. com/dictionary/presentation.

CHAPTER 5. WRITING FOR PROJECT MANAGEMENT

This chapter discusses useful documents related to project management including meeting documents, proposals and action plans, contracts and agreements, and reports. The structure, function, basic content, and writing process of each document are covered; templates and samples are also introduced.

5.1 AGENDA, MINUTES, MEMO AND MOU

This section discusses meeting and related documents: agenda, minutes, memo and memorandum of understanding (MOU). First, the role of meeting, the different kinds of meetings and their purposes are briefly introduced. Next, the greater part of this chapter is devoted to agenda, minutes, memo, and MOU. The techniques of writing effective meeting documents and the different elements that should be included are discussed. At last, templates and samples of different meeting documents are also introduced.

Meetings are where members of a group are convened for the purpose of achieving a common goal through verbal interaction, such as reaching agreement or sharing information. Meetings may occur face-to-face or virtually. It could be mediated by communication technology, such a telephone conference or a video conference.

There are different types of meetings and each type requires a different structure and supports a different number of participants. Think about the type of meeting you are planning and adjust your plans accordingly. Meetings can be classified according to the regularity with which they are held. Generally, meetings can be held on the following basis: Regular, Irregular, and Ad hoc.

A regular meeting is a meeting that recurs at fixed intervals, such as every Friday staff meeting. The meeting organizer wants the participants to attend the meeting on a constant and repetitive basis. An irregular meeting is a meeting that is held on an irregular basis without fixed intervals. For example, the Transportation Research Board Annual Meeting is held every year. However, the exact date of the meeting is different each year.

Ad hoc meetings are called when an unexpected situation, case, or issue develops. It is usually created to address a specific problem or task. For example, suppose there has been an accident in a pavement construction site work, the manager then calls all engineers together for a meeting to discuss how to respond to the press.

As to the nature of the meeting, there are different types as well. An informational meeting is to disseminate information to the participants. A reporting meeting is usually held when a project has got under way; participants need to meet on a regular basis to update each other on progress of their tasks. As a project is underway, problems are likely to emerge. A problem-solving meeting is usually held at this time to identify these problems, analyze their causes, and think of solutions to them.

Based on the kind of meeting and its objectives, the function and content of a meeting document are different as well. In the rest of the section, we will talk about agenda, minutes, memo, and MOU in details.

5.1.1　Agenda

An agenda is a list of items in the order that they are to be taken up in a forthcoming meeting or session. The heading of a meeting agenda may include the date, time, and location of the meeting. Then it is followed by a series of points. The points outline the order in which the business is conducted. Steps on any agenda can include any type of schedule or order the group wants to follow. According to different purposes of the group, agendas may take different forms and include any number of the items.

5.1.1.1　*Function/Purpose*

An organized meeting needs a well-written agenda. A good agenda will serve as a guide for participants and help a team conduct a more effective meeting by stating the participants' expectations about the meeting. An agenda should be distributed to the relevant members prior to the meeting, so they will be aware of subjects to be discussed and able to prepare for the meeting in advance.

If a meeting agenda has a specific time listed for an item, which should not be discussed before the specific time, and must be taken up when the time arrives even if other business is pending. An agenda also reminds participants of what is still left to cover if time becomes an issue.

To write an agenda for a meeting, you can create your own, work from a template, or modify one you already have. No matter what methods are chosen, a well-written agenda should outline basic information about the meeting and summarize both the objective and schedule of the meeting. A detailed and flexible agenda will help the meeting remain streamlined and focus to ensure that all the goals will be achieved in the shortest time.

An agenda should be written and distributed to all attendees in advance. This will help a meeting run smoothly. An agenda has a number of important purposes:

1) Notifies or reminds participants of date, time, and place of the meeting;

2) Focuses on the goals;

3) Indicates the items to be discussed;

4) Circulates any relevant documents for perusal before the meeting;

5) Serves as a guide for the chairperson;

6) Helps to maintain focus and time control.

5.1.1.2 *Contents*

An agenda usually has the following items:

1) The title of a meeting;

2) Date and time of the meeting;

3) Venue of the meeting;

4) Names of the invited participants;

5) Objective(s);

6) Topics (to be covered in the meeting);

7) Proposed allotment of time for each topic;

8) Name(s) of people leading each of the items.

Among the above items, the first six items are necessary and the last two are optional.

1. Title

An agenda usually starts with a title. The title should tell the readers they are reading an agenda and what topics the meeting is covering. In a business context, simple and direct titles are usually the best. You may want to use a plain, dignified font like Times New Roman or Calibri and resist fancy or large fonts. Make your title the same size as the rest of the lettering or only slightly larger.

2. Date and time

An agenda should note the date and the time. The exact date of the meeting should be included in an agenda. And the time of the meeting including both the starting and ending time should also be illustrated in the agenda. For example, the date of the meeting is Thursday, November 10, 2016, and the time of the meeting is from 2:00 pm to 4:00 pm. One thing that needs to be noticed is that sometimes the agenda only has the starting time.

3. Venue

An agenda should provide the location of the meeting. If the meeting has multiple locations, the exact address should be included in the agenda. If the meeting has just one location, the agenda should include the room (e. g., Conference Room #1).

4. Names of the invited participants

List the full names of the invited participants in the agenda. If the meeting has special individuals, such as special guests, speakers, or meeting leaders, you should list their names separately. Job titles for the participants are usually optional and not required. This section could also be labeled with "Attendees."

5. Objective

Write a brief statement of the meeting objective (s) within two sentences. Meetings without a clearly defined purpose could be a waste of precious time, as attendees will decide what to talk about. Skip a line after your heading (includes date and time, venue and attendees) and use bold or underlined text to label your objective section with a title like "Objective" or "Purpose," followed by a colon or a line break. Then, in a few concise sentences, describe the topics of discussion for the meeting. Be sure to write in broad strokes, without going into details.

6. Topics

An agenda should list all the topics covered in the meeting in a logical order. Usually, we use chronological order or list the topics from the most important to the least. The topics part is also called the schedule of the meeting. You could skip a line after your statement of the objective (s), and give your schedule a bold or underlined title, then begin making entries that correspond to the main topics of discussion. Each entry has its own line for ease of reading.

Each entry is labeled with either the time you plan for it to begin and end or the amount of time you plan for each entry to take. If possible, you could write the person who is responsible for that topic. It is better to use one system through the whole text because inconsistency looks unprofessional.

7. Proposed allotment of time for each topic

This item is optional. You can write down how long each topic should take. It requires you to calculate the time that each team needs to introduce the topic, answer questions, resolve different points of view, generate potential solutions, and agree on the action items that follow from discussions and decisions. Also, putting the time allocated against each item on the agenda will help you to ensure the meeting is running as planned, particularly for longer meetings. One thing needs to be noticed is that time allotment should be based on reality. Usually, people tend to schedule time based on the automatic 30-minute time block in their default calendar. It is better to contact the presenters before the meeting to figure out how much time each one will need for their topics. It helps to avoid embarrassing scheduling conflicts.

8. Name(s) of people leading each of the items

This item is also optional as time allotment. You can write down the presenter of each topic along with that topic. Usually, job titles are unnecessary at this time.

The following are optional items. Whether to include these items in an agenda depends on different situations. Actually, you could include the following items in a meeting without writing them in the agenda.

9. Welcome/Introduction/Warm-Up Activity

This part is particularly helpful for groups who do not meet very often. It is also a good way of getting the meeting started while making sure latecomers do not miss anything substantive.

10. Approve

Review the minutes of the prior meeting. Obviously, this part is only necessary if minutes are kept.

11. Decide on time and agenda for the next meeting

It is necessary to keep the whole meeting start and end on time. The agenda should provide some information about the next meeting if one is to take place.

5.1.1.3 *Template*

There are many word-processing programs (i.e., Microsoft Office, Pages for Mac, etc.) that have templates for both personal and professional documents, including agendas for meetings, which makes it quick and easy to produce an agenda with logical sections and a pleasant arrangement.

Alternatively, you could download a template from a third party if your word processor does not have any agenda templates but it is important to discriminate which is a good template to use.

Once you have located a suitable template, all you need to do is to fill out the blanks with necessary information, and then carefully check your work for errors. If necessary, you could make minor modifications of the agenda in order to fit your needs.

The following is an agenda sample that you could refer to.

Samples Meeting Agenda

Organization Name: Chang' an Hospital _____   **– Agenda –** Department Name: Surgical ICU Date: Wednesday, March7, 2018 Time of Meeting: 12:00 – 1:00pm Meeting Location: 4th Meeting Room
Aim of Our Microsystem: TBD
Participants: Peter, Wang, Smith, Miller, Zhang

continue

Time	Method	Item	Aim/Action
12:00-12:05		1. Clarify Objectives A. Get started with improvement! B. Determine logistics	Leader reviews objectives of this first meeting
12:05-12:10		2. Review Roles: Leader: Lucy White Recorder: David Andrus Timekeeper: Mark Stirling Facilitator: Lucy Wheeler	Use meeting role cards to help function in the meeting roles
12:10-12:40		3. Review Agenda and Times A. Welcome, introductions B. Overview, aim of improvement C. Discuss expectations C. Determine regular time/place D. Draft ground rules E. Review and discuss PACE F. Discuss communication strategy to "get everyone" in the microsystem involved and to communicate throughout the organization	Leader to move group through agenda Time keeper track time for each agenda item Recorder track action items
12:40-12:45		4. Work Through Agenda Items	Track action steps for each item to be completed during action period
12:45-12:50		5. Review Meeting Record—Action Plan	Recorder reviews with group
12:50-13:00		6. Plan Next Agenda	Leader helps group to determine next agenda based on action plan and next steps in process

Source:2004, Trustees of Dartmouth College, Godfrey, Nelson, Batalden, 09/08/03, Version 2: Rev 4/13/2004.

5.1.2 Minutes

Minutes are the instant written transcripts for a meeting or a hearing. They typically describe the events that took place during the meeting, including key points raised. Minutes may include a list of attendees, a statement of the issues or problems considered by the participants, related responses or decisions for the issues or problems, and the main points of key speakers.

5.1.2.1 *Function/Purpose*

Minutes are written as an authoritative and permanent record of proceedings. Good meeting minutes capture the essence of the meeting, including details such as: reasons for the meeting, main issues, decisions made, next steps planned, and actions agreed. However, meeting minutes are not verbatim reports that include everything said by members. Minutes provide a start point for action to be taken in the future. If a task is not performed, minutes can be referred to. Also, people who forget what was decided at the meeting can refer back to the minutes and it may be used for follow-up purposes.

Minutes are not only tangible records for participants, but also a source of information for individuals who were not at the meeting. Minutes can act as a reference when outcomes of a meeting impact other collaborative activities or projects within the organization.

5.1.2.2 *Content*

The basic format of the minutes can vary according to the standards of an organization. However, there are some general guidelines of the contents. Following are the key elements in minutes.

1. Heading

Minutes start with the name of the team or committee who is holding the meeting and may also include the time, date, and location of the meeting.

2. Attendees

It is important to clearly list people who came to the meeting, both their first and last names. Minutes should include people who sent their apologies because of absence, and who need copies of minutes. If someone was absent but what he or she did is important, he/she should be included. For example, one decision cannot be made without a particular person being present.

3. Approval of previous minutes

In some meeting minutes, the first item begins with the approval of previous minutes that notes whether the minutes of the previous meeting were approved. This section may include corrections for previous meeting minutes, or any outstanding actions and responsibilities.

4. Discussion items

This part includes key ideas of issues discussed in the meeting and all the official decisions made during the meeting. For each item, the subject of the discussion and the name of the person who led the discussion should be noted. If a formal motion is proposed, seconded, passed, or not, it should be recorded. If it is a very formal meeting, the process of how to make decision should be recorded. For example, sometimes the voting tally may be included. As for less formal meetings, only the resolutions are recorded; there is no need to keep details about the decision-making process.

5. Action items

This section includes the unfinished business from the previous meeting that still requires action, as well as all current and new items that now require action. In this case, this section should include the action itself, the person who is responsible for this action, and the required date of completion.

6. Announcements

This section reports on any announcements made by participants or people who sent their apologies, including agenda items to be discussed at next meeting.

7. Next meeting

If a follow-up meeting was agreed on, the time, date, and location of the next meeting should be mentioned. Sometimes, the name of the person who are taking the minutes should be listed.

8. Signature line

The minutes are closed with the signature and title of the person who prepared the minutes, and the date they were submitted and agreed.

5.1.2.3 *Writing Process*

1. Pre-meeting

Before the meeting begins, you should review the agenda in order to identify the main topic of the meeting. The more you know about the upcoming meeting, the more effective your notes will be. You may create a template for the minutes according to the meeting agenda.

2. In-meeting

It is necessary to bring a pen and a notebook to the meeting. If you choose to use computer to type the notes, bring your laptop to the meeting. Write down who is talking, what they are talking about, and when they say they are going to do something. If you miss or get confused about anything, you should mark it and ask someone after the meeting. Sometimes, you can ask someone right away even before the meeting is over. You could use a tape recorder or your phone to record meetings if necessary.

3. Post-meeting

Once the meeting is over, it is good to transcribe the official minutes as soon as possible. Also, check whether all decisions, actions, and motions are clearly noted. If necessary, add additional notes to clarify the points. When you are writing minutes, edit to ensure the brevity and clarity in order to make minutes easy to read.

You could use your computer to type your notes at the meeting. If you do, save your notes and begin a new file to type the minutes so you can compare the two. If there were any documents distributed at the meeting, attach them with the minutes. Be sure to check the minutes before sending to the participants, and keep all rough notes until the minutes have been approved.

Sample

Shaanxi Roads Development Project II

Appraisal Mission Wrap-up Meeting Minutes

1. The Wrap-up Meeting for the Shaanxi Roads Development Project II was

held on 11 August 2012 at the Ministry of Finance. The Mission Leader provided an introduction to the Project. This included a short presentation on cost estimates, objective, scope, international consultants time, and the concession agreement.

2. Participants:

Government Representatives

Mr. Zhang Wen—Deputy Director, IFI Division III, Ministry of Finance

Ms. Wang Fang—Project Officer, IFI Division III, Ministry of Finance

Mr. Zheng Weng—Senior Engineer, Planning Department, Ministry of Communication

Mr. Feng Shan—Loan Division I, State Development Planning Commission

Mr. Jing Feng—Senior Engineer SHEC

Mr. Yang Jinquan—Director, Shaanxi Provincial Communications Department

Mr. Li Gui—Deputy Director, Planning Division, Shaanxi Provincial Communications Department

Mr. Ma Jianxin—Chairman, Shannxi Hou-Yu Expressway Construction Co. , Ltd

Mission Members

P, Amy, Principal Economist/Project Team Leader

Choi, Sr. , Financial Analyst

S. Ferguson, Social Development Specialist

Y. Nagao, Project Engineer,

Yu Meng, Project Officer, PRCM

3. Comments received from representatives of relevant government agencies are documented in the following sections.

Ministry of Finance(Zhang Wen)

1. The draft MOU is good, and MOF has the same objective of loan negotiations by mid-October.

2. Para 26, cost estimates give a reasonable figure. It should be ensured that real needs are met.

3. Para 76, there should be no conditions for loan negotiations.

4. Para 20, the local road component has not been supported by the ADB loan. It is unclear who will be responsible for repayment and who has the allocation (MOF, Shaanxi Provincial Finance Bureau, SCD, SHEC).

5. Assurance (xx), the issue on woman and child labor is an internal issue that ADB should not be involved in.

6. Para 79, the processing schedule identifying loan negotiations by mid-October is acceptable.

7. Para 78, follow-up actions should not be in the MOU but should be attached to the minutes of the loan negotiations.

8. Mr. Wen said he understood that ADB would review the present loan agreement format starting next year, and he hoped that it would make loan negotiations more convenient under the proposed new loan agreement.

Ministry of Finance(Wang Fang)

1. Para 25, the words "county government" should be changed to "county resettlement office".

Ministry of Communication(Zheng Weng)

1. Thank you for your hard work.

2. Para 22, last sentence, what is the requirement for including 50% ensured employment? The "50%" can be replaced with "to maximize employment".

3. Para 26, what is the basis for the cost estimate should be clarified. Once detailed designs and bill of quantity are available, the cost estimates can be revised and reflected in the cost tables during loan negotiations.

4. Assurance (iii), since the PRC road construction standard ensure road quality, the maintenance of an international roughness index should be deleted.

5. Assurance (iv), the environment and migratory birds are important and they are sensitive issues. Hence all such issues must be sorted out according to the PRC environmental laws.

6. Assurance (vi) the word "ensure" should be replaced with "encouraged".

7. Assurance (vii), the term "small users" should be deleted.

8. Assurance (xi), last sentence, YEPB should be responsible for implementation and SHEC should assist.

9. Assurance (xiii), would it be possible for the ratios to be flexible during the first 3 years since they are likely to be met only after 3—4 years? Mission clarified that due to the Yellow River bridge toll collection, SHEC could meet all stated financial indicators.

10. Assurance (xix), the term "ensure" should be replaced with "encourage"

11. Assurance (xx), the issue of woman and child labor is already covered. The PRC labor laws identify pre-mature labor (16—18 years), child labor (0—16), and mature labor (above 18). SHEC will follow labor laws to reflect woman and child labor issues.

State Development Planning Commission(Feng Shan)

1. Para 76, there should be no pre-conditions for loan negotiations.

Draft MOU Issues

Three main issues regarding the draft MOU were identified during the wrap-up meeting. Two of them were related to loan negotiation conditions, and the third referred to follow-up actions.

In the draft MOU, Mission included SDPC's approval of the feasibility study as a condition for loan negotiation. However, the Government stated that SDPC approval of feasibility study is an internal issue. It is because MOF cannot request authorization to participate in loan negotiations from the State Council without the feasibility study approval of SDPC. Hence, MOF's participation in loan negotiations implies SDPC approval of the feasibility study. Mission appreciates the Government's view and agrees that SDPC approval is an internal issue. However, Mission stated that in the past there had been problems scheduling loan negotiations due to issues related to SDPC's approval of feasibility studies. In order to overcome time constraints to meet scheduled Board consideration dates, technical discussions had to be held sometimes with substantial delays in obtaining SDPC's approval.

The Government restated that there had not been a delay in transport sector loans due to a delay in SDPC's approval of feasibility studies, and in this particular Project, SDPC's approval was expected in time to schedule loan negotiations in mid-October. Thus, inclusion of SDPC's approval as a loan negotiation condition is not warranted. The Mission stated that loan negotiation is a two way process. The Government, the EA and other authorities need to receive loan documents in time to translate and prepare for negotiations. If the Government has strong reservations against including SDPC's approval as a loan negotiation condition, Mission stated that it could be considered as a condition for Mission to facilitate issuing loan documents.

In the draft MOU, Mission included the execution of the concession framework agreement (CFA) between SCD and SHEC as a condition for loan negotiation. The Government expressed strong objection to this. They stated that in recently held negotiations, such as the *Southern Sichuan Roads Project*, the execution of the CFA was scheduled two years after civil works commencement (June 2008). The Government also stated that there would be major changes in transport sector policy, regulation and laws that might have major implications for CFAs. Therefore, a delay in signing the CFA would assure a better CFA. Mission appreciated the Government's concern over unifying CFAs and supporting province-level authorities to come to such agreements with newly formed expressway companies. Such ownership of the Government would ensure sustainability of the agreements. However, Mission stated that SHEC had already been established since 2011, and the corporatization process needs to move according to the PRC Company Law. It was Mission's view that it is reasonable for SHEC to move in that direction and signing the CFA will facilitate the corporatization process. Mission agrees that signing the CFA before loan negotiation could be a very demanding requirement, although it stressed the importance of early agreement on the concession framework and requested continuous dialogue on this matter including during loan negotiation.

In the draft MOU, Mission stated two follow-up actions be taken by the Government and the EA: (ⅰ) SCD will advise ADB of the approval of the Project feasibility study; and (ⅱ) SCD will submit to ADB the final Resettlement Plan. The Government stated that the MOU should not have a section on follow-up actions. Loan negotiation minutes should instead include a letter identifying the follow-up actions to be undertaken.

The meeting adjourned at approximately 1:43 Beijing time.

This being a true and accurate record of the proceedings of this Meeting of the Board of Directors held on 11 August 2012, is attested to and signed by me below.

/s/

Secretary of Meeting

5.1.3　Memo

Memo is short for memorandum. A memo could be a note, document, or other communication that records events or observations on a topic. Memos are considered to be official documents in most organizations. Employees send memo to their supervisors, and workers send memos to one another. Memos are usually read by a large group of people within an organization. Some memos are written to only one person but are passed to people who need the information. Also, memo may be read by people outside the organization as an official organizational document. Although memos can be ten or more pages long, one to two page memos are more common and more likely to accomplish the writer's purpose.

5.1.3.1　*Function/Purpose*

The basic function of a memo is to bring attention to problems and solve specific problems. A memo can be written to inform the readers of new information, to make request, to explain a procedure or give instructions, to alert readers to a problem, to call for action, or to offer suggestions or recommendations. When written properly, memos are very effective in connecting the concern or issue of the writer with the best interests and needs of the readers.

Wisely choose the audience of the memo and ensure you send the memo to all the people who need to read it. If the issues in the memo only involve one person or a few people, do not send the memo to the entire group.

5.1.3.2 *Content*

Standard memos are written as continuous text divided into segments so that readers can find information quickly and act on it promptly. Memos begin with an introductory paragraph with several sentences, which summarizes the purpose of the memo and the major outcome, and end with a brief concluding paragraph that may summarize the findings, suggestions, or recommendations. The section between the two is the body or discussion of your memo, which includes a lot of details.

1. Heading

A memo usually has five headings at the top of the first page:

1) Company name: It usually appears on the top or is contained in the letterhead.

2) To: Full name and job title of the recipient; if your memo is sent to more than one reader, ensure that you list the readers in the order of their status.

3) From: Sender's full name and job title.

4) Date: Complete and current full calendar date.

5) Subject: Introduce the topic of the memo (highlighted in some way), be specific and concise.

2. Opening segment

The opening paragraph usually gives a brief overview about the purpose of the memo, the context and problem, and the specific assignment or task, before giving readers the details and the context. It should be brief and the length of a short paragraph.

3. Context

In this segment, the event, circumstance, or background of the issue or problem you are solving are included. Briefly give some context and use a paragraph or a few sentences to state what is necessary.

4. Task segment

Task segment is an essential part in a memo. In this part, you should describe what you are doing to solve the problem, issue, or situation. If your readers ask you about the action, you might say:

You asked me to look at...

If you want to explain your intentions for employees to consider, you might say:

We need to consider alternatives that will satisfy. . .

When the purpose of the memo is to convince the decision-makers that there is a real problem, only include as much information as needed and avoid going into more details than required. If it is difficult to describe the task in words, you may consider whether you have clearly understood the situation. You probably need to do more thinking before writing the memo.

5. Summary segment

If the memo you are writing is one page or less, a separate summary section is not necessary. However, if your analysis is fairly detailed, or your memo is longer than one page, a summary paragraph is appropriate. This segment gives a brief statement of the key recommendations. It will help your readers clearly understand the key points of the memo. It is also a good place to sum up the methods and the sources you have used.

6. Discussion segment

This segment is the longest part in the memo and is the portion in which you lay out all the details including facts, statistics, and hypotheses that support your ideas. In this segment, you should give evidences and logical reasons for the solutions you provide. Starting from the most important information and move to specific or supporting facts, this section is also the place where you make your recommendations or acknowledge others' recommendations. Also you may describe problems that might occur in the future and your suggestions to these problems. If this section has adequate information, the memo will be as effective as it could be.

7. Closing segment

Once your readers have absorbed all of your information relevant to the subject of your memo, you want to close with a courteous ending in one to two sentences and state specifically how you want your readers to respond to your memo. For instance, you might write:

I will be glad to discuss this recommendation with you later on. . .

8. Attachments

Make sure you provide necessary documentations or detailed information. You can use lists, graphs, tables, etc. at the end of your memo and refer to your attachments at appropriate points in the memo.

Each part in a memo should follow the rule of general-to-specific in content. It means starting with a topic sentence followed by several supporting sentences and ending with a concluding sentence. Supporting information is the heart of the memo, which could be explanations, statistics, facts, examples, and reasons. Feel free to use tables, charts, graphs, or bullet lists to illustrate your supporting information.

5.1.4 Memorandum of Understanding

A memorandum of understanding (MOU) is a type of document that describes a formal agreement between two or more parties. It expresses the terms and details of an understanding between the parties, and indicates an intended common line of action. MOU is not a legally binding, but it indicates that a business relationship has been established and a legal agreement such as a contract will be forthcoming. It is often used in situations where the parties cannot create a legally enforceable agreement or in cases where parties do not imply a legal commitment.

MOUs are very common and used for domestic purposes and agreements between nations. Unlike treaties, MOUs take a short time to ratify and can be kept confidential. MOUs may also be used to modify and adapt existing legal treaties. This is more expeditious than other forms of documentation.

5.1.4.1 *Content*

MOUs can vary and be tailored according to the needs of each organization or party. Usually, an MOU states or describes the following information:

1) Identification of parties: Names or titles of partners and their contact information.

2) Background: What they are going to work on, the background of the project and why the MOU is being entered into.

3) Scope of the MOU: The boundaries of the MOU- what is included and excluded in MOU, and who will use the MOU.

4) Specified activities, if already determined.

5) Implementation of activities.

6) Funding issues.

7) Joint undertakings and responsibilities: Roles and responsibilities of each party.

8) A time line, if desired.

9) Duration of agreement.

10) A signature and date of signature by all of the parties agreeing to the MOU.

5.1.4.2 *Guideline for Writing MOU*

Before discussing the structure and content of a final MOU, it is important to consider several over-arching principles:

1) Each party starts with a planning phase where a mutual desire is agreed upon

by both parties to enter into an MOU, with a shared and equal commitment to working together;

2) The provisions in the MOU should not conflict with any existing arrangements between the parties;

3) MOU often lists communication expectations to help mediate the sides;

4) The structure and content of the MOU should be clear, unambiguous, and easy to review and update, in order to guarantee decreased misunderstanding or confusion;

5) Since an MOU is a formal agreement, it should be developed with the assistance of relevant legal, financial or other relevant experts;

6) Once discussions are finished, a final MOU is drafted and signed.

Sample

MEMORANDUM OF UNDERSTANDING BETWEEN THE CHANG'AN METEOROLOGICAL SERVICE AND THE CHANG'AN DISASTER MANAGEMENT AGENCY FOR SEVERE WEATHER AND FLOOD WARNING AND EMERGENCY MANAGEMENT

This (MOU) is entered into by the Chang'an Meteorological Service (CMS) and the Chang'an Disaster Management Agency (CDMA).

The short title for this MOU will be herein referred to as the "Agreement".

1. Purpose of Agreement

This Agreement covers the roles of the CMS and the CDMA in the operation of the severe weather and flood warning and emergency management systems for Chang'an, which includes:

· Severe weather and flood advice, forecasting and warning systems;

· Rainfall, water level and flood data information collection and sharing; and,

· Effective CMS and CDMA coordination of consistent and timely information to flood-prone residents in Chang'an.

2. Objectives of Agreement

2.1　Through this Agreement, the CMS and the CDMA wish to confirm and strengthen a partnership arrangement to pursue continuous improvement and collaboration opportunities whereby both parties are working together to provide community awareness and safety in response to:

· Forecast severe weather, riverine and flash flooding;

· Broader flood awareness projects and information activities; and,

· Sharing a range of information and technologies including, but not limited

---

to, rainfall and water level telemetry systems.

2. 2 Such continuous improvement in the coordination and cooperation of the severe weather and flood warning and emergency management activities is to be achieved through working collaboratively to:

· Develop and adopt communication strategies for transmitting local severe weather and flood advice, forecasting and warning information;

· Clarify the roles and responsibilities of the CMS and the CDMA in the management and operation of flood data information systems; and,

· Adopt best practice severe weather and flood emergency management guidelines.

3. Statement of Roles and Responsibilities

3. 1 The CMS undertakes this Agreement, pursuant to its authority under the Meteorology Act, in order to carry out its functions relating to weather and flood warnings.

3. 2 The CMS is the lead agency responsible for the provision of weather and flood forecasts and warnings. Consistent with Chang'an Government legislation, the role of the CMS in respect of flash flooding (defined as rainfall to flood response time of less than six hours) is to provide advice and assistance in the development of locally based warning and response systems.

3. 3 The CDMA is responsible for the provision of functions relating to the management of flooding in Chang'an by application of the statutory powers pursuant to its authority under the Disaster Management Act.

3. 4 The CDMA, through its Flood Risk Management Strategy, is the lead agency responsible for minimizing the impact of flooding on people and property in Chang'an.

3. 5 Both the CMS and the CDMA agree to work in collaboration to deliver the following key outcomes and strategies over the life of this Agreement:

· Development of an early Flood Warning System for residents and businesses in flood-prone areas;

· Development and delivery of next generation flood monitoring systems;

· Installation and management of existing and additional telemetry gauges;

· Continual promotion of the "Flood Wise" educational campaign for Chang'an residents and industry; and,

· Undertaking site community work on the development and implementation of local flood plans.

4. Participation to the Agreement

Both the CMS and the CDMA become participants to this Agreement by completion of the declaration set out below, which becomes effective from the date of the last signature.

5. Joint Undertakings

The CMS and the CDMA agree to undertake the activities and fulfill the responsibilities as described in this Agreement in good faith, to the extent possible given prevailing operating environments. Performance under this Agreement is subject to the availability of funds and human resources to the CMS and the CDMA and to existing administrative and personnel policies, which may affect the terms of the Agreement.

6. Limitation

Nothing in this Agreement shall derogate from the CMS's responsibilities under the Meteorology Act or the CDMA's responsibilities under the Disaster Management Act.

7. Review and Amendment of the Agreement

7.1 It is agreed that this Agreement will be reviewed within three years following the date of commencement.

7.2 Supplementary guidance materials and documents may be formulated to facilitate achievement of the objectives of the Agreement. Any major revision in the objectives or scope of the Agreement outlined herein, which either party may consider desirable or necessary in the future, will be the subject of supplementary agreements.

7.3 This Agreement can be updated with amended terms and conditions as agreed in writing by each of the parties.

8. Termination of Agreement

8.1 This Agreement shall continue in effect unless terminated by one or both parties giving 90 days' notice in writing, notice to begin with the date of mailing.

8.2 Unless otherwise decided by mutual agreement, on termination of the Agreement, each party will retain possession of the equipment and resources purchased or supplied by it.

Signed by the Parties this day of _____ 2012.

Signed for and on behalf of the Changan Meteorological Service

　　Signature　　　　　　　　　　　[title of authorized signatory]

Name (print)

in the presence of:

Witness signature　　　　　　　　Witness Name (print)

Signed for and on behalf of Changan Disaster Management Agency

　　Signature　　　　　　　　　　　[title of authorized signatory]

Name（print）	
in the presence of:	
Witness signature	Witness Name（print）

Source: Guidelines for Creating a Memorandum of Understanding and a Standard Operating Procedure between a National Meteorological or Hydrometeorological Service and a Partner Agency. World Meteorological Organization, 2012.

5.2 PROPOSAL AND ACTION PLAN

5.2.1 Proposal

A proposal is a unique type of report. It is written as a persuasive description of how you can meet your audiences' specific needs. The length of proposals can be one to two pages, or even hundreds of pages if large and complex projects are involved. The audiences of a proposal could be a reader or a group of readers who are usually in position of authority, such as managers, supervisors, department heads, company buyers, or elected officials.

5.2.1.1 *Function/purpose*

The purpose of a proposal is to analyze an audience's problem, identify plans for solving the problem, and persuade the audience that the presented solution is the best possible one. It is often a kind of sales documents designed to encourage your audiences to adopt your suggestions. You can create an internal proposal, for example to your manager seeking authority to purchase a new piece of equipment or to change the procedure of a project. You can also write a sales proposal to potential customers.

In the field of project management, you must propose a plan and then get that proposal approved. For example, you can write a project proposal to your stakeholder to explain exactly what you are going to do, how you're going to do it, and what the results will be.

5.2.1.2 *Content*

The content of a proposal can vary greatly in size and scope. A proposal is determined by many variables but the main variable is whether it is a solicited or an unsolicited proposal. If it is unsolicited, then the scope and organization are up to you to decide. If it is solicited, the scope and organization are usually determined by the request for the proposal. In most documents that call for proposals, the content and order you should cover are clearly spelled out, which make it easier for them to compare and evaluate the proposals of many bidders. Different parts of a proposal will be evaluated by a team of experts from different organizations. For example, an engineer might review the technical parts of a report while an accountant might evaluate the cost estimates.

1. Proposal introduction

Start with a firm introduction. The introduction states the problem you want to solve, and gives your solution(s). The introduction of a solicited proposal should refer to the Request for Proposals (RFP); while the introduction of an unsolicited one should mention the factors that have motivated you to submit a proposal, like the mutual acquaintance or previous conversations you had with the readers.

The following is information that is commonly covered in a proposal:

1) Background or statement of the problem.

Use some background information to review the readers' situation and highlight a need for action and then state the purpose of your proposal. After the introduction, you should state the problem. If your proposal is unsolicited, convince the readers that the problem really exists. In this section, the following questions should be answered: What is the problem? What is the cause of the problem? What effects does this problem have? Why does this problem need to be solved?

2) Solution.

This section is a summary of your solution, which might have the heading of "Preliminary Analysis" or "Overview of Approach" in long proposals. This is a brief description of how your proposal will solve the readers' problem, the change you are proposing, the key selling points you are providing, and the benefits of your solution.

3) Scope.

The boundaries of your proposal, as in what you will do and will not do, are stated here. A heading for this section could be "Delimitations."

4) Report organization.

This orients the readers to the rest of your proposal by telling the readers how the proposal is laid out and calls their attentions to those divisions of significant thoughts.

2. Proposal body

This section describes the proposed solution(s) in details and gives specifics on what the expected results will be. An effective body should also cover the following:

1) Proposed approach.

This part includes information you have to offer: your concept, product or service, and may be given the heading of "Technical Proposal," "Project

Proposal," and "Issues for Analysis" or "Work Statement." This section should discuss the large impact of your ideas, focus on the strengths of your offer in relation to the needs of the readers, and emphasize the benefits of your product or service that relates to the readers' needs. Further, it should point out the advantages of your approach over other competitors.

2) Work plan.

You should provide detailed and concrete information about how you will accomplish the solution you are proposing unless you are providing a product that is a standard, off-the-shelf item. You need to explain: the steps that you are providing, the timing and method of these steps, and the resources you will use; as well as the person(s) responsible. State the specific date that you envision the project to start, the date of completion, and if there will be any follow-up work involved. In the solicited proposals, ensure that your dates match the dates required in the RFP. Meticulous work shows that you have done all of your homework and will not waste your readers' money and this will give your readers a sense of confidence. It is important not to promise more than what you are able to offer or achieve within the given period.

3) Statement of qualifications

This section describes the experience, personnel, and facilities of your organization in relation to the needs of the readers. This can be an important selling point and must be carefully taken care of.

4) Costs

In this section, you should state the costs of your proposal, show the readers how you come to the total costs, and break them down in details. Make sure that your proposal has financial sense. If you quote too high of a price, you could lose the bid to your competitors. If you quote too low, you could lose money with the project.

In an informal proposal, some of the above elements can be combined together and presented in a letter format. However, the discussions of these elements will be rather long and thorough.

3. Proposal closing

In the closing, mirror your introduction and summarize the main points of your proposal. Emphasize the benefits that the readers will obtain from the solutions, and summarize the benefits of your approach. Re-emphasize why you and your organization are the people for the job and thank them for their considerations and time. The closing is the last chance for you to persuade the audiences to accept your proposal, so you should be succinct, assertive and confident in the closing.

5.2.1.3   *Guidelines for Writing a Successful Proposal*

As mentioned earlier, the main purpose of a proposal is to persuade the audiences to do something such as fund a project or purchase goods. Consequently, methods used in writing a proposal are similar to those used for writing a sales letter. The proposal has a purpose to sell your products, service, ideas, methods or company to the audiences. The AIDA (an acronym that stands for Attention, Interest, Desire and Action) plan is also used when writing proposals as persuasive sales messages. It is used to arouse attention, build interest, intensify desire, and finally motivate action.

The following are additional strategies that can be used to strengthen the argument in a proposal:

1. Define your audiences

Before writing, you need to be sure of what your audiences already know. It will help you to present your ideas effectively. Even though the proposal you offered will benefit your readers, do not be overconfident that they will accept it. Any errors and inconsistencies may lead your audiences to reject the proposal.

2. Demonstrate your knowledge

Show your readers that you have conducted in-depth research and evaluations to understand the problem, and possess the knowledge and experience to solve the problem.

3. Provide concrete examples

You can support your proposal by using evidences and explanations. Hard facts are the most convincing so avoid vague and unsupported generalizations. Be detailed in describing your plan and how it will work.

4. Define your solution

Your proposal needs to define a problem and offer a corresponding solution that will convince the uninterested or skeptical readers to support it. You need to prove that your solution is workable for the audiences and within their capabilities to achieve.

5. Research the competition

You need to become familiar with your competitors' product lines, services, prices and strategies, have a fair idea about their market costs, and be able to show how your work is better overall.

6. Package your proposal attractively

Your proposal should fit a certain style and write in plain and direct language without errors, inconsistencies, or omissions.

Sample Project Proposal

Purpose and Justification

Project Requestor:

Allen Smith, Professor of Rodent Studies: 213-4455 allen. amith@ changan. edu

Statement of the Problem or Need:

CAware is used by the Rodent Studies department to support both its research and its teaching activities. The software is used by researchers to track, record, and analyze data on various facets of rodent life cycles. For example, the software was used during research through which we were able to identify that rodents existing on an extremely high sodium diet experienced a significant reduction in the number of offspring.

All students in the department are taught how to use the software and many of their assignments are required to be done using CAware. Since CAware is one of the leading applications used by private sector organizations involved in this field, we feel that having experience with the software gives our graduates a leg up.

The server on which the CAware software runs has been unsupported by the manufacturer since December of 2018. Support is currently being received through a contract with CAware Authorities, Inc. (CAAU) The contract expires at the end of the next calendar year. We have been warned by CAAU that there will be a significant increase in the support fees under any new contract.

In addition, the process of backing up data from the existing server is extremely cumbersome. We have experienced a number of occasions where data has been inexplicably lost and had to be re-entered. As a result, we are keeping reams of printed reports in the research labs.

Project Deliverables and Beneficiaries:

At the end of the project we hope to have the current software running on a new, faster and more stable server. In addition, all of the existing data should have been moved from the old server to the new. All of the current functionality should still exist. Access to the system should still be controlled through the use of user IDs and passwords, which are administered by the department of Rodent Studies.

· Students of the department will continue to benefit from the hands-on experience of working with CAware software. Less of their class time will be wasted waiting for server performance issues to be resolved.

· Researchers will benefit from the increased speed and reliability.

· Both the department and Ithaca College will benefit from a cost savings gained through the increased efficiency. No longer will time and effort be required for multiple reboots and the redundant entry of data that is lost during backups.

Strategic Context:

Because the software running on the server supports both research and instructional activities within the department, the project is in direct support of Chang'an College's initiative to incorporate the use of technology in education.

Time Factors:

We would like to have the server replaced as quickly as possible. The current server is becoming more and more unstable. It locks up numerous times during the day and has to be shut down and restarted.

The cost of the replacement server has been included in this year's fiscal budget so we are ready to go.

Special Provisions:

None.

Related Projects:

This is a follow up to the CAware Research Project (Project ID # 2016-11). The CAware Research Project evaluated servers currently available on the market and identified the best option to replace the existing server on which CAware is currently running.

Project Assumptions and Constraints:

Assumptions:

· The new server will be able to be placed in the same location as the existing server.

· The new server will not require any modifications to the power supply.

· The existing network data transfer rate will be sufficient.

Constraints:

· It is important that the application be available during normal classroom hours.

Project Risks:

· There is a risk that the old server may stop functioning prior to installation of the replacement.

Project Expenses:

Implementation Expenses:

We have received a quote from the vendor of $60,000.00 for the new server. This includes charges for shipping and insurance during shipment. The funds have been approved and are available from the Department of Rodent Studies current fiscal year budget.

Post-implementation Expenses:

The vendor includes one year of maintenance and support in the purchase price. Beginning in year two maintenance and support are available from the vendor at $16,000.00 annually. The Department of Rodent Studies will fund any ongoing maintenance and licensing expenses.

Project Champion:

Susan Miller, Director of Rodent Studies: 213-5566 <u>susan. miller@ changan. edu</u>

Primary Contact:

Allen Smith, Professor of Rodent Studies: 213-4455 <u>allen. amith@ changan. edu</u>

Major Stakeholders:

Olivia White, Manager of Rodent Studies Lab: 213-6677 <u>olivia. white@ changan. edu</u>

Emma Brown, Assistant Dean of Rodent Studies: 213-7788 <u>emma. brown @ changan. edu</u>

Source: Project Proposal, Cheezewiz Server Placement, Ithaca College.

5.2.2 Action Plan

An action plan is a detailed document listing necessary steps or activities that should be taken to achieve a specific goal. The purpose of an action plan is to clarify what resources are required, and to formulate a timeline for when the tasks need to be completed. An action plan has benefits for both individuals and businesses. In project management, a well-developed action plan can serve as a blueprint for the project manager or any member of the group to monitor their progress and break a large project down into more manageable tasks.

The advantage of writing an action plan is to give you and your group a structured step-by-step schedule to achieve the goal. It provides appropriate foundations to the team; therefore, the amount of time spending on each task is prioritized. This will prevent any distractions that may occur. Lastly, it helps members of the team be fully aware of their roles, and provides the necessary information to guarantee success.

5.2.2.1 *Content*

An action plan has a number of action steps or changes. Each of them usually includes the following information:

1) What actions or changes will occur.

2) Who will carry out these actions or changes.

3) Before what time and date they will take place, and for how long.

4) What resources (i. e. money, staff, equipment) are needed to carry out these actions or changes.

5) Communication (who should know what?).

There are many different models of action plan. In real life, it is not quite as simple as this and the process is more complex with overlapping stages. Your plan must be changed or revised during execution.

5.2.2.2   *Guidelines for Writing an Action Plan*

There are some guided steps that need to be followed in order to ensure success when creating action plans, however, the structure can be altered in the process. The following lists the main steps to create an action plan:

1) Set a clear goal of your action plan.

2) Make an outline regarding what you want to achieve.

3) Consider possible problems that may occur and make preparation with sufficient amount of skills, resources, and issues related with your targets.

4) Set measurable milestones. Create milestones easily by starting from the end (the accomplishment of the goal) and working backwards to present day and current circumstances.

5) Break the tasks down into steps and focus on one step at a time.

6) Put timeline in place. Specific timeline and deadline will help avoid delay.

7) Make every effort to solve the issues of each step.

8) Review and revise your progress to achieve final success.

5.2.2.3   *Tips for Writing an Action Plan*

Make sure your goals are SMARRT. Here is a basic definition that can make your plan more executable.

1) Specific: Make sure your goal is clearly defined with as many details as possible. For instance, compare saying, "I want to make more money," "I want to make $10,000 per month" is better.

2) Measurable: You need to be clear whether the goal is obtainable and how far away the completion is.

3) Achievable: The goals you defined need to be realistic and achievable.

4) Realistic: Within the availability of resources, knowledge, and time.

5) Relevant: Your goal should matter to you and align with other relevant goals.

6) Time: Goals should be linked to a time frame that creates practical sense.

Sample

ACTION PLAN MY OBJECTIVE IS: To choose my future career! TO ACHIEVE THIS I NEED TO: List the steps I need to take. Be detailed and specific, such as "Find email addresses of 3 local employers everyday" instead of "I'll contact some employers".	Date I expect to complete this step by
I will tell my plan to: my three best friends and my parents	
I will start my action plan on (date):	3rd May
Step 1. I will use the computer guidance system to help me to identify jobs of interest	4th May
Step 2. I will use the Find Job website to find out what jobs graduates from my subject can enter	6th May
Step 3. I will pick up booklets from the Career Service on some of the careers suggested and browse through these	9th May
Step 4. I will use the Careers Network Website to communicate with a graduate in the Career that I are interested in most	10th May
Step 5. I will see my careers adviser to discuss the ideas I have got from the above and to narrow these down	By 12th May

Potential problems I am likely to face. What will I do to overcome these?

Fear of life after university. Have procrastinated too long and now realize that I must take action or miss opportunities.

Will I be able to find a suitable graduate in step 4? If nobody suitable in the Careers Network Website, may have to contact companies directly for help

5.3　CONTRACT AND AGREEMENT

A contract is a voluntary arrangement between two or more parties that is enforceable by law as a binding legal document. The requirements for a valid contract include:

1) The parties must possess legal capacity to enter contract;

2) One party must have made a binding offer and the other one must accept it;

3) The contract must be supported by consideration;

4) The resulting agreement must be a genuine one;

5) Some contracts must be made in a particular form;

6) The object of the contract cannot be disapproved of by the law.

A contract is a result of mutual understandings between two parties on a subject matter, where two parties agree to enter in a contract and finalize the terms and conditions. The purpose of making the contract as perfect as possible is that it may be used at any time in the case of dispute as evidence. The purpose to bring an understating into written form is to keep proof and evidence of that understanding in documentary form.

5.3.1 Commodity Sales Contract

5.3.1.1 *Introduction*

In international trade, the seller and the buyer will reach an agreement through negotiation. The general practice of international trade is that the two parties sign a formal contract as a constraint on both sides of the legal basis.

The contract defines the rights and obligations for both parties. It stipulates the concerns related to both parties and includes the production quality and quantity, unit price, time period, location, liability for breach of contract, solutions for disputes, packing method, inspection standard, testing method, and the method of payment.

5.3.1.2 *Composition*

The head of a contract usually includes name and number, date, location, two party's names, address, contract information, etc.

1. Name and number of contract

E. g., Purchase Contract, Commodity Sales Contract, Lease Contract, Shipping Contract, etc. Usually the word "Original," or "Copy" is marked in the upper right corner.

2. Name of Buyer and Seller

E. g., President; Board of Directors; CEO/general manager; Department manager; Corporation Ltd. (Co. Ltd.); Branch; Subsidiary.

3. Preface

E. g., this contract is signed by and between the Buyer and the Seller, according to the terms and conditions stipulated below.

4. Main Body

This part includes commodity and specifications; quality; quantity; price; time of shipment; insurance; packing; shipping mark; guarantee of quality; inspection and claims; terms of payment; terms of shipment; force majeure; late delivery and penalty; arbitration, etc.

5. End

This part includes effective date, law applied, signature and note.

5.3.1.3 *Case Study*

Commodity Sales Contract   Original/Copy

 Data:

 Contract No. :

 The Buyers: The Sellers:

This contract is made by and between the Buyers and the Sellers; whereby the Buyers agree to buy and the Sellers agree to sell the under-mentioned goods subiect to the terms and conditions as stipulated hereinfter:

  (1) Name of Commodity: (2) Quantity: (3) Unit Price:

  (4) Total Value: (5) Panking: (6) Country of Origin:

  (7) Terms of Payment: (8) Insurance: (9) Time of Shipment:

  (10) Port of Lading: (11) Port of Destination:

Within 45 days after the arrival of the goods at the destination, should the quality, specifications, or quantity be found not in conformity with the stipulations of the contract except those claims for which the insurance company or the owners of the Vessel are liable, the Buyers shall, have the right on the strength of the inspection certificate issued by the C. C. I. C (China Commodity Inspection Counceil) or the relative documents to claim for compennsation to the Sellers.

  (12) Force Majeure:

The Sellers shall not be held responsible for the delay in shipment or non-delivery of the goods due to force majeure, which might occur during the process of manufacturing or the course of loading or transit. The Sellers shall advise the Buyers immediately of the occurrence mentioned above the within fourteen days thereafter. The Sellers shall send by airmail to the Buyers for their acceptance a certificate of the accident. Under such circumstances the Sellers however, are still under the obligation to take all necessary measures to hasten the delivery of the goods.

  (13) Arbitration:

All disputes in connection with the execution of this Contract shall be settled friendly through negotiation. In case no settlement can be reached, the case then may be submitted for arbitration to the Arbitration Commission of the China Council for the Promotion of International Trade in accordance with the Provisional Rules of Procedure promulgated by the said Arbitration Commission. The Arbiration Committee shall be final and binding upon both parties, and the Arbitration fee shall be borne by the losing parties.

  The Buyers: XX Investment Co. Signature/Chop

  The Sellers: YY Limited   Signature/Chop

5.3.2 Equity Transfer Contract

5.3.2.1 *Introduction*

Equity Transfer Contract defines the rights and obligations in the equity transfer activity between assignor and assignee of the share (or stake). Due to the complexity of equity transfer act, the assignor and assignee sign an equity transfer contract in order to avoid unnecessary disputes.

5.3.2.2 *Factors in Consideration*

First, we need to know the stock sharing structure. It includes business license, tax registration certificate, contract, board of the company, and stockholders of the company. Be sure the seller has the authority to sign the contract. To assess the asset, the asset assessment could be obtained by national certified company.

In addition, we need to be aware of the warrants of seller. These include their authority, amount of share, rights, stipulations of agreement legally protected, no third party involved (otherwise, ask them to provide other certificates involved, e. g. , land use right, estate ownership.), indebtedness, etc.

5.3.2.3 *Main Contents*

The main content of an equity transfer contract is listed below:

1) Amount and percentage of share transferred;

2) Unit and total price;

3) Effective time of the agreement;

4) Effective time of the transfer;

5) Payment method;

6) Obligations of buyer and seller;

7) Statements and warrants of the seller;

8) Rights and obligations after transfer;

9) Dismiss clauses;

10) Confidentiality clauses;

11) Settlement of disputes;

12) Breach responsibility;

13) Miscellaneous.

5.3.2.4 *Vocabulary*

Hereafter = after this time	Hereby = by means/reasons of this
Herein = in this	Hereinafter = later in this contract
Thereafter = after that time	Thereby = by that means
Therein = from that	Thereinafter = later in the same contract
Whereby = by what/which	Wherein = in what/which

5.3.2.5 Case Study

Equity Transfer Contract

The parties hereinafter include:

Party A:Peter Investment Co. Ltd.

Party B:White Global Architecture Inc.

Party C:Mr. William Weeks

ID No. :490135 19650315 7293

Address:320 Torgerson Hall,Hendricks St. ,Richmond,Virginia

Whereas Party A legally owns 100% shares of Peter Investment Co. Ltd ("Peter"),Which is registered in the Washington,D. C. ;

Whereas Peter,registered in Washinggtion,D. C. on Jan 1,2001,legally owns 80% shares of Newton Braking System Co. ,Ltd(i. e. ,Limited Company, abbreviated as the "Company");

Whereas Party A intends to sell the legally-owned 100% shares of Peter,wheraeas the Company is 20% owned by White Global Architecture Inc. (incorporated),and they have certain pre-emptive regarding the shares in the Company;

Whereas Party C intends to buy the whole shares of the company held by Party A and B,adhering to the principals of equality and mutual benefit,the parties have reached the following agreement(the "Agreement")after friendly consultations regarding the Equity Transfer matters:

Article 1 Price of the Shares

After the Company repays RMB 400 million of payables due to Party B or its designed agent,subject to the terms and conditions in the Agreement,Party A hereby agrees that it will transfer and convey to Party C its shares of Company at the price of 200 million US Dollars and Party C agrees to purchase the shares of the Company held by Party A at this price. At the same time,Party B agrees to transfer to Party C the title of its remaining receivables from the Company at the price of 100 million US Dollars and Party C agrees.

Article 2 Representations and Warranties

Party A represents and warrants to Party C that it legally owns the Shares subject to Article 1, as well as the right to deal with the shares entirely and effectively;and that prior to any transfer it will obtain all necessary consents such that Shares can be tranfered to Party C at the effective time of the transfer, free and clear of liens and encumbrances whatsoever.

The Company consents to and agrees that he shall arrange the Company to pay RMB 100 million in accordance with in the Article 1 to Party B or the designated agent before the date of March 1, 2012, and the remaining RMB 300 million of the repayment of payable dues referred in Article 1 shall be paid to Party B or the designated agent in two equal installments of RMB 150 million before September 1,2012 and September 1. 2013, respectively. Party C consents to pay Party A and Party B the purchase price of 200 million and 100 million US Dollars respectively before December 1, 2013 to purchase the said receivables at this price.

Article 3 Allocation of Shareholder Rights and Indebtedness

Article 4 Equity Transfer Arrangement and Cost

Article 5 The Company's Management and Confidentiality Obligation

Article 6 Breach Responsibility

Article 7 Application of Law and Settlement of Disputes

Article 8 Miscellaneous

The Agreement is signed by the authorized representatives of the parties on Jun 1,2011.

Party A: Peter Investment Co. Signature/Chop

Representative: Signature/Chop

Party B: White Global Architecture Inc. Signature/Chop

Representative: Signature/Chop

Party C: Mr. William Weeks Signature/Chop

Date: _____

5.3.3 Contract for Technology Transfer

5.3.3.1 *Introduction*

Technology transfer (or transfer of technology) is the process of transferring skills, knowledge, technologies, methods of manufacturing, samples of manufacturing and facilities into new products, processes, applications, materials, or services. It includes patented technology, trademarks, and non-patented technology, such as proprietary technology, biodiversity, business management methods, etc.

Commercial technology transfer activities inevitably involve technical, financial, marketing and law, and many other aspects of content.

Many companies, universities, and governmental organizations now have an Office of Technology Transfer (also known as Tech Transfer) dedicated to identifying research that has potential commercial interests and strategies for exploiting it.

5.3.3.2 *Main Contents*

1) Definition

2) Object of the contract

3) Contract price

4) Delivery of the technical documentation and software

5) Technical service and personnel training

6) Acceptance of the contract products

7) Guarantees and claims

8) Infringements and confidentiality

9) Taxes and duties

10) Performance bond

11) Force majeure

12) Settlement of disputes

13) Effectiveness of the contract and the miscellaneous

14) Legal addresses

5.3.3.3 *Case Study*

Object of the Contract

2.1 The Licensor has agreed to transfer to the Licensee and the Licensee has agreed to obtain from the Licensor the technical know-how for the design, manufacture, assembly, installation, test, inspection, adjustment, operation and maintenance and management of the Contract products. The name, model, specifications and technical indices of the Contract Products are detailed in Annex _____ to the Contract.

2.2 The Licensor has agreed to grant the Licensee the license and right to design, manufacture, use, sell in the PRC the Contract Proucts. The license and right are non-exclusive and non-transferable.

2.3 The Licensor has agreed to provide licensee with the Technical Documentation and Software related to the Contract Products. The contents, copies and time of delivery of the Technical Documentation and Software are detailed in Annex _____ and Annex _____ to the Contract.

2.4 The Licensor has agreed to dispatch his technical personnel to the Contract Factory, for Technical Services. The specific contents and requirements for the Technical Services are detailed in Annex _____ to the Contract.

2.5 The Licensor has agreed to give the Licensee's personnel technical training in Licensor's factories and at the Contract factory, to ensure that the Licensee's technical personnel shall master the above technical know-transferred to the Licensee. The specific Contents and requirements of technical training are detailed in Annex _____ to the Contract.

2.6 The Licensor has agreed, upon the request of the Licensee for a period of ten years after the date of validity of the Contract, to supply the Licensee at the

---

most favorable price with the parts, components, raw materials and accessories which are necessary for manufacturing the Contract Products under a separate contract to be signed in due time.

2.7 The Licensor has agreed, upon the request of the Licensee for a period of ten years after the date of validity of the Contract, to supply the Licensee at the most favorable price with equipment and software which are made or developed by the Licensor and necessary for manufacturing the Contract software which are made or developed by the third party and necessary for manufacturing the Contract Products.

2.8 The Licensor has agreed to grant the Licensee the license and right to use, on the Contract Products manufactured by the Contract Factory, the word "made in China under license of" followed by Name of the Licensor, at the option of the Licensee, provided the Contract Products can meet the technical and quality requirements as specified in Annex _____ of the Contract.

Contract Price

3.1 The total Contract price, which is based on the contents and scope stipulated in Article 2 to the Contract and Licensor's fulfillment of his obligations under the Contract, shall be _____ EUROS, (SAY: _____ EUROS ONLY) details as follows:

3.1.1 Price for Technical Know-how: _____ EUROS (SAY: _____ EUROS ONLY). The breakdown prices of the technical know-how are as follows:

A. Technology transfer fee is: _____ EUROS (SAY: _____ EUROS ONLY).

B. Technical documentation and software fee (CIF Beijing Capital International Airport is _____ EUROS (SAY: _____ EUROS ONLY).

C. Personnel training fee is _____ EUROS (SAY: _____ EUROS ONLY).

D. Technical service fee is _____ EUROS (SAY: _____ EUROS INLY).

3.2 The above-mentioned total Contract price shall be firm and fixed price for the Licensor's obligation under the contract including all expenses incurred for delivery of Techical Documentation and Software CIF Beijing Capital International Airport China.

5.3.3.4   *Processing Trade Contract*

Abundant and cost-efficient human resources is an important factor in China to attract foreign processing trade orders, so we often have such trade cooperation with European and American countries. The trade is a win-win for both sides and mainly refers to processing and assembling small and medium-sized compensation trade and feed processing trade. This collaboration involves cost of process, taxation, and material damage rate as well as other details. All of these factors need to be addressed in the contract.

5.3.3.5 *Compensation Trade Contract*

Compensation trade refers to a party on the basis of credit, large machinery, equipment, technology, raw materials, or services from the other party abroad. The party amortizes the loan to its products, goods, or services within a certain period of time.

With the rapid development of multi-national companies, cooperation of production enterprises across different countries has become common. Many companies take advantage of compensation trade and use it as a mean of exaggerating sales of capital goods, and thus gain double profits. Therefore, compensation trade contract documents become very important.

5.3.3.6 *Counter Trade Contract*

Counter trade means exchanging goods or services which are paid for, in whole or part, with other goods or services, rather than with money.

Barter: Exchange of goods or services directly for other goods or services without the use of money as means of purchase or payment.

Switch trading: Practice in which one company sells to another its obligation to make a purchase in a given country.

Counter purchase: Sale of goods and services to one company in another country by a company that promises to make a future purchase of a specific product from the same company in that country.

Buyback: It occurs when a firm builds a plant in a country—or supplies technology, equipment, training, or other services to the country—and agrees to take a certain percentage of the plant's output as partial payment for the contract.

Offset: Agreement that a company will offset a hard-currency purchase of an unspecified product from that nation in the future. Agreement by one nation to buy a product from another, subject to the purchase of some or all of the components and raw materials from the buyer of the finished product, or the assembly of such product in the buyer nation.

Compensation trade: Compensation trade is a form of barter in which one of the flows is partly in goods and partly in hard currency.

5.3.4 Sales Agency Agreement

5.3.4.1 *Introduction*

A Sales Agency Agreement is signed between the principal and agent, defining the authority, rights, and obligations of both sides.

5.3.4.2 *Main Contents*

Agency authority: if the agency is the only one in a region, the principal (seller) cannot directly or indirectly sell the product in the region.

Agent product: define the product item and type. The agent has authority to sell all or part of the products from the seller.

Agent region: China and the US have different region divisions (Country/province/city/town vs. Country/state/county/city); the agent should obey the local laws and regulations.

Minimum agent amount: fixed or subject to change according to the market demands. A solution to a breach of contract would also be clearly stated here.

Commission and payment: this part defines the sales quota, invoice amount, or the sales ratio, as well as the payment date and method.

Business report: this part defines the report period, report format, and content. For example, commercial activities, market information, local laws, foreign exchange, and customs.

Intellectual property rights and protection: intellectual property rights abroad shall be inviolate.

5.3.5　Chinese-Foreign Equity Joint Venture Contract

5.3.5.1 *Introduction*

This contract is signed in the case of joint venture of a Chinese enterprise and a foreign enterprise.

5.3.5.2 *Main Contents*

1) The contract terms;
2) Total amount of investment;
3) Registered capital;
4) Cooperative production and management of project;
5) Sales quota at home and abroad;
6) Cooperation period;
7) Scope of business;
8) The joint venture's operation and management;
9) Financial management;
10) Labor management;
11) Liability for breach of contract clause;
12) Law terms and conditions, etc.

5.4 **REPORT**

This part provides a general introduction to write and organize a clear and well-structured report. It also includes a typical structure and a step-by-step guide for producing reports. Writing a good report requires you to use and combine many of the writing skills and research strategies you have already learned in the previous chapters. Additionally, this part briefly introduces some different types of reports that students usually use in the university.

5.4.1 Writing a Report

A report is an orderly objective document where specific information and evidences are presented. It is usually written for a clear purpose and to a particular audience. Reports come in all shapes, sizes, and lengths and may be conveyed through a written medium, oral speaking, television, or movie. In the professional field, reports are the most important and common types of communication. Depending on the scenario, reports can be official or unofficial, and can be listed publicly or only available privately. The information in a report is presented in a clearly structured format with use of sections, headings, and sub-headings, so that the information is easy to locate and follow.

5.4.1.1 *Content/Structure*

The main features of a report are described below and this is only a general guide. These should be used in conjunction with instructions or guidelines. The following are commonly covered.

1. Title Page

The title needs to briefly but explicitly describe the topic or purpose of the report. Other details such as your name, the submission date, and for whom the report is written is also included in the title page. Other details are not needed on this page.

2. Terms of Reference

In this part, you could include a brief explanation to the audience, the purpose of writing, and the method used in writing this report by using the form of a subtitle or a single paragraph.

3. Summary

The summary can be also called the "Abstract," or "Executive Summary." It should briefly describe the content of the report and is an overall summary of the entire report. The length of a summary is usually a paragraph or two and always less than a page but it will depend on the extent of the work reported. This is the first section to be read but one of the last things to be written. The summary should provide the audiences with a clear and helpful overview of the content. A good summary should include the following items:

1) The topic and purpose of your report;

2) The method you use for your research;

3) The main findings and conclusions reached as a result of your research;

4) Recommendations for future action.

4. Table of Contents

The table of contents, also called "content," should orderly list the different chapters and/or headings together with the relevant page numbers. The main purpose of this table is to help readers quickly scan the list of headings and find a particular part of the report they may be looking for.

5. Introduction

This section sets the context for the report, provides the background information, and introduces topics and the thesis for the readers. In this section, you should explain the aims and objectives of the report in details so that the readers know what the report is going to be about, what key questions the report is trying to answer, and what it is trying to achieve. Any problems or limitations in the scope of the report should be identified here.

6. Methods

In this section, you need to state clearly how you carried out your investigation and explain why you used this particular method. This part includes: a list of equipments and materials used; explanations of procedures followed; reference to problems encountered, and subsequent changes in procedure.

7. Results

The results section should present the findings of the investigation or experiment as simply and clearly as possible, with necessary diagrams, charts, graphs or tables that support your results. You should choose just one format and present the results in a logical order without comments. Label your figures and tables clearly, give each of them a title, and describe what the figure and table demonstrates. However, the interpretation of your results should not be listed in this section but rather should take place in the discussion section.

8. Discussion

This section is probably the longest section where you discuss your material. The facts and evidences you have gathered in your introduction and previous research should be analyzed and discussed with specific reference. You need to discuss not only what the findings show but also the reasons behind it and use evidences to back up your explanations. Your points should be organized logically and easy to follow. If your discussion is too long, you could divide it into sections with headings, sub-headings, and minor sub-headings to create a clear structure.

Use bullet points to present a series of points in an easy-to-follow list.

9. Conclusion

The conclusion summarizes the major findings that can be drawn from the previous report. It effectively attempts to remind the readers of the most important points which appear in the report and answer the key questions stated in the introduction section. However, in this section, no new arguments or evidences should be introduced and the conclusion usually uses present tense.

This section may also include:

1) Recommendation for actions;

2) Suggestion for future research.

10. Recommendation

Recommendations can be listed as part of the conclusion section. However, if required, recommendations should be included separately from the conclusion section. Recommendations should tell the readers what actions should be implemented based on the information in the body and conclusion section, and never contain any new evidences. These could be listed in bullet points or small paragraphs.

11. Reference

This section is also called "Reference List" or "Bibliography." A reference is a list of all the published sources referred to in your report, in alphabetical order by the author's name. The list includes the full publication details of all books, articles, websites, and other sources used to write the report. Each reference in the list needs to contain all of the bibliographic information from a source. As for the texts you consulted but did not refer to directly, these could be grouped under a separate heading such as "Background Reading" and listed in alphabetical order using the same format as in your reference list.

12. Appendices

The appendices include information that is supplementary but not necessary or essential to explain your findings. If these materials were inserted into the body of the paper, the readers' attentions would be detracted from the orderly and logical presentation of the whole work. Appendices might include visual supporting documents such as tables of raw data, graphs, charts, imagines, questionnaires, surveys, or transcripts of interviews. All appendices must be separated, labeled, and referenced where appropriate in the main text. Each separate appendix should be lettered or numbered, such as Appendix A, Appendix B, or Appendix 1, Appendix 2, etc. The order is based on when the content of the appendix appears in the previous text.

13. Acknowledgement

This section is usually the last section of a report. It allows the author to acknowledge the support or assistance from a particular organization or people like colleagues who offered material, suggestion, advice, or help.

5.4.1.2 *Writing Process*

There are many different types of reports, including business, scientific, and research reports, but the basic steps for writing them are the same. All of the reports need to be clear, concise, and well structured. Before writing, allocating time for planning and preparation will help you write effectively. With careful planning, the writing process will be much easier. The following guidelines will help you write any report successfully.

1. Understanding the problem and purpose of your report

The first step is also the most important one. You need to read your instructions or other information you have been given, and make sure you understand the problem and purpose. Once you have determined the purpose of the report, it will be easier to define your audiences and the information you need to collect.

2. Gathering and selecting information

After clearly understanding the purpose of your report, you need to find information for your report. There are a variety of sources you can use to gather information, but make sure the information you decide to use is relevant and appropriate , which depends on the requirements and guidelines of the report. The procedure of collecting information includes: reading relevant literature, visiting libraries or searching the library's database for any books or material, and using the Internet to find reputable information. You can also use other forms of information such as questionnaires, surveys, etc. When you are gathering information, you need to assess its relevance to your report and select it accordingly. It is better for you to write down each source you use so that you can easily create your reference list.

3. Organizing your material

When you have gathered enough information, you should decide what will be included in your report and in what sequence it should be presented. All of the materials you should refer to the thesis of the report. When organizing your research, group together information that is related and cut information that is not relevant to the report.

4. Prewriting for your report

Before writing the first draft of your report, create an outline to help you visualize how your report will look. You may want to make notes on the points you will make, the conclusion you will draw, or the limitations you will have in your report. Additionally, deciding the structure of your report depends on the topic, type, and the length of report. For example, if your report is about a person, it makes sense to structure your report in chronological order.

5. Writing the report

After organizing your material into appropriate sections and headings, you can begin to write the first draft of your report with clear and concise points. The abstract and contents page are usually written at the end. Chapters, sections, and even individual paragraphs should be written with a clear structure. Do not forget to format your report at the end according to the instructions. If there are no formatting instructions, format your report with a clean and classic style.

6. Finalizing your report

Try to read through your report from the perspective of your readers. Consider these questions: Is your report easy to follow and well structured? Are the points in your report clearly explained and supported by relevant evidences? If possible, get someone else to read your report to make sure your points are clear enough. Finally, check for spelling, grammar, and punctuation errors.

5.4.2 Types of Reports

There are two types of reports: short reports and long reports which are based on different formats, styles, depths, and lengths. A short report is also called an informal report and a long report is sometimes called a formal report.

A short report is often no more than a one page statement including facts and figures in a concise manner. The style of a short report is often casual, relaxed, and it is an organized presentation of relevant data on any topic. There are the seven most common types of short reports:

1) Periodic reports;

2) Sales reports;

3) Progress reports;

4) Employee activity/Performance reports;

5) Trip/Travel reports;

6) Test reports;

7) Incident reports.

Long reports are major studies that provide an in-depth view of problems or ideas. A long report usually has several pages with a title, introduction, body, and then conclusion. These reports sometimes contain a cover letter that mentions all the details that are included in the long report, a bibliography, and an appendix at the end of the report. Long reports examine a problem in detail, while short reports cover just one part of a problem. Long reports require much more extensive research than short reports. As for the format, long reports are detailed and complex, and the above sections explain some of a long report's key elements.

The scope and style of reports vary widely. At university, students may be required to write several types of reports.

5.4.2.1 *Technical Report*

In industry, technical reports are formal reports used to convey technical information in a clear and easily accessible format. It describes the process, progress, or results of technical research and may include in-depth experimental details, data, and results. The audiences and purpose of the reports are important considerations for preparing technical reports. These factors determine the degrees of technicality of language and concepts involved.

At a university, students in the engineering and applied sciences department often use technical reports. These students are usually required to combine theory and real world situations and present the information in a structured and accessible format. For example, engineering students may be asked to solve a design problem and evaluate the solutions; computer science students might be asked to develop a program for a specific issue or company.

5.4.2.2 *Business Report*

At a university, business reports are required in disciplines like finance, accounting, management, marketing, and commerce. Writing business reports requires students to analyze a real world situation or a case study by applying business theories to produce suggestions for improvement. For example, accounting students may be asked to analyze a company's financial data and write a report stating their findings; project management students may be asked to report on the progress or management structure of a project and make recommendations for future actions.

5.4.2.3 *Field Report*

Field reports are usually used in disciplines such as law, industrial relations, psychology, history, and education. These reports usually require students to combine theories studied in the course and practice observed in the real world. The function of field reports is to describe an observed person, place, or event and analyze that observation. For example, law students may be asked to have a court observation; education students may be asked to report a teaching observation.

5.4.2.4 *Scientific Report*

Scientific reports, also called laboratory reports, are used to communicate the results of your experiments. They are frequently used in all the sciences and social sciences studies at a university. These reports use a formal structure describing methods, results, and conclusions to report upon a particular experiment. It could give you valuable practice in combining theoretical and empirical knowledge.

5.5 EXERCISES

1. Read the Equity Transfer Contract in Section 5.3.2.5 and then answer the following questions.

1) How much percentage of shares of Newton Braking System Co. Ltd. do Party A and arty B own, respectively?

· Answer: 80% , 20% .

2) How much money does the Company owe to Party B? The Company agrees to pay the payable to Party B before or after Party C make the purchase of the Company?

· Answer: RMB 400 million; before.

3) If, beside Party C, Party B also wants to purchase the equity of the Newton Braking System Co. Ltd, who has the priority to make the purchase?

· Answer: Party B.

4) Before what date does the Company agree to make the first, second, and third payment to White Global Architecture Inc. , respectively? And how much for each of them?

· Answer: RMB 100 million before March 1, 2012; RMB 150 million before September 1, 2012; and RMB 150 million before September 1 2013, respectively.

5) How much money does Party C spend in total in order to obtain the ownership of the Newton Braking System Co. Ltd completely?

· Answer: 300 million US Dollars.

2. Read the business contract samples carefully. Be familiar with the expressions of the clauses (objective). Be able to translate these.

The HR department of Chang'an Company will have a general meeting on the morning of next Monday at 9:00. This meeting will be held in the 1st meeting room. The HR manager will host this meeting, and the chairman, recruiting supervisor, training supervisor, and performance evaluating team head will attend this meeting. The objective of this meeting is to discuss the application requirements of opening positions for a new branch, consider the four applicants for the post of general manager, and propose the next meeting.

Write a meeting agenda according to the information above. The information gives you a brief description of the meeting and you will need to add more information with enough details to make a specific meeting agenda.

3. Read the Sample Meeting Minutes (Sample 5.1.2.3) and then answer the

following questions.

1) When and where was the meeting?

2) Who attended?

3) What general topics were discussed?

4) What detailed content of each topic was discussed and decided?

5) Is a follow-up meeting scheduled? If so, when? Where? Why?

4. Read Sample 5. 2. 1. 3 carefully. Identify the purpose and content in this proposal. Decide whether it is a successful proposal.

5. Write an action plan for yourself. It could be an action plan preparing for your final exam or an action plan related to your daily life.

6. Read two reports carefully.

First, work on the structure of the reports you select and show the framework of the reports in a flowchart. Then, answer the following questions:

1) How is the writer successfully limiting the scope of the report?

2) Where and how does the writer use visuals well?

3) How does the writer introduce, summarize, and draw conclusions from the expert opinions he/she cites in order to substantiate the main points?

4) What functions does the conclusion serve for readers? Cite specific examples from the report.

5.6 BIBLIOGRAPHY

1. KOLIN P C. Successful Writing at Work[M]. 4th ed. Boston: Cengage Learning, 2011.

2. LI K C. Effective Business Communication in English: A Practical Approach[M]. 2nd ed. Singapore: Prentice Custom Pub. , 2007.

3. STARKEY L, Good-proof Business Writing. 1st ed. New York: Learning Express, 2003.

4. World Meteorological Organization. Guidelines for Creating a Memorandum of Understanding and a Standard Operating Procedure between a National Meteorological or Hydrometeorological Service and a Partner Agency [M], Switzerland: World Meteorological Organization, 2012.

5. WESTLAND J. Project Proposal: A Beginner's Guide[OL]. [2018-07-04]. https://www. projectmanager. com/blog/project-proposal.

CHAPTER 6. WRITING FOR THESIS

This chapter will introduce the normal structure of the thesis and how to write it. The basic structure of a thesis is listed in section 6.2. Tips on how to write each part of the thesis will be introduced in section 6.3. What needs to be clarified in advance is the difference between thesis and dissertation. Under different educational systems, usage of these two words may indicate different writing works. In the British education system, "thesis" means the writing work for pursuing a doctoral degree, while "dissertation" is the writing work for pursuing a master degree. However, in the American education system, they are the opposite. "Thesis" is the writing for the master degree, while "dissertation" is the writing for the doctoral degree. A writing work for pursuing a doctoral degree is usually a long piece that includes almost all necessary parts in an academic writing. Other types of academic writing or research papers often just include some parts of a doctoral writing. The requirements of the detailed information provided by other academic writings and a doctoral writing are different. Other academic writing is shorter than a dissertation. Here in this chapter, the meaning of thesis and dissertation are based on the British education system. The section introduced later in this chapter addresses a doctoral thesis. For writing a master's dissertation or a small piece of academic writing, it may not be necessary to include all the sections introduced here. We suggest you ask your adviser or instructor for clarification of what parts are needed in your personal academic writing.

6.1 BASIC GUIDELINES FOR WRITING A THESIS

For general academic writing, the writer should have a clear purpose. The purpose can be a report of a research project or an answer to a theoretical question. It can also be a discussion of a widely interested subject with a personal opinion. There are several types of academic writing like notes, essays, theses, or small research papers and these are the common formats for student assignments.

Students commonly use notes to help them remember or understand something. These are written in a fairly casual writing style with almost no requirements of format. The content and editing style can be very personal because the main aim of notes is to record the main points of a text or lecture for personal use. Thus, it does not need to abide by common rule and can even be written in a "personal language" by using special signs.

Essays are the most common type of writing used as student assignments. Essays are more formal in style than notes and can ask for the students' personal views about an issue or a question. Essays may require reference and analysis, but do not necessarily need to be very long.

Theses belong to long academic writings and can be called as research papers. Writing a research paper is a procedure of solving a problem. To solve a problem, the first step is usually searching for information related to the problem. Try to find out if there are candidate methods that are possible to solve the problem. Then, students can try those candidate methods one by one and see whether the problem has been solved based on the derived results. When the problem has been solved, it is the time to write the thesis and describe the procedure. It will include how you search for the information, what methods are used to solve the problem, what the final results are, and why the issue can be solved in this way.

The above procedure is not only for a thesis, but is relatively common for all types of research papers aiming for reporting a project. For those whose research is to answer a question (this type is typically popular with social research and theoretic research), the procedure might be slightly different. The first step for all research papers is always the same, searching for information on the chosen subject. Then take a stand on your own opinion, back it up with the opinions, ideas, and views of others to support your own opinion, and defend your opinion with full evidence.

6.2 BASIC STRUCTURE AND OUTLINE OF A THESIS OR DISSERTATION

1) Abstract: a short and brief summary of the main information of your thesis or dissertation;

2) Keywords: a short list (usually around five) of words that can reflect the main tasks or problems this thesis addresses;

3) Table of content: outline of the content;

4) Acknowledgement;

5) List of figures & tables;

6) List of abbreviations;

7) Introduction;

8) Literature review;

9) Methodology;

10) Results;

11) Discussion;

12) Conclusions;

13) Reference;

14) Appendix.

6.3 MAIN ELEMENTS

6.3.1 Abstract

6.3.1.1 *Abstract vs. Summary vs. Executive Summary*

Abstracts, summaries, and executive summaries share some of the same purposes. Firstly, they aim to provide the readers a miniature version of an entire thesis or paper so that readers can identify key information quickly and accurately. Secondly, they play the role of a navigational tool for the whole document. The main information in an/a abstract/ summary/ executive summary is the overview of the entire document it describes. It is very important in helping the readers understand and access the information in the long document. The overview of the information will help the readers determine if they need to read the whole document. A specific example is that the conference abstract will help the conference organizers to decide if they will invite the authors to present a paper in the conference.

Even though abstract, summary, and executive summary hold some similarities, they are still different from each other.

An abstract is written for a professional audience and assuming that its readers have the professional background in the related discipline. An abstract is usually required for a thesis, journal paper, conference paper, or poster.

A summary is written for a less-professional audience. A reader without much professional background in the related field should be able to obtain the general idea of the paper and understand the main features and findings.

An executive summary aims for an executive audience who may have no professional background in the related discipline. It is generally longer than a summary and the content should be more specific than that of a summary. The language in an executive summary may not be scientific or technical but needs to be clear and easy to understand. An executive summary is often required in a management or consulting document, particularly for the management personnel of an organization.

Typically, there is an abstract before the main body of a research paper. It is important for readers to quickly grasp the main information provided in the main text and the abstract helps readers understand the whole document. The sentences in an abstract should be short, brief, and clear enough to cover all the necessary information. So what information should be included in an abstract? It depends on what type of abstract is required. Generally, according to different types of content, abstracts can be categorized as descriptive and informative.

6.3.1.2 *Types of Abstract: Descriptive vs. Informative*

The descriptive abstract is also called the indicative abstract. This type of abstract should be avoided for writing a thesis because it mainly describes the structure of the whole document without any indication of the findings and conclusions. It is more like an outline instead of an overview of the document. There is an example listed below to show the structure of a descriptive abstract.

Example

> *This study aims to propose a method which can derive the land surface temperature with a higher accuracy than the traditional single-band method. The structure of the proposed method is given in the article and the comparison between the single-band method and the new method has been done as well. The comparison results are illustrated in the context and conclusions for the new method are provided, together with suggested recommendations for possible improvements of the proposed method in the future.*

It can be seen that the above abstract mainly describes the structure of the entire document with no specific details given of the main findings and conclusions; there is no detailed description of the analysis of the results. For example, what parameters are used for the analysis of the comparison? What is the standard for the analyzing parameter? In a descriptive abstract, it just mentions the information is derived or given but does not provide the exact content. For instance, in the example, it says the conclusions based on the comparison between the single-band and the new methods are given in the context but does not provide details about what the conclusions are.

In contrast, informative abstract provides not only the information given by a descriptive abstract but the detailed information from the main findings and conclusions . A research paper such as a thesis or journal usually requires this type of abstract. Informative abstracts often use academic wording style and avoid stock phrases of a descriptive abstract/summary. Usually, for experimental investigation, specific and quantitative information on methods, as well as results and conclusions need to be provided. For other documents, specific information on the topic under investigation should be provided, including hard facts and the main conclusions. The difference between informative and descriptive abstracts can easily be seen from the following example.

Example

> *This study aims to propose a method which can derive the land surface temperature with a higher accuracy than the traditional single-band method. An improvement has been done for the single-band method that reduces the requirement on the input data. In addition, an optimization algorithm has been used firstly to the input of single-band method enhancing the accuracy of the final output predicted land surface temperature. The accuracy assessment has been done for both the new method and the traditional method by using the relative coefficient. Visual comparison between the predicted LST and the reference LST map has also been done for accuracy analysis. Through the comparison of relative coefficient, the new method obtained a much higher coefficient, which indicates a higher accuracy, than that of the traditional method. Similarly, the visual comparison suggests that the LST map predicted by the new method has larger coverage area.*

In the above example, it can be seen that the detailed information about the newly proposed method, how the comparison is made, and how to analyze the results are mentioned in the informative abstract. It is quite obvious that the information given in an informative abstract is more detailed than that of the descriptive abstract.

Typically, for a long thesis, the commonly used abstract is a detailed version of an informative abstract that provides readers both the descriptive information (e. g. what you have done, what results you have got), and the informative information. This information includes the explanation of the analyzing procedure, results, and the causes and effects if applicable. Due to the length of information found in a thesis, these abstracts are long because they include both key points and related findings with their explanations. Likewise, its abstract contains more information than the abstract of a journal paper. For a journal paper, the abstract often presents the key points of research (not all the findings like in a thesis) and is shorter.

6.3.2 Keywords

This is a short list (usually around five) of words that are relevant to the work reported in the thesis. This list is usually required by a thesis, journal paper, and conference paper. These words are provided for online information searching by readers who look for the relevant topics. If you want your paper to be read by relevant people, it is critical to work out the words those readers are most likely to use. Here are some examples to show the relationship between keywords and the title.

Example

> · *Title*: Enhancing the spatial resolution of satellite-derived land surface temperature mapping for urban areas
>
> *Keywords*: thermal sharpening, urban remote sensing, urban heat island, super-resolution mapping, super-resolution reconstruction.
>
> · *Title*: Subretinal electronic chips allow blind patients to read letters and combine them into words
>
> *Keywords*: Subretinal neural-prosthetics, retinal implant, retinitis pigmentosa, blindness, artificial vision, bionic vision.

6.3.3 Table of Content

The table of content plays a role very much like an outline of the whole document because it includes at least the second level subheadings. The chapter headings and subheadings are followed by corresponding page numbers in the table of content. The main role of the table of content is not only to outline the text, but also to be used as a navigational tool.

Examples of table of content can be found in almost every book (including this textbook). Additionally, an example of the table of content in a Ph. D. thesis is given in Figure 6.1.

Table of contents

Figure 6.1   Gas components: An example for the table of content in a Ph. D thesis

There are three common difficulties in writing a table of content: layout, formatting, and page numbers. For layout, it is important to determine something appropriate to provide readers enough information. Do not make the table of content too "thin," or too "fat." Formatting should be consistent within the whole table of content which means that the font, size, and all the spacing in each row should be consistent. For instance, if the second level subheadings have a space of four characters before the words, then all the second level subheadings need to be written with a four characters' space at the beginning (like shown in the example in Figure 6.1). Finally, pay attention that the page numbers for the corresponding headings are correct. All the above difficulties can be solved by computer software (e. g. word processor) that automatically builds the table of content with set headings and subheadings. The most commonly used word processing software are Microsoft Word and WPS Word. These software that build the table of content have been introduced in the previous chapter so no more details will be provided here.

6.3.4 Acknowledgement

This section aims to convey thanks and appreciations to all the people who helped you complete the thesis. Examples:

1) Provided the materials for your research

2) Provided the technical help in your lab/computer work

3) Shared their views or ideas about the issue relevant to your work

4) Introduced you to some other experts in your field or people who may have been helpful to your research

5) Provided you the spiritual support, particularly your family

There are some commonly used examples when writing the acknowledgement:

· *I would like to thank the following people...*

· *I would like to show my thanks/appreciations to...*

· *I would like to express my sincere gratitude and thanks to my supervisors...*

· *Without anyone of them, I could not finish my study and this thesis.*

· *I would like to convey my great thanks to...*

· *I am particularly grateful to...for...*

· *Special thanks to...*

There are some points to be concerned with when writing the acknowledgement:

1) Make sure to use not only the surname, but also the first name of the person you are thanking in the acknowledgement.

2) Do not make mistakes on the title of a person you are thanking (Dr., Associate Professor, Ms., Mr. and so on). If you are not sure, find out by

searching or telephoning their institutions.

3) Do not forget to provide the department of the person when he/she is mentioned in the acknowledgement.

6.3.5 List of Figures & Tables

The function of this section is very similar to the table of content, key items in this list are also in the same format: page number, and layout. The layout is particularly important because sometimes, the caption of a figure is very long. Questions as to maintain the entire caption of a figure or table, and how to arrange the layout for the list, are issues when building the list of figures and tables. If the captions of certain figures and tables are too long, use only the first two or three sentences in the list of figures and tables. This is because the long captions usually include lengthy descriptions and explanations of specific points in the figures and tables. However, only one sentence at the beginning of the caption is needed to introduce the general idea or function of the figure or table. It will make the list clear and tidy but also provides necessary information for navigation. Figure 6. 2 shows an example of a list of figures and tables where each item of the list has kept the first sentence of the caption.

List of Figures

List of Tables

Figure 6. 2   An example of list of figures and list of tables

6.3.6 List of Abbreviations

This list is sometimes needed in a research paper, especially for long research papers such as a thesis. It is used to define special terms, symbols, and abbreviations used in the main text to provide convenience to readers when searching any abbreviations or special items in the text. It is relatively common to use abbreviations in a research paper when long names are proposed or frequently used. In addition, when a large number of formulas are used or inferred in a long document, the meaning of a letter representing a variable can be easily confused in different places in the document. For example, if the commonly used letter, T, is used in the first chapter of a thesis to represent one variable, it should always indicate the same variable throughout the entire thesis.

The format of the list of abbreviations is a table where one column gives the abbreviation and the second column provides the corresponding full name. The format may vary among specific documents, but the information that needs to be included should at least include what is introduced here. An example for list of abbreviation is given in Figure 6.3.

List of abbreviations

ANN	Artificial Neural Network
ASTER	Advanced Spaceborne Thermal Emission and Reflection Radiometer
ATSR	Along Track Scanning Radiometer
AVHRR	Advanced Very High Resolution Radiometer
CBEM	Classification-Based Emissivity Method
DCT	Discrete Cosine Transform
DFT	Discrete Fourier Transform
DisTrad	Disaggregation procedure for radiometric surface temperature
DN	Digital Number
EM	Emissivity Modulation
ETM+	Enhanced Thematic Mapper Plus
GOES	Geostationary Operational Environmental Satellite
HNN	Hopfield Neural Network

Figure 6.3   An example of list of abbreviations

6.3.7   Introduction

From here we go into the main text body of a thesis. An introduction is always an important section for the whole document, as it provides the background knowledge for all the key points throughout the entire document. A good introduction could ensure readers with a less professional background feel more comfortable with the ideas of the author without consulting extra literature. However, the length of the introduction should be an adequate level and not too lengthy.

It is always good to think through some questions before beginning the introduction. First of all, what topics should be included in the introduction as the background knowledge, and how much detail for each? The reason to consider these questions is because research, especially research reported in a thesis, usually includes a large amount of information and several related topics will be proposed in the context. In addition, though a thesis is written with a specific topic in mind, it should be understood by almost anyone. So even though some professional concepts seem simple for people who work in similar research fields, these concepts may still need to be explained in the thesis for people who are not familiar with it. Many details still need to be provided to ensure everyone can understand what is introduced in the thesis. Therefore, deciding how many references to include and keeping the length of the introduction in mind is one of the main considerations when writing an introduction.

Another tip for a good introduction is to write a good starting sentence for each paragraph. This will help your writing work sound impressive. It should not be a banal statement of a general knowledge, but be an overall introduction that specifies the particular issue for each key point.

6.3.7.1 *Background Knowledge*

As mentioned before, providing the background knowledge is the main task of the introduction but keep in mind that a thesis is not a textbook. Do not just list all the basic knowledge one by one in the introduction section; there should be a logical flow in the introduction to the relevant background. Start with a broad view, for example, if your thesis is trying to develop new material for road pavement, the introduction might start at road engineering and move to pavement engineering and finally the particular pavement material. Nevertheless, for a bachelor thesis, the starting point for your introduction may be the same but the details for each section can be simpler than a Ph. D. thesis. There should be a logical flow. The commonly used flows for a technical introduction is the development of a specific type of technology in a research field. However, introducing an entire research field may be too complicated for an introduction section. Usually an introduction needs only to achieve the following aims: 1) provide the background knowledge in the relevant research field; 2) lead the readers to the current status of the development in the relevant field; 3) analyze the advantages and disadvantages of the current techniques; and 4) clarify the particular issue this thesis addresses.

6.3.7.2 *Objectives/Aims*

As introduced above, there should be a flow from the introduction to the related background and the final aim is to find the research gap based on the introduction, summary, and analysis of current status in the related research field. A research gap means a problem or issue that has currently not been solved yet. A research gap can be used as the problem needs to be solved for your research. If this gap cannot be solved based on current techniques, any process that could help solve the found research gap can be used as the basis for your research.

To describe the aims or objectives of your study, use brief and concise language. This might be the most important but difficult section to write in the entire thesis because it is the finishing touch of the whole document.

For a long research document such as a thesis, it is recommended to state the main aim first and then provide a series of specific objectives. The objectives play a role similar to the sub-aim for each stage of the whole research project. An example is given below; the general format to write objectives is also demonstrated in the example.

Example

Aim: *In this thesis, a method is proposed to enhance the spatial resolution of satellite-derived LST maps that does not require a fine spatial resolution input and does not rely on any spectral indices of land covers to sharpen the LST. This research creatively used two image processing techniques which were used to enhance image spatial resolution: superresolution mapping (SRM) and superresolution reconstruction (SRR). Neither technique has been used in thermal sharpening before.*

Objectives:

1. To enhance the spatial resolution of emissivity map, which is a necessary input to LST estimation methods, using a SRM technique to aid the derivation of a spatial resolution enhanced LST map.

2. To increase the spatial resolution of thermal radiance and atmospheric profiles, which are necessary inputs to LST estimation methods, using a SRR technique to aid the enhancement of spatial resolution of an LST map.

3. To explore the accuracy of the proposed thermal sharpening method using different data sources, including the coarse or very coarse spatial resolution data (MODIS) and the medium spatial resolution data (Landsat ETM +).

4. To analyse the accuracy of both the proposed and other currently popular thermal sharpening methods from two perspectives: the similarity of the statistical nature (e. g. histogram distribution) and the similarity of spatial pattern of the sharpened LST map to the reference data.

5. To explore the impact of using different zoom factors on the accuracy of the proposed thermal sharpening method.

---

6. 3. 7. 3 *Structure of the Thesis*

For a long thesis, it is better to provide the readers a brief description of the structure of the whole document. It provides the readers understanding of the entire document as well as a general introduction to each chapter. Readers can directly jump to the chapters they are concerned with. An example is given for this part in the introduction section.

Example

> *This chapter introduced the background knowledge for the research, including principles of thermal remote sensing and its applications to urban areas. Then, based on the limitations of current technologies for the derivation of LST with fine resolution in both spatial and temporal dimensions, the aim and objectives of this project were proposed. The second chapter reviews the key concepts of thermal remote sensing, LST estimation from satellite-derived data and thermal sharpening techniques. Chapter 3 reviews the two key techniques that this project is based on-SRM and SRR. Chapter 4 introduces the structure and principle of the proposed thermal sharpening method, super resolution thermal sharpener (SRTS), in details. A coarse spatial resolution data, MODIS, is used as the example to show how to implement SRTS. Also the superiority of combining use of SRM and SRR in SRTS will be demonstrated by a comparison of the LST sharpened by SRM only, SRR only and the SRTS. Therefore, Chapter 4 introduces the data sets used throughout the thesis and the study areas. Comparison for LST sharpened by different methods is conducted in two aspects: the similarity between the sharpened LST and the reference data on the statistical nature and the spatial pattern. Also, whether the accuracy of a thermal sharpening method is stable has been tested by using thermal data in different seasons. Then the accuracy of the SRTS is further validated by comparing with other currently popular thermal methods in Chapter 5 by using the same data as Chapter 4. The same analyses are conducted for LST sharpened by different methods. Chapter 6 analyses whether using different zoom factors for the proposed method will impact its accuracy, while Chapter 7 illustrates the flexibility and simplicity of the proposed method for use on different data sources. Landsat imagery is used as another example to show how to implement SRTS for it in detail. Finally, Chapter 8 summarizes all the findings from the experiments reported in Chapter 4—7, including the advantages and limitations of the proposed method and the future work for this research.*

6.3.7.4 *Schedule*

This part is usually required for a research proposal, thesis, or report from a project team. Schedules are commonly made in a table format with the time and work that needs to be finished; it could be considered an allocation of responsibilities. An example is given in Table 6.1.

Table 6.1　An example of the schedule in a research proposal

Months \\ Tasks	12	2017												2018										
		1	2	3	4	5	6	7	8	9	10	11	12	1	2	3	4	5	6	7	8	9	10	11
Data collection of testing area	■																							
Image processing		■	■																					
Improvement of the SRTS				■	■	■	■	■																
Data collection of all study area									■	■	■													
Road network extraction												■	■											
Extraction of the road edge																	■	■	■					
Organizing the results of the project																							■	

6.3.8　Literature Review

This section is usually required for a research paper. In a thesis, literature review can be its own separate chapter or put in the beginning of each chapter. The location depends on the writing habits of the writer and the topic chosen. For journal and conference papers, a brief literature review is necessary in the introduction in order to emphasize the significance of the main objectives of the paper. Sometimes, supervisors may require literature reviews when you begin your research to help you familiarize yourself with the topic and related academic fields.

6.3.8.1　*Why the Literature Review is Needed*?

Literature reviews provide a series of benefits to the writer no matter what stage of writing you may be in.

First of all, writing a literature review forces you to familiarize yourself with the topic you are working with. You must do a lot of research to guarantee your literature review covers enough materials in the related field, and shows the readers the reliability of your work. To conquer the amount of research necessary, your ability to search for information will be challenged. Furthermore, your ability to summarize will improve and you will gain a comprehensive consideration of various areas relevant to your topic.

6.3.8.2　*Requirements for Writing a Literature Review*

To write a literature review, there are some requirements for the writers to keep in mind.

1) Be familiar with the citation systems such APA, MLA and other commonly used systems.

2) As a kind of original contribution, not only introducing what others did in the past, but also showing the link between various areas related to the topic. To summarize the correlations, contradictions, ambiguities and gaps in the knowledge.

3) To show the advancement of a technique or method at a certain time and its limitations later.

4) After the comparison and analysis, a list or summary of the currently available techniques and materials needs to be produced.

6.3.8.3 *Difficulties When Writing a literature Review*

1) The overwhelming amount of literature available for research.

2) The lack of research on a particular subject.

3) Difficult to get started. It is easy to feel overwhelmed with all the things that need to be done to start research and your writing and one of the reasons for this is not knowing where to start.

4) Determine the range of review. Looking too broad will make a lot of work for you that you may not finish, while being too narrow will not be convincing enough for readers.

5) Selection of the useful information. To make your work concise, useless information should be disregarded during your research. It is equally important to keep a record of the work that may initially seem irrelevant to your topic because you may find there are some areas that are potentially related further along. Thus, the literature you find needs to be constantly reviewed.

6.3.8.4 *Comparison between a Poor & a Good Review*

1. What is a poor review?

Typically, a poor review will be a list of who-did-what-and-when, without any or very little comment on the relevance and quality of the work. It does not show original work and contribution to the topic, but only indicates your limited understanding of the purpose of a literature review.

2. What is a good review?

1) Shows the issues that have been dealt with in the past, present, and what needs to be addressed in the future.

2) Shows the correlations, contradictions, ambiguities, and knowledge gaps that exist within the field.

3) Shows the conflicts between competing research groups.

4) Provides an analysis and commentary that make it clear you contributed original work to the topic.

6.3.8.5 *Suggestions for Writing a Literature Review*

Literature review can be a part of a thesis or a journal paper or an independent research paper to be published. Here we will provide you some suggestions on how to get started and finish a literature review.

1) It is always recommended to use literature management software when you have a large body of papers. This type of software not only helps record key information for citations (e. g. author names, published year, published journal, etc.), but also generates the citation and reference list automatically according to the citation information.

2) An easy start for information searching is to search currently published relevant literature reviews. These papers may not have exactly what you need for a narrow topic, but can provide background information for the broad disciplines and general ideas of what might be relevant to your topic.

3) Try to find the KEY journal papers in the reference list of a published literature review. Generally, a review paper will provide a large list of sources at the end of the paper. Those papers cover a wide range of disciplines and may not all be relevant to your topic, but determine which are the most helpful and utilize this resource.

4) When the KEY papers are determined find other relevant papers through the reference list of these key papers. This procedure is actually an enlargement of your literature database for your own topic and research. From now on, all the papers you read should be exactly related to your topic and some might be commonly cited in your literature review.

5) Try to form your own story by using these papers as support to your own ideas. At this stage, the logical flow of the review needs to be seriously considered. Pay attention that your review is not a list full of others' works. What is the potential clue of which links all the evidences together? Why are you writing this review? What is the final purpose at the end of this review? Every literature review demonstrates the procedure of exploring and finding a research gap. Particularly in a thesis, literature review not only provides relevant background information it leads to the current research gaps. After the literature review, the next section would be the aim and objectives of your own research.

6) Treat the writing of literature review as an iterative process. The whole procedure needs to repeat or redo some work or refresh the database. As your understanding of the topic increases, it is natural that you read more papers and update the literature review. Do not plan to finish a literature review in only one pass; it is more like a read-write-revise procedure.

6.3.8.6 *Common Mistakes*

1) Finish the literature review before fully understanding the topic.

2) A who-did-what-and-when list

3) Miss a clear logical thread running through the entire review, including those in the sub-headings of the review. It will lead the review to be a who-did-what-and-when list.

4) Did not point out research gaps or knowledge gaps in the literature review.

5) No analysis or commentary is made. Did not show your involvement and contribution.

6) Referencing errors.

6.3.9 Data and Methods

Both the introduction and the literature review sections mainly provide and summarize the work of others. After these sections, your own research and commentary are what matters. Whether an answer to a theoretical problem or a report for a research project, your own opinion and research are what this paper is about. It is just like telling people what dishes you will cook before providing them a list of materials you will use for the dishes. In that case, the readers will have less possibility to be lost in the journey of exploring your story.

6.3.9.1 *Purposes of This Section*

This section aims to enable the readers to judge whether your experiment is real, reasonable, and valid. The details of the experiment must be provided in this section to allow other professional readers to repeat your work. It not only proves that you have done this work in a lab, but also proves your work can be applied, repeated, and furthered by others.

6.3.9.2 *Requirements for This Section*

Compared with other sections, this part is easier to write and recommended to be the first part to write in a thesis. It is because, considering the length of a thesis which is tough to finish, it will make the writing easier to get started if the writing starts from an easy part. Generally, this part requires you to list and introduce the materials and methods you used in your research with clear, brief, and straightforward language covering all aspects that needs to be provided.

6.3.9.3 *Suggestions*

For experimental work, logically describe the steps of your experiment to enable other professionals to repeat the procedure. Also, the extent of how much detail needs to be considered. If the methods used in your experiments are published or established ones, there is no need to provide details about the method; just summarize the steps and provide citations and references for those methods if any reader who would like to know more about those established methods. Make sure that the cited papers actually have detailed descriptions of these rudimentary methods. In contrast, for the novel method developed or proposed by yourself or your research team, much more details must be provided in the description. Sometimes, illustration for the general flow of steps or for the principles might be helpful for readers to quickly grab the idea of the novel method. For both established and novel methods, description of the materials, such as the sources of chemicals, model numbers of equipment used, should always be listed. This information is critical for your work to be evaluated by others through repeating your work.

1) There is a possibility that you think you have provided enough details but actually it lacks essential descriptions on your experimental procedures. It is simply because you are too familiar with the techniques and unconsciously suppose some information is common knowledge. Thus, it is suggested that give your written work to your colleagues to proofread.

2) Explain why you designed your experiment the way that you did. The explanations can range from the introduction section until the data and method section. This section is needed for readers to understand why you chose these materials and methods for the experiment and explore the research gap questions. Avoid making this section a list of materials and experimental steps.

3) Do not mention any results in this section; this is a common mistake for an inexperienced author. Remember to separate the section of methods and materials clearly with the section of results.

4) Another common mistake for an inexperienced author is to arrange this section chronologically, especially for the description of the methods. Make sure the introduction of methods is not a diary of what you did but a detailed description with commentary and reasons.

5) It is suggested for experimental work to use the past tense when describing your steps. However, some descriptions of morphological, geographical, or geological features that are common phenomena without change, the present tense can be used.

6) The language should be clear and brief. There is no need to show your fabulous writing skills like a literary work. Long and complex sentences may lead the readers to confusion and ultimately frustration. A scientific paper, especially in this section, needs short and straightforward sentences because you are proposing a newly developed method and you want it to be accepted by other people. To accomplish this, your readers must be able to understand what you are trying to say without straining to read complex sentences.

6.3.10 Results

This section is used to present your results but not the place to discuss them.

This may give readers a chance to generate their own analysis and conclusions about your work based on all the results you have provided. It can be a challenge to decide how much detail needs to be provided here.

Suggestions:

1) It is very important to use illustrations to show your work. Illustration is always a useful tool to help people quickly grab key information unless the illustration itself is not well presented. If the illustration is presented well, it will help readers understand what your methods can do and what the advantages and limitations of your work are. For example, if your result is a comparison between six sample sets, it might be a good idea to use a bar chart to clearly illustrate and compare the results.

2) Write the text of the result section near the illustration to guide readers in the right direction. A reader will get bored or even angry if they do not know what you are referring to or if they have to keep turning pages over and over to find the relationship between the text and the illustrations.

3) Plan the illustration well in advance to make sure all the illustrations support and emphasize the points you are trying to make. Each illustration should convey at least one obvious message. Carefully choose the title or caption of the illustration and try to make a summary of the information contained in the illustration. Sometimes, it might be needed to emphasize some key information in the caption as well, but keep the whole caption short.

4) In the text, choose the most important aspects to write in the results section. There might be loads of information conveyed by the illustration but to provide a logical thread and lead the readers to the point you prefer are your critical task. Providing a clearly logical thread and emphasizing the aspects you valued in your work when describing the results.

5) It is relatively common to have repetitive data in the results. In that case, it needs to be dealt with; maintain the representative data that can be used in later discussion. Explain why this data is representative but do not discuss it here in this section.

6.3.11　Discussion

This section is the core section of a thesis or a journal paper, as it verifies whether the experiment is designed reasonably, and whether the results prove and support the assumptions you made. This section is the place to show how to reach the conclusions from the results where you can finally derive clear conclusions. The main task here is explanation; explain why the conclusions can be derived based on the results and show the significance of the results and how those results support the derived answers to the research gap. A common mistake is to confuse the discussion with the results. The reason is that it is easy to provide the description of what the results show without inferring from the results or providing explanations to why the results appeared like that. One tip to distinguish the results and discussion is that descriptions of illustrations or tables are the results, and the explanations of illustrations/tables are the discussion.

The above difficulty may partly be the difficulty of being unsure where to start. Discussion is often written in the same section with results and it is reasonable that when the results are described, the discussion of those results immediately follows. However, for some inexperienced authors, it is easy to be confused about what the explanation or deduction is and what the "further description" of the results is. Sometimes, they thought they explained the reasons why the results show like that and actually those explanations are not the original reasons for the phenomena and some "further descriptions" that can be deduced from the most apparent results.

There are some words commonly used in the sentences that belong to a discussion section of a paper, including "show," "demonstrate," "indicate," or "suggest." These words are representations of the discussion sentences and infer that the content is deduced from the previous results.

Suggestions:

1) Conclusions should be clearly given. There might be a series of conclusions derived in the discussion section; make sure they are arranged with supporting evidence. If there is a logical thread in the conclusions, link the discussion sections in that logical thread as well (e. g. one followed by one).

2) Each conclusion should have strong support behind it that includes all the evidences/results and the explanation to the evidences/results.

3) It is common to do comparisons in a research paper but always be objective, fair, and accurate when describing and explaining the results of others. Be brave to defend your conclusions while respecting others' work.

4) Keep your speculation of results reasonable without any far-fetched hypotheses.

5) To be objective to your own work. Do not ignore some of your results that might reflect the limitations or some incorrect results. It can be the evidence of limitations of your work.

6.3.12 Conclusions

This section is used to present all the main conclusions of your work. It acts like a highlight and summary of the discussion; extracting the main findings from the discussion section.

Suggestions:

1) Summarize the conclusions derived and stated in the discussion section. Any new findings should not appear in the conclusion section; if you derived a new finding, it can be brought into the discussion section to describe and explain.

2) Language in a conclusion section should be brief, as each conclusion has already been explained and stated before. There is no need to repeat any redundant content.

3) Even though this section acts as a summary, future work for this research, or criticisms this research may receive is also required to be provided here.

4) If you would like to summarize the conclusions as a list, list the main conclusion or the most significant conclusion first and then follow likewise.

5) In a thesis, sometimes you may need to point out the innovations of this research. It is recommended to use the numbered or bullet-pointed list to summarize them and make the contribution clear and persuadable.

6) Avoid using vague and generalized statements in the conclusion section, especially when summarizing the main conclusions of the work.

7) Similar to the introduction section, conclusions can be written for each chapter of the thesis or as one final conclusion chapter.

6.3.13 Reference

The Reference section is usually just behind the last chapter of the main body. This section is essential in a research paper because it not only shows the reliability of your work (to show you have referred to a large amount of literature), but also provides the readers a chance to access the sources related to your work. It also shows the acknowledgement or respect to the works done by other researchers. Any work you quoted from other works should be put in the reference list.

It might be noticed that sometimes in a book, there is a section that provides the referencing sources after the main body of the text, called a bibliography. There is a small difference between references and bibliography. A bibliography is a list of all the sources you have consulted during your writing, whether you cite them in the text or not. In contrast, every source provided in a reference list is a list of the sources source that is actually cited in the document.

Details about types of referencing and how to cite them have been introduced in previous chapters. What needs to be emphasized here is the location of this section and what kind of information should be included.

6.3.14 Appendix/ Appendices

For research with a complicated or very long Method & Materials section, long descriptions can interrupt the flow of the document if inserted in the text. These can be put at the end of the whole document as an appendix or appendices. These complex materials can be the raw data, detailed illustrations of equipment, evidences, software coding, specifications, product descriptions, charts, and so forth.

An appendix is not just adding related research materials to the document. There should be a specific purpose to point out for which part the appendix is used. In addition, appendices should be well organized; grouping the related materials into different groups and giving each of them a numbered or lettered title (e. g. Appendix I: Raw data, Appendix II: Specifications; or Appendix A: Raw data, Appendix B: Specifications). Every appendix should be included in the table of contents.

6.3.15　Summary of This Chapter

This chapter introduced the sections of a thesis. Sometimes, they may not have to be written in the order as introduced. Also, for different disciplines, it is possible that not all of the sections introduced are needed (e. g. a social science research). Or some sections may have similar content with a different title and some can be put in the beginning of the document and at the end of the document (e. g. acknowledgement). Some sections might be an independent chapter in a thesis or a sub-section in each chapter (e. g. introduction, conclusion, literature review).

6.4　EXERCISES

Please read the following small research paper and write a descriptive abstract and an informative abstract.

Children of Poverty: Can They Succeed?

A problem that should be of deep concern to society is the question of how children from low socioeconomic groups can raise their status and success level by hard work and higher education. On the surface it would seem that our schools offer equal learning opportunities for all students. Yet, as a counselor and a teacher, the author has seen children from this class who, while initially having lofty goals, follow in the same path as their parents and grandparents before by failing to achieve them. It seems as if social class mobility is very rare and that the lower class tends to perpetuate itself from generation to generation. In this paper, some of the reasons for this phenomenon will be explored.

So why children cannot take hold of the educational opportunity available to them and change their social and economic status for the better? Several environmental factors decrease the possibility of this happening. Perhaps the first matter to consider is the characteristics of the family system itself. Families commonly seek *homeostasis*—the tendency of any group of relationships to continually strive to preserve the principles of its existence. The family strives for a kind of balance in order to foster the continuity needed to maintain its identity. In other words, families tend to resist change. The creative thinker who disturbs the balance will often be ignored or rejected (Friedman, 1985).

In their study concerning the effects of poverty on children, Guang Guo and Kathleen Mullan Harris (2000) have demonstrated that poverty has a measurable effect on children's development and school achievement, bringing with it risk factors that can predispose children to perform poorly. A recent study has isolated five such factors: the child's ill health at birth, poor health in childhood, cognitive stimulation, parenting style, and physical environment (Guo & Harris, 2000).

Poor mothers are much more likely to have minimal prenatal care, if any at all, in sharp contrast with mothers from a higher economic plane. They do not know about nutrition and other factors that will affect their babies. Poor nutrition and lack of health care, along with a higher chance of exposure to lead and other contaminants, attack the healthy development of the growing child (McLoyd, 1998).

Studies on children residing in economically shattered neighborhoods independently predict lower scores on intelligence tests, lower levels of school achievement, and more socio-emotional problems. The results of these studies also coincide negatively with completed years of schooling. The cognitive stimulation that is so vital to developing children is often absent in poor homes (McLoyd, 1998). According to one study, enriched learning experiences are crucial during the "windows of opportunity" which occur in the young growing child, and if these critical times are not taken advantage of, the child is not even adequately prepared for preschool (Begley, 1996).

Parents from these homes are often driven by stress, and they tend to be harsh and punitive with their children (Guo & Harris, 2000). These parents face many more stressful life events and have less social support than do parents who have more money. There is often a single parent in the home, but even when both parents are present, they usually have to work long hours for minimal wages and can spend little time with their children. Sometimes they lack basic skills of literacy and math and cannot supply the training that children need when entering kindergarten (McLoyd, 1998).

The physical environment in which poor children find themselves can be one of abuse and alcoholism. Also, poverty contributes to a high incidence of teenage pregnancies, drug abuse, and pervasive violence within the neighborhood. This makes every child a victim. Many children are so afraid that they actually stay home from school, adding truancy to the problem (Kelly, 1994).

Another real factor is the issue of housing. Our nation has one of the highest mobility rates of all developed countries—annually about one-fifth of our people move. This especially affects low-income families who are often displaced when rents increase or rental markets tighten. According to one study in 1994, 41% of all third-graders from low-income families have attended at least two schools. And nearly 20% of all third-graders have attended three or more schools. Children who move frequently face disruption in their lives and their education. And many times they are not helped to adjust to this disruption. The rates of family mobility correlate directly with student underachievement. Children who have moved often are more likely to have behavioral problems as well (Kaptur, 2001).

Also to be taken into consideration is the attitude of the teachers. It appears that all students do *not* receive equal preparation in schools. Teachers of high-risk students tend to use ineffective instructional approaches. They have negative attitudes and low expectations for these students (Jones & Watson, 1990). According to McLoyd (1998), instructing teachers about normative behaviors such as speech patterns among lower class children and affirming the legitimacy of those behaviors may be prerequisites to raising teachers' expectancies of these children.

This study has discussed the problems and barriers those children and youth from low-income homes face environmentally and educationally. Some strides toward helping to solve some of these problems have been made, but much remains to be done. People who work directly with such children can make a real difference in their lives. Although faced with an uphill battle, these children can succeed. That would be a legacy of which all Americans could be proud.

6.5 BIBLIOGRAPHY

1. BAILEY S. Academic writing: a handbook for international students[M]. 4th ed. London and New York: Taylor & Francis Group, 2014.

2. HACKER D, SOMMERS N. Rules for writers-with writing about literature [M]. 7th ed. Boston, New York: Bedford/St. Martin's, 2011.

3. WINKLER A C, METHERELL J R. Writing the research paper: a handbook [M]. 8th ed. Boston: Cengage learning, 2011.

4. BRAUSE R S. Writing your doctoral dissertation-invisible rules for success [M]. 1st ed. London and New York: Taylor & Francis Group, 1999.

5. HEATHER S. Writing for science and engineering-papers, presentations and reports[M]. 2nd ed. Amsterdam: Elsevier, 2012.

CHAPTER 7. WRITING FOR ENGINEERING DRAWING

The design process of a highway project usually includes preliminary design and final design. Preliminary design plays a key role in time-effectiveness, cost-effectiveness, and environmental responsibility, in which the project location and design concept are generally determined. The final design clearly includes the preparation of construction plans and detailed specifications for construction works. Documents of the final design include the overall design statement, alignment design, subgrade and pavement surface design, bridge and culvert design, tunnel design, drainage and protection work design, intersection design, traffic facility design, environment protection, and landscaping design, etc.

The designs expressed in graphical language are engineering drawings used to fully and clearly define requirements for engineered items and form an essential part of highway construction projects.

On a sheet of an engineering drawing, there is a border line enclosed area in which there are usually three views drawings of a construction. Figure 7. 1 provides an example of the general layout of the drawing sheet. For application in a specific project, the layout should comply with related engineering specifications and standards. Usually the three view drawings are composed of the front view (or elevation), side view (or profile) and plan (or top) view. To provide internal information of constructions, the cross-section views may be needed.

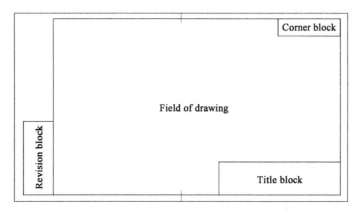

Figure 7. 1   Layout of a typical engineering drawing

Cross-section views are usually related to other views on the same drawing sheet. As shown in Figure 7.2, in the TYPICAL DETAIL PLAN view, there are three section lines (A-A, B-B and C-C), and the corresponding section views are shown on the same sheet respectively as the Section C-C and Section B-B.

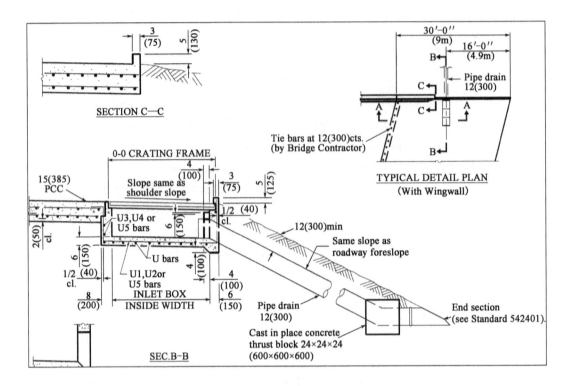

Figure 7.2   Relationship between the section views and other views

For some large-sized constructions, small scale should be adopted to make sure all parts can be drawn inside the field enclosed in the border line. This, however, makes some of its parts be insufficiently shown. Hence, another type of graph, usually called Detail X, is used. Here X is the numberings of the parts illustrated with detailed information. For example, in Figure 7.3, the local part of a connection in Section G-G, marked as "see DETAIL A", is specifically shown in the drawing of Detail A.

Except the views and graphs in the field of drawing, text notes lists are commonly used in the drawing to provide information to users of the drawing by conveying any information that the graphical expressions did not show. Traditional locations for the notes can be placed anywhere along the edges of the field of the drawing.

The content of notes can be general notes applying to the user of the drawing or specific notes applying only to certain part numbers, surfaces, or features.

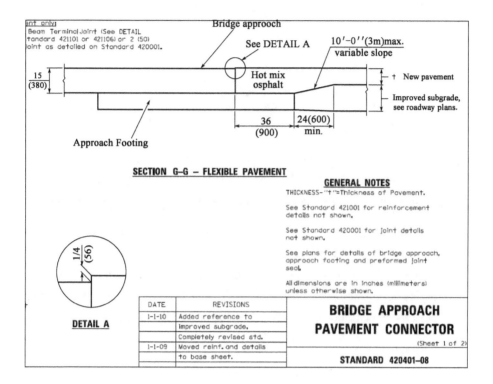

Figure 7.3   Relationship between the detail graph and its related view

7.1   DIMENSION INFORMATION

The measurement unit is an indispensable note in the engineering drawing to define the dimensions, where the numerical values used to describe the theoretically exact size, profile, orientation, or location of constructions. The commonly used sentence for measurement unit of drawing can be, "All dimensions are in millimeters unless otherwise noted."

Although metric system is the internationally adopted decimal system for engineering drawing, it is appropriate to use the imperial units or the United States customary units by the designers in overseas projects. In the case of dual units used in the drawing, clarification should be made with parentheses as shown in Figure 7.4a), or the note, "the dimensions in parentheses are in millimeter and that outside the parentheses in inches".

In addition to units for length, other information related to dimension can also be provided in the notes [e.g. the slope ratio in Figure 7.4b)].

GENERAL NOTE

Reinforcement bars shall be No. 3 (No. 10) unless otherwise specified.

A 2¾x12⅛ (70x310) shadow box with beveled edges, and a 3/16 (5) thick indentation may be used with the standard lettering shown.

All dimensions are in inches (millimeters) unless otherwise shown.

a)

GENERAL NOTES

All slope ratios are expressed as units of vertical displacement to units of horizontal displacement (V:H).

All dimensions are in inches (millimeters) unless otherwise shown.

b)

Figure 7.4　Examples for notes clarifying dimension information

7.2　RELATIONSHIP WITH OTHER DRAWINGS OR DOCUMENTS

Sometimes one graph in the drawing is related to or sharing information with other drawings of a project. In that case, notes need to clarify the number of the related drawing so that readers could find the related information [as shown in Figure 7.5a) and c)]. If the details can be found in some other documents, they need to be clarified in the notes [as shown in Figure 7.5b)].

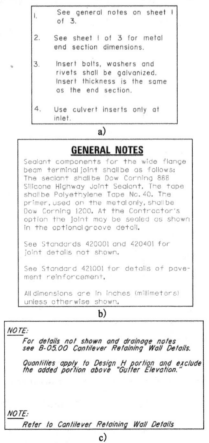

1. See general notes on sheet 1 of 3.

2. See sheet 1 of 3 for metal end section dimensions.

3. Insert bolts, washers and rivets shall be galvanized. Insert thickness is the same as the end section.

4. Use culvert inserts only at inlet.

a)

GENERAL NOTES

Sealant components for the wide flange beam terminal joint shall be as follows: The sealant shall be Dow Corning 888 Silicone Highway Joint Sealant. The tape shall be Polyethylene Tape No. 40. The primer, used on the metal only, shall be Dow Corning 1200. At the Contractor's option the joint may be sealed as shown in the optional groove detail.

See Standards 420001 and 420401 for joint details not shown.

See Standard 421001 for details of pavement reinforcement.

All dimensions are in inches (millimeters) unless otherwise shown.

b)

NOTE:
For details not shown and drainage notes see B-05.00 Cantilever Retaining Wall Details.

Quantities apply to Design H portion and exclude the added portion above "Gutter Elevation."

NOTE:
Refer to Cantilever Retaining Wall Details

c)

Figure 7.5　Examples for notes clarifying relationship with other drawings

7.3 CLARIFICATION INFORMATION ABOUT THE MATERIALS

Sometimes, it may not be suitable to illustrate the material of some constructions in the drawings, then the clarifications can be made with notes (as shown in Figure 7.6).

6. Precast bases shall have No. 13 reinforcing bar on 300 mm centers each way for depths under 6 m and No. 16 reinforcing bar on 150 mm centers for depths of 6 m and over.

7. Poured in place concrete bases shall be 200 mm thick for depths less than 4.5 m and 300 mm thick for depths 4.5 m or greater.

a)

GENERAL NOTES

Joint configuration and dimensions of flat slab top shall match and fit the riser joint detail.

Lifting devices shall be approved by the Engineer.

Bottom slabs shall be reinforced with a minimum of 0.34 sq. in./ft. (720 sq. mm/m) in both directions. with a maximum spacing of 11 (280).

Bottom slabs may be connected to the riser as determined by the fabricator; however. only a single row of reinforcement around the perimeter may be utilized.

See Standard 602701 for details of manhole steps.

All dimensions are in inches (millimeters) unless otherwise shown.

b)

Figure 7.6   Examples for notes clarifying information about the materials

7.4 INSTALLATION INFORMATION

In the drawings for transportation facilities, the notes may be needed to provide detailed descriptions on the information for their installation or construction (as shown in Figure 7.7).

As aforementioned, the notes in engineering drawings play an important role for readers to get full understanding of the engineering design. Writing notes varies due to the demand of drawings and requires large number of technical terms and expressions.

NOTES.

1. Where it is not practical to install final pavement markings conforming to the Alaska Traffic Manual before a road segment is opened for public travel, install interim pavement markings as shown here.

2. Interim markings may be used for no longer than the period (in calendar days) shown in the table below. After that, markings shall conform to the Alaska Traffic Manual.

3. Dimensions in parentheses apply to curves with a radius less than 350m.

4. Where R4-1 "DO NO PASS" signs are used, install them at the beginning of no passing zones and at no more than 450m spacings within the zones.

5. Install high level warning devices on all "Do Not Pass" and "Pass With Care" signs.

6. Install interim lane-dividing lines on multi-lane roads as follows:

Striping: 1.2m long 100mm wide stripes with 11m gaps (0.6m stripes with 5.5m gaps where the radius is less than 350m).

Temporary Raised Pavement Markers: Three markers at 0.9m o.c. with a gap of 10.4m between marker groups (two markers at 0.6m o.c. with a 5.5m gap where the radius is less than 350m).

Figure 7.7   Example for notes clarifying installation information

7.5   EXERCISES

1. How many kinds of notes are included in engineering drawing, and what their purposes to be used?

2. How to write a note for the unit of dimensions if dual measurement system used in a drawing?

3. What are the other types of graphs or drawings in addition to the three view drawings?

4. Please translate the following sentences into English.

1)所有尺寸标记都是以毫米为单位计。

2)除其他特殊说明外,图中所示钢筋均为 8 号筋。

3)参照 3 页中第 1 页上的概要说明。

4)没有显示的接合处细节参照 GB42001。

5)参照第 1 页的挡土墙设计细节。